ERASMUS AS A TRANSLATOR OF THE CLASSICS

This first full-length study of Erasmus' translations of classical literature examines his approach to translation and, more generally, his role as a transmitter of the classics. It traces in chronological order the progress of his Greek studies and the publication history of his translations from Greek into Latin; these included selections from the works of Libanius, Euripides, Plutarch, Lucian, Galen, Isocrates, and Xenophon. It also illustrates Erasmus' methods with appropriate examples from his own texts and from those of his predecessors and contemporaries. In so doing it provides an overview of the state of Greek literature in the Renaissance.

Erasmus shifted from literal translation to a more liberal approach – a change in attitude that was accompanied by a redefinition of his role as a translator. In his early work he had pursued private goals, regarding his versions from secular authors as practice pieces for his magnum opus, the New Testament. In later years his approach became more reader-oriented. He saw his work in terms of a service to scholarship – making Greek literature accessible to Latin readers and acting as their guide to classical thought. He was concerned not only with the mechanics of conveying the factual contents and literary qualities of the original, but also with the applicability of its moral content to Christian philosophy.

This book includes a chapter on Erasmus' New Testament version; by allowing a fuller evaluation of Erasmus' contribution to philology, this subject adds an important dimension to the book. Erasmus' translations of Greek texts reflect two concerns that dominated his life. As an educator he wanted to see classical philology firmly established in the curriculum of schools; as a Christian humanist he wanted to convince biblical scholars that it was an indispensable tool of their profession.

ERIKA RUMMEL is Executive Assistant to the Editorial Board of the *Collected Works of Erasmus*.

Erasmus Studies

A series of studies concerned with Erasmus and related subjects

Erika Rummel

Erasmus as a Translator of the Classics

University of Toronto Press
Toronto Buffalo London

© University of Toronto Press 1985
Toronto Buffalo London
Printed in Canada

ISBN 0-8020-5653-9

Canadian Cataloguing in Publication Data

Rummel, Erika, 1942–
Erasmus as a translator of the classics

(Erasmus studies, 7; ISSN 0318-3319)
Bibliography: p.
Includes index.
ISBN 0-8020-5653-9
1. Erasmus, Desiderius, d. 1536.
I. Title. II. Series.
PA8518.R86 1984   199.492   C84-099475-3

Contents

⚜

Preface

꽃

Erasmus' career as a translator of classical literature spanned thirty years and won him wide acclaim among his contemporaries. Some of his publications remained popular for several decades, others fell into disuse even during his lifetime – partly, as Erasmus himself liked to think, because the revival of Greek studies decreased the demand for translations, partly because literary tastes changed and new translations captured the mood of a new generation. The single most important development affecting the publishing history of the translations was, however, the gradual replacement of Latin by vernacular languages. In modern literature Erasmus' versions from the classics have received scant attention because, unlike his original works, whose spirit is alive and whose appeal remains constant, the translations have outlived their original purpose. When Latin ceased to be the universal language of scholars, Erasmus' texts no longer functioned as effective vehicles for the dissemination of Greek literature.

The substance of Erasmus' translations may be obsolete, but other dimensions of his work as a translator deserve our continued attention. The most obvious of these is the historical aspect of his publications and the questions related to their genesis. How did Erasmus acquire his knowledge of Greek, what do we know about the chronology of his publications and the circumstances surrounding their composition, what motivated Erasmus to choose a particular Greek author? The answers to these questions shed light on biographical details of his life, form a commentary on the availability and condition of Greek texts, and illustrate the literary tastes and preferences of a generation, as circumscribed by Erasmus' need for self-education and his publishers' view of the market. Erasmus' work also reveals his attitude towards classical literature. He treated his sources with respect and admiration, but always reserved judgment, rejecting unquestioning loyalty and mindless imitation. Moreover, his relationship to the classics was characterized by a utilitarian element. He approached his sources with the idea of adapting their impressive knowledge and their admirable skills to contemporary needs, to place them into the service of education and Christian philosophy.

Apart from the historical dimension, we must also consider the linguistic aspects of Erasmus' work. His statements on methods of translation and the practices observed in his compositions reveal a surprisingly modern, or rather timeless, approach to the task. Of course the problems confronting translators have remained the same. They continue to face the challenging task of conveying to the reader not only the thought and ideas of the original but also its aesthetic appeal, of providing a cognitive as well as a formal equivalence. Like the modern translator, Erasmus pursued a twofold goal: to promote in his readers an understanding of the factual content and to elicit in them an emotional response to the literary qualities of the text. We also note that Erasmus shares with contemporary translators the dilemma of choosing between a literal and a liberal translation – or rather, the difficulty of steering a middle course between their extreme forms. He faced the task of defining his role as an intermediary between Greek source and Latin readership, of drawing the line between his responsibility towards the Greek author, which obliged him to convey the meaning of the original faithfully and accurately, his considerations for the needs of the reader, which prompted him to adopt the role of a commentator, and the demands of his own literary persona, which he was unable to suppress completely. Moreover, we are able to observe the skilful translator at work. We recognize Erasmus' mastery of rhetorical devices, his creativity and resourcefulness in choice of words, and his versatility in adapting his style to the poet's flowing language, the satirist's biting wit, and the orator's solemn gravity. Finally, a study of Erasmus' translations illustrates the respective values he assigned to secular and ecclesiastical sources. Our findings bear out his own designation of the translations as *parerga* or preliminaries to the more important task of restoring and elucidating biblical texts.

They confirm the essentially Christian orientation of his work. Theology was the queen of sciences, and to her Erasmus dedicated the fruits of humanistic learning and classical scholarship.

Acknowledgments

✣

The author wishes to express her gratitude to Professor James K. McConica and Dr Ron Schoeffel for their encouragement and support; to Professors Clemens Bruehl and Paul Grendler for their useful comments and advice; to D.S. Harris for proofreading an early draft; to Professor Alec Dalzell for proofreading the final version with special attention to the Greek; to the readers appointed by the Press whose suggestions have been incorporated in the book; and to the copy-editor, Judy Williams, for the careful attention she has given to the manuscript.

This book has been published with the help of a grant from the Canadian Federation for the Humanities, using funds provided by the Social Sciences and Humanities Research Council of Canada, and a grant from the Andrew W. Mellon Foundation to the University of Toronto Press.

ERASMUS AS A TRANSLATOR OF THE CLASSICS

First Steps:
Erasmus' Greek Studies

ℵ

'No Latin expression,' said Erasmus in the *Copia*, 'can approach the charm of a Greek one when we allude to a passage or remark of some author.'[1] His appreciation of the evocative qualities of the language and its subliminal appeal was, however, coupled with the recognition of its value as a currency in the learned world. He recognized its exclusive character. Greek could be used as a password to establish instant rapport between scholars or as a secret code to keep the uninitiated at bay.[2] To know Greek meant to belong to an inner circle, and Erasmus embarked on his studies seeking both a literary experience and a place among the acolytes of New Learning.

As he advanced in his studies, as Greek literature opened up to him its store of historical, philosophical, and scientific learning, he discovered the instructive value of the Greek classics. He became conscious of the restrictions placed upon the Latin reader, the limitations imposed on his progress in learning, and formed the conviction that a well-rounded education must include a knowledge of Greek. This appreciation of its didactic value gave a new dimension to Erasmus' studies: he no longer pursued them for the gratification of his literary tastes alone, or for the membership they gave him in a select circle of Philhellenes, but with the conviction that Greek literature was the fountainhead of all learning: 'For whereas we Latins have but a few small streams, a few muddy pools, the Greeks possess crystal-clear springs and rivers that run with gold.'[3]

Soon, however, the call *Ad fontes!* acquired a new meaning for Erasmus. In the course of his theological studies he came to prize Greek not only as the key to classical learning, but also as a valuable aid in the restoration and interpretation of sacred texts. He endorsed the 'handmaiden' theory, which designated philology as an auxiliary science and zealously promoted the idea of applying philological principles to scriptural texts. Thus he regarded his translations from the classics not as an end in themselves but as a means of perfecting his skills, as a useful exercise preparing him for the greater task of editing and interpreting ecclesiastical texts. Although the translations from the classics therefore occupied a subordinate position among Erasmus' projects, they played a necessary role in his career. Their usefulness, to both Erasmus and his readers, was undeniable. Not only did they provide the author with a practice ground for his skills, they made Greek classics accessible to a Latin readership and contributed to the dissemination of Greek literature in northern Europe.

In Erasmus' youth a reading knowledge of Greek was a rare accomplishment and instruction was not readily available. While Greek studies had been an integral part of higher education in Italy for some time and Greek was taught, for instance, at the schools of Guarino in Ferrara and Vittorino in Mantua, it had barely found its way into the curriculum of northern schools by the end of the century.[4] Only limited opportunities presented themselves to the student of Greek in Erasmus' native country, and the youthful aspirant had to demonstrate exceptional strength of character to hold out against unsympathetic educators who tended to view pagan literature as a temptation sent by the devil. The school at Deventer which Erasmus entered at the age of nine was no exception to the rule. In Erasmus' words, it 'was in a state of barbarism' and breathed the spirit of the Dark Ages. He acknowledged, however, that conditions improved towards the end of his stay, that a fresh breeze swept through its halls 'after Hegius and Synthen had begun to introduce something of a higher standard as literature.'[5]

Hegius belonged to the first generation of northern humanists who rallied around Rudolf Agricola. On becoming headmaster at Deventer he initiated a classically oriented curriculum and prepared his own teaching aids. He attributed considerable importance to Greek studies, a view he expressed in a poem significantly entitled 'On the Utility of the Greek Tongue.'[6] Unfortunately his innovations came too late for Erasmus, who left the school on completing five of eight grades. Since the headmaster only taught the senior form, Erasmus had little opportunity to benefit directly from his instructions, but he gleaned what he could from older schoolmates and was a keen listener when Hegius addressed the whole school on feast-days.[7] Although these occasions were infrequent, they left a deep impression on the young Erasmus and filled his mind with a love of classical learning. He remained in touch with Hegius in later years and paid homage to him on several occasions, acknowledging his educational influence and praising his saintly character and devotion to the cause of humanistic learning.[8]

In a short biographical sketch Beatus Rhenanus tells us that Erasmus learned the 'rudiments of both languages under Alexander Hegius,'[9] but just how much Greek the youngster acquired at Deventer is not clear. From Erasmus' own reminiscences we may surmise that he learned no more than the letters of the Greek alphabet and the meaning of single words contained in such textbooks as Eberhard Bethune's *Graecismus*, Alexander de Villa Dei's *Doctrinale*, and John Garland's 'half-Latin, half-Greek disticha.'[10] The Greek words that appeared in these texts were mostly technical terms in transliteration and often fitted with Latin case endings. A typical example is the section on rhetorical figures in the *Doctrinale*, lines 2365–8:

> Hinc sunt exempla: pleonasmos, acyrologia
> et cacosyntheton et eclipsis, tautologia,
> amphibologia, tapinosis, macrologia,
> perissologia, cacenphaton, aleoteta.

Here are examples (of what should be avoided): exaggeration, impropriety of speech, bad composition, ellipse, tautology, ambiguity, lowly style, lengthy speech, wordiness, impropriety, and a heaping up of words.

One assumes that the teacher explained these terms to the class and pointed out the primary meaning of the constituent parts of these composite nouns. In John Garland's textbook a running translation or paraphrase is usually provided. For example, he explains: *'atomus' est indivisibile corpus* (the atom is an indivisible body); *'logica' ... est sermocinabilis vel disputabilis scientia* (logic ... is the science of what can be put into words or disputed); [*'philosophiae'*] *interpretatio est sicut 'amor sapientiae'* (philosophy interpreted means the same as 'love of wisdom'). Bethune's

Graecismus contained a whole chapter on loan-words with Greek roots, listing some three hundred Greek words in transliteration, explaining their meaning, and putting them into context, pointing out a Latin derivative. For example: *'coenum' commune sit, coenobium probat illud* (*coenum* means 'common'; *coenobium*, 'monastery,'* shows that); *dic 'xeron' siccum, probat illud xerofagia* (say *xeron*, 'dry'; *xerofagia*, 'asceticism,' shows that).[11] Hegius may have provided additional examples or tendered his own etymological explanations,[12] and his lessons may have been reinforced by educational games such as the one described in *De pronuntiatione* in which Latin words were matched with Greek ones.[13]

However rudimentary and unstructured the knowledge was that Erasmus acquired at Deventer, he elevated it to almost mystical significance. Thus, when he addressed a poem to his friend Cornelis Gerard, he wrote his name in Greek letters at the top of the page, offering the symbols as a token of their secret fellowship and joint devotion to the Muses.[14] He repeatedly described his love for the classics as a mystical experience: he was 'driven to good literature as if by some hidden force of nature.' It was a 'miraculous power' that drew him to the temple of the Muses 'like one possessed by spirits.' Only divine inspiration could account for this enthusiasm, this love of humane studies which evinced a judgment beyond his age, a precocious discernment of wisdom and beauty.[15]

After the death of his parents, Erasmus attended the school in s'Hertogenbosch.[16] His stay there contributed little to his learning in general and nothing to his advancement in Greek, as his disparaging remarks make clear. In his opinion, the Brethren were 'suffering from a lack of the best authors' and were in no position 'to give the young a liberal education.' In fact, he believed that he himself 'knew rather more than his teachers.'[17]

Similar conditions greeted him at the monastery in Steyn where he prepared to take his vows. He remembered with abhorrence 'the conversations so cold and inept ... the gatherings at mealtime so profane in their spirit.'[18] In these days of intellectual deprivation, reading was his only source of comfort, but classical literature was so unpopular at Steyn that he was forced to pursue his studies surreptitiously and at night.[19] The paranoid fear with which the Brethren rejected anything to do with Greek literature can be judged from an anecdote recounted by Erasmus in a letter to Botzheim. Providing background information for his catalogue of works. Erasmus wrote: 'Many years ago I composed a sapphic poem on the archangel Michael ... Although I so restrained my style that it could be taken for prose, the prior did not dare to post it up because, in his words, "it was so poetical it might have been written in Greek."'[20] This pronouncement, which could have passed for praise in another age, turned to criticism in the mouth of the conservative prior, who obviously regarded 'Greek' as an epithet of sinister connotations.

The Brethren's animosity towards the New Learning was also on Erasmus' mind in 1514 when he explained his prolonged absence from the monastery as a reaction against the hostility he had encountered there, 'the envy of many, the contempt of all';[21] but when he had first obtained leave to become secretary to the bishop of Cambrai and was subsequently given permission to study in Paris, he found the atmosphere there no different from at home. He was still obliged to conceal his interest in the classics, to pursue them furtively, and to apologize for them. Thus he reported from Paris to the abbot of St Bertin: 'I had the good fortune to come upon some Greek books and am secretly engaged day and night in copying them.' This admission was followed by a lengthy apologia for his interest in learning Greek.[22]

Public opinion and the concomitant fame or neglect are powerful agents in directing the efforts of a generation, and Erasmus rightly observed that 'it matters a great deal when you write and where; who are your judges, who your competitors; for a distinguished rival sharpens your wit, and Honour nourishes the Arts.'[23] Such incentives were absent in Erasmus' youth. The negative attitude he found, especially in clerical circles, had a demoralizing effect on him, reduced his self-confidence, and at times undermined his resolve to study classical literature. On more than one occasion he was at the point of surrender, ready to yield to the majority and to swear off his love for the Muses. At the nadir of his feelings he wrote to Cornelis Gerard: 'I observe literature, which once won benefits and fame for its devotees, causing loss and disrepute among the men of today, since things have come to a pass where the more educated a person is the more he is pursued by misfortune and derision. Accordingly, my dear Cornelis, I saw no reason to spend my life idly in the study of literature, with the result that I have long since completely given up its pursuit.'[24]

When his hopes of accompanying the bishop of Cambrai to

Italy were disappointed, he was thrown into a depression: 'Nothing is fit for me but to weep and wail,' he wrote, 'and through these distresses my brain has already so lost its edge and my heart so wasted away that I have come to take no joy at all in my former studies. I find no pleasure in the poets' Pierian charm, and the Muses, who were once my love, repel me now.'[25] But he always recovered from these bouts of depression, rescued by the encouraging letters of one or two intimate friends who shared his love of the Muses.

Having a sense of belonging, winning the acceptance and support of his companions, was important to Erasmus, as it is to any sensitive human being. At Steyn he had actively sought the fellowship of like-minded men, trying to form an inner circle to protect himself against his hostile environment. Thus he had encouraged Servatius Roger, a young monk and fellow inmate at Steyn, to join him in his studies; and when Cornelis Gerard expressed a similar yearning for companionship, Erasmus was elated at the prospect of sharing his interests and profiting from mutual encouragement, friendly criticism, and scholarly competition. He replied with alacrity: 'I am glad to echo your remark and make it my own: "Suffice it to say that my supreme desire is to join with you in a single bond of brotherhood, a single devotion to the literary pursuits we share ..."'[26]

In Paris, too, it was the community of friends with whom he could share his love of learning that made life agreeable, rekindled his zeal for humane studies, strengthened his scholarly commitment, and allowed him to remember the city as a place where he had spent 'some delightful years with freedom to study the best authors.'[27]

The colleagues he met and the young men to whom he was both tutor and companion brought into his everyday life an exuberant joy and devotion to learning. He described the atmosphere in a letter to Christian Northoff, a pupil from Lübeck: 'Our talk is of letters at the noonday meal; our suppers are made exquisite by literary seasoning. In our walks we prattle of letters and even our frivolous diversions are no strangers to them; we talk of letters till we fall asleep, our dreams are dreams of letters, and literature awakens us to begin a new day.'[28]

It was in Paris that Erasmus first entered a more congenial society and renewed his contacts with the humanistic movement, befriending the royal poet Fausto Andrelini and approaching the distinguished French humanist Robert Gaguin. It was in Paris that Erasmus felt encouraged to take up Greek studies once more. Letters written during this period bear witness to his progress, for he keenly displayed his new accomplishments, using Greek words and phrases in addressing his correspondents. The earliest letter to contain a significant number of Greek expressions dates from the year 1497[29] and is addressed to Thomas Grey, a student to whom Erasmus had formed a strong attachment. Their relationship was, however, frowned upon by the young man's guardian, an 'elderly humbug,' as Erasmus described him, who eventually took steps to remove his charge from Erasmus' care. The separation caused Erasmus acute grief. He protested that his friendship with Grey had been based, not on 'any youthful whim, but an honourable love for letters.' Their joint studies had brought them together, for 'between good and studious men there is a kind of impersonal, but very firm link forged by their enthusiasm for similar things.'[30] He continued to correspond with Grey and dedicated to him in 1497 an early version of *De ratione studii*, fondly graecizing the young man's name and addressing him as 'my Leucophaeus.'[31] Greek also occurred in a contemporary letter to Richard Whitford, companion of Erasmus' pupil Mountjoy and a mutual friend, whom he called ὁμοτράπεζος, 'mess-mate.'[32] A third letter containing Greek quotations and dating from the early Paris years is the protreptic epistle addressed to the ten-year-old Adolph of Burgundy, heer van Veere, first published in the *Lucubratiunculae* (Antwerp 1503) under the title 'Epistola exhortatoria ad capessendam virtutem ...' In this highly rhetorical composition Erasmus congratulated the boy on his linguistic accomplishments and portrayed him in a bucolic scene as the Muses' 'nursling ... who with lisping and as yet scarcely controlled tongue practises words in the Greek as well as the Latin language.' Exhorting Adolph to persevere in his studies, he addressed to him a Homeric line, quoting it in Greek 'since you are already learning that.'[33]

Among Erasmus' contacts in Paris, the man most instrumental in promoting his studies was Robert Gaguin. The aging scholar, who had acquired his knowledge of Greek in Italy, possessed a large library, which he put at Erasmus' disposal.[34] It seems that he also acted as his monitor and literary critic, for it was he who described the first edition of the *Adages* as jejune and admonished Erasmus to seek a broader base for his knowledge in Greek literature.[35]

We do not know if Erasmus also relied on the services of a professional teacher to guide him in his studies. In *De pronuntiatione* he speaks of the benefits of 'hiring a native Greek ... for that native and authentic quality of sound' and in a letter to Antoon of Bergen written in 1501 he announced his intentions of hiring a tutor, 'a genuine Greek he is, or perhaps twice over; for he is always starving and charges an exorbitant fee for teaching.'[36] In later accounts, however, he denied having received professional help, saying that Georgius Hermonymus was the only teacher available at that time and describing him in disparaging terms as a man 'who could not have taught if he had wanted to, and would not have wanted to teach if he had been able to.' He reported that he was obliged to be his own teacher and resolved to translate classical authors as an exercise in self-discipline, to force himself to concentrate on the text before him. In a letter to Choler he described his situation in similar terms: 'I translated some dialogues by Lucian and two tragedies by Euripides, for no other reason than to practise Greek on my own, since I did not have access to a teacher.'[37] Accordingly, he advised others who found themselves without professional instruction to follow his example, pointing out the alternative to formal instruction in *De ratione studii*: 'If by chance no teacher is available, the next best thing is to read authors.'[38]

If we draw up a balance at this point in Erasmus' life and consider what we know of his Greek studies before 1499, the year in which he left Paris for a six-month stay in England, we note a surprising lack of direct evidence for this preliminary stage in his career as a Greek scholar. Most references to Erasmus' initial efforts take the form of reminiscences. They are comments made in retrospect, autobiographical notes written fifteen or even twenty-five years after the fact. Erasmus' early educational writings, the *Copia*, *De ratione studii*, and *De epistolis conscribendis*, contain references to the importance of Greek studies, but the relevant passages appear in later editions and are not documented in draft versions composed during the Paris days.[39] The letters written between 1495 and 1499 make no specific mention of Greek studies, although the use of Greek attests to the writer's pursuits. The nature of our evidence changes significantly over the next years, however, as pertinent references become more frequent and Greek studies emerge as a topic of some prominence in the letters.

In the summer of 1499 Erasmus was invited by Lord Mountjoy to visit England. The contacts he made during the following six months gave a new impetus to his Greek studies. He befriended Grocyn, who had learned Greek in Florence under the direction of Demetrius Chalcondyles and who taught Greek first in Oxford, then in London. He met Linacre, who had worked for Aldo Manuzio on the Greek edition of Aristotle and had just published a translation of Proclus' *Sphere*. He initiated his lifelong friendship with Thomas More, who was to share his enthusiasm for Greek literature and become his fellow translator.[40] And he came under the influence of John Colet, who presented him with an alternative to the frigid scholastic method taught at the faculty of Paris.

Colet had been to Italy but, unlike his compatriots, had not studied Greek. In fact, at this point in his life, he denied that classical languages held any importance for the theologian. A polemical statement in his *Lectures on Corinthians* expresses this view, but also shows that it went by no means uncontested. Addressing an anonymous opponent, Colet set forth his opinions defiantly: 'Now if anyone should say – as is often said – that to read heathen authors is of assistance for the right understanding of Holy Writ, let them reflect whether the very fact of such reliance being placed upon them does not make them a chief obstacle to such understanding ... Those books alone ought to be read in which there is a salutary flavour of Christ, in which Christ is set forth for us to feast upon ...'[41]

It is likely that Erasmus participated in the debate on the merits of ethnic literature and took a stand on the issues involved. In fact, we know that he had discussed the problem and points related to it with Gaguin in Paris, for he cited his mentor's opinion in the prefatory epistle to William Hermans' *Silva Odarum* (Paris 1497). In this letter, which is addressed to the bishop of Cambrai, Hendrik of Bergen, Erasmus defended the Roman poets, his 'former darlings,' and asserted the value of non-Christian literature, saying he would not even reprehend anyone for applying 'Egyptian trimmings' though he was against the 'appropriation of Egypt in its entirety.'[42] In such cautious terms and with due respect for the sensitivity of the issues involved Erasmus commended the form rather than the content of pagan literature, pointing out that rhetorical skills could be learned from classical models and be used to embellish or elucidate Christian themes. The point made was carefully delineated: he was not praising the substance of ethnic literature but only its linguistic virtues, which could be pressed into the service of Christ. His glory need not be tarnished by barbaric language; it could be illuminated with classical splendour.

The debate with Colet and other English friends may well have been the crucible through which Erasmus' thoughts passed before he reached the conclusion that a knowledge of Greek was not only a desirable accomplishment for scholars, but a necessary one for theologians. This conclusion was hastened by his own experience with sacred literature: the discrepancies he noted between the Greek and Latin Psalms, the difficulties he encountered when he began work on Paul and Jerome, the feelings of frustration and inadequacy when he realized that he needed more Greek to accomplish what he had set out to do, and finally the discovery of Valla's *Annotationes*, which demonstrated the importance of consulting Greek manuscripts to establish biblical texts.[43]

The shift in Erasmus' views from regarding Greek as a feather in the scholar's cap to recognizing it as a tool in the theologian's hand is apparent from a letter written to Colet during his stay in England in which he renounced studies in literature for pleasure's sake and substituted another, more profound, motive: the necessity to acquire a sound linguistic basis for his theological studies.[44] He had come to realize that linguistic skills were more than optional gear: they were essential equipment. In an expanded statement to the abbot of St Bertin, Antoon of Bergen, he therefore explained that he had resolved to concentrate on learning Greek, not only because of the encyclopedic knowledge to be drawn from such sources, but because it was impossible 'even to put a finger on that part of theology which is specially concerned with the mysteries of the faith unless one is furnished with the equipment of Greek.'[45]

On his return to Paris at the end of 1500 Erasmus began to study Greek with this new purpose in mind. The letters from the years 1500–2 reflect his determination to succeed, but also attest to the many difficulties he faced: the scarcity of teachers, texts, and funds with which to obtain them. Thus he wrote to Jacob

Batt, a young man who shared his enthusiasm for classical literature: 'My readings in Greek all but crush my spirit; but I have
no spare time and no means to purchase books or employ the
services of a tutor.'[46] And a month later to the same friend: 'I have
turned my entire attention to Greek. The first thing I shall do, as
soon as the money arrives, is to buy some Greek authors; after
that, I shall buy clothes.'[47] And again from Orleans where he had
fled to escape the plague: 'My mind is burning with indescribable
eagerness to bring all my small literary works to their conclusion
and at the same moment to acquire a certain limited competence in
Greek, and thereby go on to devote myself entirely to sacred
literature.'[48]

Although this higher goal was now firmly established in
Erasmus' mind, his appreciation for the charms of the Greek
language remained undiminished. He took much pleasure in his
readings, however difficult, declaring himself overwhelmed by
the beauty of Homeric poetry: 'Indeed my affection for this
particular author is so warm, that even though I should fail to
understand him, I should still derive refreshment and sustenance
from the very sight of his work.'[49] The text in question had been
loaned to Erasmus by Augustine Vincent, his sometime host.
When asked for its return, Erasmus displayed reluctance to part
with the book. In the end he sent off only one part, so as not 'to be
wholly bereft of solace.'[50]

At this time Erasmus began to promulgate his belief in the
importance of Greek. He tried to convert his friends and to make
them the companions of his studies. With varied success he
approached William Hermans, his old friend and companion;
Jacob Batt, at the time tutor to Adolph of Veere; Nicolas Bensrott,
a former pupil; and Jacob Voogt, his host in Orleans. From
Orleans he wrote urgently to Batt: 'I am very anxious that you
should know Greek, both because I find that a Latin education is
imperfect without it, and also to heighten the pleasure we take
in each other's society, as would happen if we both enjoyed
precisely the same range of study.'[51] He began to insert Greek
words into his letters to Batt and begged him to support him in
his efforts to persuade William Hermans to join them in their
endeavours.[52] But a year later he reported to Voogt that he had
made little progress in his efforts to draw others into the Greek
circle: 'I am practising Greek, but alone, for Batt has too little time,
and moreover is fonder of Latin.'[53]

The mission undertaken to win over William Hermans had similarly failed: 'I have gone as far as Haarlem (and whether it cost me more in expense or effort or danger I cannot yet tell) on purpose to visit my friend William, or rather to make a Greek out of him, taking a huge bundle of books with me; but all my trouble and all my money were wasted.'[54] Subsequently Erasmus demanded back his books in a clipped tone: 'Please send back those Greek fables now that you need them no longer, since we are very hard up for Greek books here.'[55]

With Voogt, who would have been a more promising candidate for joint studies, Erasmus was never able to form a close association. Their relationship lacked warmth and spontaneity, and he pointedly described the terms on which he lived with his host as amounting to 'solitude.'[56]

An exchange of texts and perhaps of ideas was taking place, however, between Erasmus and Nicolas Bensrott, who had been at various times his and Augustine Vincent's pupil. In 1501 Erasmus sent him 'a Euripides and an Isocrates' and invited him in turn to send along any Greek texts available in his part of the world: 'If any new Greek books have arrived, load the bearer of this with a bundle of them – and myself with kindness at the same time.'[57] In the same breath he invited Bensrott's scholarly cooperation: 'I wish, dear Bensrott, that we might combine our literary efforts.'[58] But nothing more transpires to suggest that this idea was put into practice, and it seems that Erasmus' friendly suggestion – like his other efforts to promote a team spirit – came to nothing.

Erasmus' own progress in Greek was paralleled by an increased use of Greek in his correspondence. Not surprisingly, the preface to his *Adagiorum Collectanea* (Paris 1500), one of the first books north of the Alps to contain words in Greek font, was sprinkled with quotations from that language.[59] Greek also occurred in letters addressed to Jacob Batt, to the physician d'Angleberme, who was taking lessons in Greek at the time, to the steward of St Bertin, Antoon of Luxembourg, and the abbot Antoon of Bergen, to Erasmus' patroness Anna of Borsselen, his hosts Jacob Anthonizoon and Nicolas Ruistre – that is, in about half the letters we have, dating from the years 1501–3.[60] In fact, Erasmus apologized to Antoon of Bergen for his overt display of learning: 'If your lordship will bear with me when I perhaps overdo Greek in a letter to the point of absurdity, since I am a recent and green beginner in that language.'[61] Such modesty in describing his accomplishments was, of course, perfunctory. Before equals Erasmus did not disguise his satisfaction with the success of his studies. Thus he wrote to William Hermans in 1502: 'I have made such good progress that I am capable of expressing my meaning in Greek with reasonable proficiency, and what is more, extempore.'[62]

Four years later he declared himself satisfied with his achievements, writing to Servatius Roger: 'I have made up my mind to be content with my present undistinguished fortune especially since I have acquired as much Greek as I need.'[63] The remark must be taken with a grain of salt, however, for only half a year later he informed the same correspondent that he was going to Italy 'mainly to learn Greek.'[64] Both statements, the earlier expression of self-satisfaction and the subsequent commitment to further studies, no doubt represent genuine feelings, but show Erasmus in different frames of mind. He was speaking at one time with just pride, at another with intellectual humility. In truth he was never fully content with his achievements and had no intentions of passing up an opportunity to further his knowledge. At this time Italy was offering him an opportunity to establish contact with native Greek scholars, to benefit from their learned advice, and to gain access to Greek manuscripts.

Erasmus embarked on the journey in 1506, no longer a tyro in his field, but the author of several successful publications, among them translations from Euripides and Lucian.[65] The fact that the prestigious publishing house of Aldo Manuzio, whom he approached during his stay in Bologna, agreed to reprint his Euripides translations[66] clearly shows that the days of his apprenticeship were over and that he had emerged as a master of the Greek tongue. We may therefore conclude our observations on this first stage in his career, returning to a theme touched upon repeatedly in the course of tracing his progress: Erasmus' motives for learning Greek.

Three stages may be distinguished in Erasmus' attitude towards Greek studies, perhaps paralleling the stages in a man's life, for he seemed to have been motivated, successively and cumulatively, by pleasure, usefulness, and necessity.

As was to be expected from a spirited young man with scholarly ambitions, Erasmus threw himself with enthusiasm into the vogue of classical learning, battling against the conservative notions of his elders. At Deventer he was first drawn into the sphere of humanistic learning. At that time reading the classics was a gratifying and elating literary experience to be shared with a few intimate friends in a tryst to defy the opponents of the Muses. In his earliest references to classical, and in particular Greek, authors Erasmus therefore often spoke of the 'delight' and the 'pleasure' he experienced in reading them. 'Charm' (*lepos*) became a catchword to describe the captivating powers of Greek literature.[67] Accordingly, he promoted his first translations by promising his readers 'a vast degree of pleasure.' Lucian's works were gay blossoms picked 'from the precinct of the Greek Muses whose gardens bloom even in the depth of winter'; he praised Euripides for his 'exquisite and delicate' diction and the 'honeyed sweetness' of his style.[68]

During his stay in Paris, however, Erasmus' outlook gradually changed, acquiring a new dimension; he recognized the usefulness of his studies and came to value Greek literature for its 'rich subject matter and vocabulary,' asserting that 'almost all knowledge of things is to be sought in Greek authors.'[69] Thus he commended his translations not only for their gratifying literary qualities but also for their instructive, and finally their inspirational, value. Lucian could be read 'with a certain amount of profit'; Plutarch was not only 'most learned' but also a 'most sacred writer, second only to the Scriptures'; and Xenophon and Isocrates presented models worthy of imitation by Christian princes.[70]

Erasmus' final evaluation of Greek studies was based, however, not on the literary appeal of Greek authors, nor on their instructive qualities, but on the supporting role Greek philology played in theological studies. He came to regard a knowledge of Greek as a necessary prerequisite for biblical scholarship. The new note, first struck in the dedication of Cornelis Gerard's *Odes* to the bishop of Cambrai (Ep 49, Paris 1496), in which he defended the study of ethnic literature as a preparatory discipline, was further developed in a letter to the abbot of St Bertin (Ep 149, Paris 1501). The points made in this apologia of his interests foreshadow the arguments he presented in the great controversy following the publication of his New Testament in 1516. Because of its position in the history of Erasmus' defence of liberal studies, the letter deserves closer examination.

Erasmus began by reporting to Antoon of Bergen his efforts to acquire a knowledge of Greek. He expressed his regret at not having had an opportunity to do so earlier on in life, for only now could he see the truth of the statement: 'Latin scholarship, however elaborate, is maimed and reduced by half without Greek.'[71] The student of sacred literature, especially, could not go about his task unless equipped with a knowledge of Greek, for the available standard translation of the Bible was so literal as to be obscure. In support of his views Erasmus cited the authority of Clement v and the decrees of the council of Vienne which instructed universities to engage teachers of Hebrew, Greek, and Latin because 'Scripture could not be understood, much less discussed, without them.'[72] He then described his current project, the preparation of an edition of Jerome's works, which were a case in point: they had been corrupted for lack of philological skills, 'through ignorance of classical antiquity and of Greek.'[73]

The letter to Antoon of Bergen contains in a nucleus Erasmus' position on the role of classical philology in biblical studies. Of similar programmatic importance for this early period in his life is the letter to Colet (Ep 181, Paris 1504) accompanying a presentation copy of the *Enchiridion*. In this letter Erasmus explained that he was held up in his theological research by a lack of linguistic skills, for he 'needed Greek at every point.'[74] He reported that he was reading Greek authors for an enlarged edition of his *Adages*, but immediately pointed out that these labours were incidental to a higher goal: 'While I linger within the garden of the Greek I am gathering by the way many flowers that will be useful for the future, even in sacred studies; for experience teaches me this, at any rate, that we can do nothing in any field of literature without a knowledge of Greek, since it is one thing to guess, another to judge; one thing to trust your own eyes, and another to trust those of others.'[75]

Work on the edition of St Jerome, begun in 1500, had strengthened Erasmus in the view that Greek was not only desirable but necessary for the theologian; the discovery of Valla's *Annotationes* confirmed him in his beliefs. In the preface to his edition of this work (Ep 182, Paris 1505) he referred to the controversial nature of Valla's undertaking and methods, justifying his application of linguistic principles to scriptural texts: 'Tell me what is so shocking about Valla's action in making a few annotations on the New Testament after comparing several old and good Greek manuscripts? After all it is from Greek sources that our text undoubtedly comes; and Valla's notes had to do with internal disagreements, or a nodding translator's plainly inadequate renderings of the meaning, or things that are more intelligibly expressed in Greek or, finally anything that is clearly corrupt in our text.'[76] In this letter Erasmus also proclaimed the 'handmaiden' theory of classical philology: 'But I do not really believe that Theology herself, the queen of all the sciences, will be offended if some share is claimed in her and due deference shown to her by her humble attendant Grammar; for, though Grammar is of less consequence in some men's eyes, no help is more indispensable than hers.'[77]

As in his earlier apology to the abbot of St Bertin, Erasmus cited the decrees of the council of Vienne in support of his views.[78] In rendering his verdict on the role of philology in theological studies, he was in league with Christopher Fisher, an Englishman in the papal service to whom the edition of Valla's *Annotationes* was dedicated: 'So, most learned Christopher, you are absolutely right when you remark, as you frequently do, that those who venture to write, not merely on the Scriptures, but on any ancient books at all, are devoid of both intelligence and modesty if they do not possess a reasonable command of both Greek and Latin.'[79]

After the edition of his New Testament was published, Erasmus found that he had to repeat in his own defence what he had previously said to exonerate Valla. In 1519 his position was attacked by the Louvain theologian Jacques Masson, who wrote a dialogue *De tribus linguis*, subtitled 'Whether a knowledge of the three languages is necessary for a theologian.'[80] In his answer, published without delay, Erasmus defended his position, again referring to the council of Vienne and declaring: 'I have never said that anyone with linguistic skills will right away understand the mysteries of sacred literature, I said that it is a great help in arriving at an understanding of Scripture; and I have said that this can be achieved through many means, and not only through the help of linguistics. But just as the philologist does not instantly attain an understanding of the innermost mysteries, so – all other things being even – the man who is ignorant of languages is rather far away from understanding them.'[81]

Having realized the importance of Greek for an interpretation of the Bible, it became Erasmus' lifelong quest to convince fellow theologians of the validity of his cause. Although he fought the reactionaries with arguments, eloquence, and satire, the idea of applying philology to sacred texts did not carry the day during his lifetime. Erasmus remained at the centre of the controversy surrounding the issue and was engaged to the end of his days in battling those who proclaimed that linguistics were the 'spring from which heresies flow' and insisted that there was 'no difference between knowing Latin and Greek and being a heretic.'[82]

In examining Erasmus' motives for promoting Greek studies we have anticipated later developments in his life, and must now return to the early stages of his career.

We begin our survey of his translations from the classics, taking as our point of departure the year 1501 in which Erasmus left Paris to return to his native country.

The Years of Apprenticeship: Erasmus' Translations from Libanius and Euripides

꙼

In the spring of 1501 Erasmus fled Paris to escape an outbreak of the plague and spent the following months visiting friends at Steyn and Haarlem, then staying at Tournehem and St Omer. By the autumn of 1502 he had taken up residence in Louvain and a year later he brought forth the first-fruits of his Greek studies, his translations from Libanius.[1] The fourth-century-AD rhetorician had taught a number of distinguished Christian authors, among them John Chrysostom, Basil, and Gregory of Nazianzus. He was regarded as a model of style, both in Christian Byzantium and in Renaissance Italy.[2] Filelfo, Guarino, and Bessarion, among others, possessed manuscripts of his writings, and some of his orations appeared in print in Ferrara, 1517. Apart from these speeches, which treated of political and cultural questions, Libanius' works included rhetorical declamations and character sketches. Erasmus chose for his translations three short model speeches on literary themes: Menelaus demanding the return of Helen, Medea contemplating the murder of her children, and Andromache addressing Hector.

In November of 1503 Erasmus presented a manuscript copy of the versions, together with a transcript of the Greek text, to Nicolas Ruistre, bishop of Arras and chancellor of the University of Louvain.[3] In the dedicatory letter he described the translations as the test of his linguistic achievements, 'determining how far I have made any considerable progress in the knowledge of both these tongues.'[4] Explaining his choice of author, Erasmus cited the rhetorical skills of Libanius, 'to whom the verdict of scholarship awards a leading place among the practitioners of Attic style.'[5] In particular, he praised the author's dexterity in portraying character and adapting his style to the person of the speaker. Tempering his praise, however, Erasmus noted that style was the author's chief merit and that form rather than content commended him to his readers. He therefore added apologetically: 'Of course the whole exercise is somewhat trivial; yet I thought it might be suitable for attempting my first ventures in this kind of work, in order, of course, to avoid "learning the potter's art on a great jar."'[6] He also hinted at a more practical reason for choosing Libanius' speeches as his subject matter: their availability.[7] Indeed, this may have been the determining factor at a time when Greek texts were hard to come by, and the translator's choice was further reduced by the need for considering a particular piece's suitability to serve as a literary offering to a prospective patron.

Erasmus' translations were not printed until 1519, that is at a time when Erasmus had established his reputation as a translator of classical texts with versions from Euripides, Lucian, and Plutarch.[8] In this first edition (Louvain: Martens 1519) several errors and omissions contained in the manuscript version were corrected. Another, more thorough, revision was undertaken in 1522. In this second edition (Basel: Froben 1522) most of the remaining mistakes were eliminated and a number of passages were given a clearer, more accurate form. For example, 'Glauke,' which had been translated literally as *noctua* (owl) in the manuscript version and in the first edition, was now recognized as a proper name. In another passage where the manuscript and the 1519 edition had the faulty rendition *ut quae nostra erant aufugiens asportares* (fleeing, to bring away what was ours), the 1522 edition read correctly *ut a nostris temperares* (to keep away from what is ours).[9]

Examples of changes to make the translation more accurate are: the substitution of the more meaningful and appropriate verb *favente* (favouring) for the colourless *presente* (being present) in the phrase *Fortuna vel virtute presente vincere* (either Fortune or bravery bringing about the victory, translating ἢ τῆς τύχης ἢ τῆς ἀρετῆς νικῆσαι); the replacement of *Fortuna invida* (jealous fate) by the neutral *Fortuna* to translate δαίμων εὐδαιμονίας (demon Luck); and the switch from a deficient *conspiciendo* (looking on) to *propugnante* (defending), which carries the full impact of προβεβλημένου.[10]

A few mistakes remained, however, even in the second edition, among them the sentence 'he covered up his lie with a crime,' which does not make sense in the context and should have been turned around to read 'he covered up his crime with a lie,' and the phrase '[courted] among neighbours' which should read '[courted] among princes.'[11] In addition to such obvious mistakes we find garbled translations betraying Erasmus' difficulties with a corrupt text. In one passage, for example, Erasmus has Medea say *hic in vos per me adigendus est* (I must plunge this [sword] into you). The Greek means, however, 'he [Jason] plunges this [sword] into you through me'; that is to say, Jason forced Medea's hand.[12] Similarly obscure is the sentence *Manu tenebam adhuc trementem* (I held the trembling [Jason] by the hand), where the Greek clearly means 'He [Jason] held the fleece in his trembling hand.'[13] In the latter example, at least, variants in existing sources suggest that Erasmus' distortion of the meaning was due to difficulties in his text. This explanation may also be extended to a number of omissions, none of which are substantial or affect the understanding of the text.[14]

Even in this 'apprentice work,' as Erasmus called it,[15] this first attempt at translating a classical text, he gave proof of his linguistic skills and his native rhetorical powers. If 'nothing is harder than to turn good Greek into good Latin,'[16] Erasmus succeeded admirably in devising natural and idiomatically correct versions for difficult Greek phrases, as the following examples will demonstrate.

In translating εἰς ἔργον ... καθίστασθαι (come to blows) by *ad manus venire* he conveyed the sense of the Greek idiom, but cast it into a new mould, substituting for the Greek notion of 'taking action' the Latin idea of 'laying hands on' someone; rendering εἰ μὴ τοὺς προσήκοντας λόγους τὰ πράγματα λάβοι (literally 'if deeds do not get their proper account') into Latin by an appropriate native phrase, Erasmus wrote *nisi negotium ut gestum est ita narretur* (unless the matter is told as it happened); in a similar manner he naturalized the phrase ἥκει δὴ πρὸς ἔργον ὁ φόβος, literally 'my fear became fact,' translating it into Latin as *evenit quod timebam* (what I feared came to pass); and in the same way he conveyed the meaning of the Greek idiom ἔξω φόβων (beyond fear) by the corresponding Latin idiom *in tuto* (safely).[17]

In each of these cases Erasmus could not render the text word for word because the idea was expressed in a manner peculiar to the Greek language. A literal translation into Latin would have been jarring or even incomprehensible to the Greekless reader.

The ability to spot potentially obscure phrases, to refrain from a literal translation where it would not serve the purpose, and to substitute a Latin idiom conveying in a manner familiar to Latin readers the contents of the original phrase is one of Erasmus' greatest virtues as a translator and a quality that gives his translations their smooth and polished character.

In some instances it was not a whole phrase but a single word that lacked a parallel grammatical form in Latin and obliged Erasmus to employ an expanded phrase. The following examples will demonstrate this process. Ἄρχοντες (the offending party, literally 'those initiating the hostilities') is expressed by the phrase *iniuriae authores* (the originators of the offence); the unstated object of συνειδότες (those realizing or being conscious of) is revealed in the phrase *eius rei testes* (witnesses to this deed); and the participle ὑβρισμένοι (the offended party), which has no exact equivalent in Latin, is unfolded into the phrase *iniuria lacessiti* (those harrassed by the offence).[18]

In each of these cases Erasmus conveyed the full meaning of the Greek by giving an interpretation or explication rather than a literal translation. This is a feature which we shall encounter frequently in his translations. He prefers to give an expansive and circuitous version rather than to fall short of conveying the full implication of a term or phrase. His endeavour to do justice to the meaning and content of each word is particularly obvious from his careful rendition of δίκαιον (that which is just), a keyword in Menelaus' plea for Helen's return. Erasmus used no fewer than eight different word combinations and variations to translate this Greek term, which encompasses all aspects of justice. In an effort to convey the particular nuance required in a certain context, but also taking pleasure in variation, he translated δίκαιον variously as *rectum, iustum rectumque, quod ius est, aequitas, aequi bonique ratio, aequi honestique ratio, citra culpam,* and *quae par est.*[19] In this manner he made use of a whole range of Latin expressions to parallel the scope of the polysemous Greek word.

If a Greek term had entered the Latin language in classical times, Erasmus used the loan-word in its naturalized form; for example, *xenia* and *plaga.*[20] The word *philanthropia*, on the other hand, does not occur in his text in its familiar latinized form, but is translated by Latin terms proper, once as *comitas*, and elsewhere as *humanitas.*[21] While the selective retention of Greek loan-words indicates that Erasmus made general usage his criterion, the fact that he avoided a facile translation of φιλανθρωπία shows his desire to give the text an entirely Latin garb.

Occasionally Erasmus abandoned the obvious translation for a more creative choice, surprising the reader with an unexpected version. Thus he conveyed the negative element suggested in a particular context, rendering τῶν τυχόντων (the first-comer) by the phrase de plebeiorum ... sorte (one of the common lot); in another case he translated ἀνηδία (unpleasantness; unwillingness) more pointedly as iniuria (offensiveness); similarly he replaced οἶμαι (I think; in my opinion) with auguror (I divine; I suppose) which weakens the speaker's point; elsewhere he introduced a subtle change of meaning by translating τὰ δέοντα (that which ought to be done) as utilia (that which is useful).[22] In these cases Erasmus manipulated the Greek term, either by increasing its force or by selecting one particular nuance from a range of possible meanings. In the examples cited, Erasmus' changes did not significantly affect the content of the phrase; in other instances, however, they introduced a considerable shift in meaning. For example, a critical reader might take offence at Erasmus' liberty, when he translates φυλοκρινεῖν (to distinguish [between guilty and innocent]) as parcere (to spare [the innocent]) or ἐπαιρόμενος (proud of) as potitur (in possession of).[23] The capricious spirit or indulgence in his own preferences, noticeable even in this first translation which Erasmus described as accurate rather than bold,[24] becomes more prominent in his later versions in which he does not shrink from playing the censor and imposing his own construction on the Greek text.

In a number of cases Erasmus' free translations or unconventional choice of words have tangible stylistic or semantic reasons. For example, when he translates τῶν ἀδυνάτων ... γενέσθαι κρείττω (to master the impossible) as invincibilia vincere (to gain a victory over the invincible), he obviously selected this particular wording for the sake of the rhetorical figure; in choosing the word preoptare to translate προαιρεῖν he reproduced the structure of the Greek word which, like its Latin counterpart, consists of the prefix 'pre' and the verb 'elect'; in translating ἀξιοῦν by dignari Erasmus revealed the primary meaning common to both words: 'to deem worthy.'[25]

As a further means of preserving the rhetorical flavour of the Greek original in translation, Erasmus frequently rendered one Greek adjective by two Latin ones. The instances in which he used this device are numerous, but a few examples will suffice to make the point: ψιλή (simple) is translated as *simplex nudaque* (simple and unadorned); ὕπτιος (lying on one's back) by *oscitabundus et supinus* (yawning and lying on one's back); χρηστός (good) as *probus frugique* (good and honest).[26] Similar constructions involve the coupling of synonymous verbs or nouns, such as *cavendum nobis prospiciendumque* (we must be careful and circumspect) or *suspicimus et observamus* (we look up to and respect);[27] *praesides et conciliator* (guardian and promoter) or *religio ac numina* (religious observance and divine spirit), and other paired expressions where the Greek original has only one term.[28]

In these cases Erasmus used rhetorical devices familiar from Cicero's speeches and appropriate to the epideictic genre of Libanius' writings. Stylistic considerations may also account for Erasmus' tendency to be more expansive and elaborate in his expressions than the Greek original. Thus he did not employ a simple Latin adjective to translate Greek δυσμενής (hostile) or δυσχερής (unpleasant), as he might have, but instead used relative clauses, conveying the sense in a more circuitous, but typically rhetorical, manner: *quicum tibi inimicitiae intercedebant* (with whom you had a hostile relationship), *quod animum tuum offenderit* (what offended your spirit).[29] In some instances the expanded version was not a matter of the author's choice: the Greek allowed a brevity of expression that could not be duplicated in Latin. In such cases Erasmus was obliged to supply the words which were understood or implied in the Greek idiom. The following examples will illustrate this practice: We find *nihil habes quod adferas* (you have nothing to allege) for ἀλλ'οὐκ ἂν ἔχοις, which does not state the object; *effusas tanto numero* (spread out in such great number), which elaborates on the Greek participle κεχυμένους (spread out); *hoc e filiis solatium* (this comfort derived from his sons), which establishes the context of παραμυθία (comfort).[30] In these cases Erasmus added what was needed to complete the sense, to clarify the meaning, or to satisfy the rules of Latin grammar.

It is proof of Erasmus' remarkable talent and industry that he could produce a translation of this quality after only four years of study undertaken in difficult circumstances, without a proper supply of texts, without regular professional supervision, and during an unsettling period that saw several changes of residence. Erasmus himself did not cite extenuating circumstances when he invited his patron Ruistre's judgment, nor did he have need to do so. Commenting on his working methods he explained: 'I have followed Cicero's old rule; in translation I thought it my duty to weigh the meaning, not the words. However, as an apprentice-translator I have preferred to err on the side of accuracy rather than of boldness. But others must judge the success of my efforts.'[31] Ruistre was well pleased with Erasmus' work and rewarded him with a dinner and ten gold pieces; modern readers, too, will applaud Erasmus' success in producing this elegant translation which gives Libanius' rhetorical exercises their proper Latin guise.

Erasmus' reference to Cicero's 'rule' echoes a passage in Jerome's letters with which he was no doubt familiar. Defending himself against accusations that his version of a letter by Epiphanius was biased and inaccurate, Jerome rejected literal translation as being a form of κακοζηλία, slavish imitation.[32] In support of his views he quoted Cicero's remarks on his translations of Demosthenes and Aischines: 'I have not turned them into Latin as a translator, but as an orator, adapting the words to our own usage in phrase, structure, and figure. There was no need here to render the text word for word, rather I preserved the general style and force of the words; for I thought the reader should *not count the words, but weigh their meaning.*'[33] The key phrase of this passage which is quoted by Jerome to counter Pammachius' criticism is repeated by Erasmus to characterize his own approach to translation.

In voting for a liberal translation Erasmus broke away from the medieval ideal of the *fidus interpres* who would render every word of the original text and keep close to its grammatical structure. Instead he followed a tradition popularized by the Italian humanists.

The expression *fidus interpres* was coined by Horace in the *Ars poetica* (133–4), where it is used in a disparaging sense: to achieve a name of his own an author must not copy the ideas of Greek writers; he must rise above slavish imitation. In the Middle Ages, however, when scholars focused on biblical translation, it was considered a sacred duty to be a *fidus interpres*. Thus Boethius, and in his wake John Scotus Erigena, defended this role on the basis that in translating the Bible 'one must not write for rhetorical appeal, but express the unadulterated truth.' In approaching this task a scholar must take care not to exceed his mandate which was to be 'a translator ... not a commentator.'[34] When the first generation of Italian humanists began to translate secular Greek literature into Latin, they waived the medieval rule which was based on religious scruples. In a letter to Antonio Loschi dating from 1392 Coluccio Salutati expressed the new (or rather, revived) Ciceronian ideal: 'I want you to consider the content, not the words.'[35] While it was acknowledged that special considerations applied to biblical translations,[36] Italian humanists generally followed the Ciceronian precept that one should not 'count the words but weigh their meaning.'[37]

Erasmus was acquainted with the works of at least two of the advocates of liberal translation: Lorenzo Valla and Leonardo Bruni.[38] In the preface to his translation of Demosthenes' *Pro Ctesiphonte*, Lorenzo Valla lays down a number of principles of successful translation that are manifest in Erasmus' versions: the translator must demonstrate rhetorical skills; Greek has a greater range of expressions and grammatical structures than Latin and the translator must therefore have a fertile and creative mind to discover suitable equivalent modes of expression. 'Often the Greek character of speech must be abandoned and a new figure of speech must be created and devised.'[39] Bruni, who was moved by his critics to defend his methods of translation in a treatise *De interpretatione recta* (ca 1420), insisted that even when a literal translation was required the evocative quality and the full meaning of individual words and phrases must be preserved. Ideally the content should be complimented by the appropriate rhetorical form: 'the meaning should not suffer through lack of words, the words themselves should not suffer from a lack of neatness or rhetorical style.'[40] Faced with the dilemma of choosing between an exact transference of linguistic devices from the source into the receptor language and their approximate representation by equivalence, Erasmus, after some vacillation, favoured the liberal approach. Even in his earliest translations he did not hesitate to depart from the Greek text for the sake of purity and clarity, a tendency which was increased in later years by a desire to adapt pagan teaching to the contingencies of a Christian life.

Erasmus remained in Louvain until the autumn of 1504. During his stay, he not only completed the Libanius versions, but also began work on a translation of Euripides' *Hecuba*, as he reported in his first catalogue of works: 'Some years before going to Italy when I was residing at Louvain [ie between 1502 and 1504], I translated Euripides' *Hecuba* for the sake of practising my Greek since there was no teacher available.'[41] He recounted the circumstances in similar terms in a letter to John Choler in 1535, saying that he translated Euripides to improve his linguistic skills, since he could not obtain professional instruction, 'for in this part of my studies I have been completely αὐτοδίδακτος, self-taught.' Describing his working method, he admitted that he wrote the translation in a desultory manner, sometimes dashing off a hundred verses at a time.[42]

The famous fifth-century playwright whom Erasmus chose for this exercise in translation had gained both fame and notoriety in his own time. The moral scepticism displayed in his dramatic dialogue scandalized Greek audiences, but the masterful portrayal of characters, the dialectical acumen, and the style of the dialogues, which cleverly concealed the poet's artifice, won him universal recognition and account for his abiding success with later generations.

Several circumstances combined to stimulate Erasmus' interest in translating Euripides. From a letter to Bensrott in 1501 we know that he had an (unspecified) text in his possession; the publication of the Aldine editio princeps in 1503 may have renewed his interest in the author.[43] Another incentive may have been his discovery of Filelfo's translation of the prologue to *Hecuba*, a version which he considered a challenge to do better.[44] Finally, he was encouraged in his enterprise by Jean Desmarais, orator at the university of Louvain, in whose house he was staying at the time.[45] Thus he went to work on a task which no humanist before him had accomplished: the task of translating a complete tragedy in verse.[46]

During a second visit to England in 1506 Erasmus presented a manuscript copy of the completed version to William Warham. The archbishop rewarded his efforts with a modest sum of money, and Grocyn, who had encouraged Erasmus to dedicate the work to this patron, suggested, perhaps jokingly, that the reward was kept small because it was common practice for authors to present the same literary gift to more than one patron. Angered by these aspersions on his integrity, Erasmus prepared a second translation, a version of Euripides' *Iphigenia in Aulis*, dedicating it to Warham as well.[47]

Both translations were published almost immediately by Bade (Paris, September 1506). The edition sold well, but was so 'chock-full of errors'[48] that Erasmus, dissatisfied with Bade's services and having more ambitious plans for the future, approached Aldo Manuzio and proposed a revised edition. Uncertain how his request would be received by the famous printer, he was at pains to offer attractive terms. Not only would he supply the copy free of charge, he was also willing to take a number of books on commission.[49] Aldo agreed to print the translations, and a subsequent exchange of letters shows Erasmus concerned with points of revision and emendation, politely soliciting Aldo's advice on variants in readings and giving him a free hand in correcting obvious errors.[50] Further revisions *ex autoris recognitione* were undertaken by Froben in his editions of 1518, 1524, and 1530.

In the dedicatory letter to William Warham, Erasmus explained that he embarked on the translations in preparation for greater tasks. He had made similar remarks about the Libanius translation, but was now more specific about his long-range goals: no doubt Euripides was superior to Libanius in his power of expression, no doubt he posed a greater challenge to the translator, but like the sophist he treated of secular topics. Erasmus had his sights set on more exalted goals, the translation and interpretation of scriptural texts. For this reason he spoke humbly of his task even though it was a serious scholarly enterprise, belittled its importance, and called it a mere rehearsal, a trial piece to perfect his techniques before embarking on a task too sacred for experiments. 'Euripides,' he said 'was hard enough to afford me good practice, but any mistake I made would be at the cost of my intellectual reputation alone, causing no harm to Holy Writ.'[51]

Erasmus' remarks seem calculated to slight Euripides and to gainsay his merits, but the value judgment is only relative, indicating his ranking of ecclesiastical above secular literature. Among secular authors, however, Euripides held a high place in Erasmus' opinion. He persevered in the task of translating the plays in spite of the many problems he encountered and pressed on, inspired by the poet's brilliant style and powerful argumentation.[52] Erasmus had critical words only for the choric parts of the play, but this was a reservation he extended to classical drama in general. 'Through excessive striving for novelty of utterance,' he wrote, 'the authors destroyed clarity of expression, and in the hunt for marvellous verbal effects their sense of reality suffered.'[53] Erasmus disapproved of such deliberate obscurity. The annoyance it caused him surfaced in his remarks on the genesis of the translation. He listed as factors contributing to his difficulties the corrupt text, the lack of commentaries, the range of Greek words which required great versatility from the translator, and to cap it all, 'the choruses, which are so obscure, because of some sort of deliberate artifice, that they need an Oedipus, or Delian prophet, rather than a commentator.'[54] The remarkably accurate translation which Erasmus produced seems to belie this expression of impatience. Indeed, he was now drawing back from his earlier, liberal, position on translation, taking a somewhat sterner view of the translator's task, promising 'as far as possible to reproduce the shape and, as it were, the contours of the Greek poems, striving *to render verse for verse and almost word for word* [my italics], and everywhere trying zealously to adapt the force and effect of the meaning to Latin ears, with all fidelity.'[55] In doing so he held out against the temptation to reshape the material before him and rejected the alternative method open to the translator of verse, that of metempsychosis, the recreation or transfusion of a poem into the corresponding genre of the recipient language. Defining the translator's role in narrower terms than before, Erasmus refused to create a Latin tragedy in the style of a Seneca and insisted on transferring the meaning in a form that reflected the stylistic peculiarities of the original: 'I have chosen to reproduce the concise clarity and neatness of my original rather than the pomposity that does not belong to it and in which I take little pleasure in any case.'[56]

As for Euripides' metrical pattern, Erasmus made an attempt to preserve it as much as possible in the *Hecuba*, but simplified his approach in the *Iphigenia*, explaining to Aldo Manuzio: 'when I saw that neither Horace in his lyric verse nor Seneca in tragedy imitated the great confusion or freedom (whichever it is), I thought it foolish for me to try to do so amidst all the difficulties I had to face. Accordingly I was content with somewhat fewer metrical patterns.'[57] He repeated this explanation in the preface addressed to Warham, adopting a more apologetic tone: 'I have to some extent reduced the metrical diversity and licence of the choric parts, hoping that scholars would take my difficulties into account and pardon me for this.'[58] No doubt the difficulties mentioned played a major role in Erasmus' decision to follow a pattern of his own choice, but technical problems were not the only factors involved. A translator's pledge of loyalty to his original entails necessarily an act of self-denial and it seems that Erasmus' aversion to the extravagance and concomitant obscurity of the choral parts made such a commitment and the ensuing abnegation of critical rights unbearable. It was therefore as much an emotional as a practical decision to deviate from the original form, which was alien to his spirit, and to impose a new form that was more congenial to his own taste. In fact, Erasmus declared that in any future translations of tragedies he would no longer feel bound by the restrictions normally placed on a translator and would alter not only the form but also the content of the choruses, replacing them with 'some commonplace or deviating into some agreeable digression, rather than wasting effort upon what Horace calls "melodious trifles."'[59] This rather bold plan was never put into practice, however, and thus the modern reader is deprived of an interesting literary experiment: the joining of creative powers to produce a classical dialogue with Renaissance lyrics.

The gradual relaxation of self-imposed rules which character-izes Erasmus' treatment of metre in the *Hecuba* and *Iphigenia* respectively is evident also from his graduated pronouncements on principles of translation. In the preface to his Libanius translations he had explained that he was following Cicero's advice in considering the meaning rather than the words of the Greek text. Nevertheless he committed himself to a certain degree of accuracy. He reiterated this pledge in the preface to *Hecuba*, promising once again 'to run aground occasionally through hugging the shore, rather than to suffer shipwreck and be left swimming in the ocean';[60] indeed, he now applied even stricter standards of accuracy than before, retracting his declaration of allegiance to Cicero and commenting instead: 'I do not fully share the freedom in translating authors that Cicero both allows others and (I should almost say excessively) practises himself.'[61] Com-mitted to producing a faithful version, he refused to facilitate his task by styling his work a 'paraphrase,' a label which he considered a sign of cowardice, a shirking of responsibilities, and a cover-up for ignorance.[62] In the *Iphigenia*, however, we notice a return to the liberal position coupled with an emancipation from the novice status. Newly confident in his abilities, Erasmus abandoned the primary, self-seeking goal of exhibiting his skills and turned outwards to face his audience's needs. Acknowledging the reader's twin expectations of enlightenment and entertainment, he stated in the preface *Ad lectorem*: 'I have given up some of the old attention to exactitude and paid somewhat more regard to attractiveness and clarity.'[63] He indicated that he was now granting himself more freedom than in earlier works and had ventured to translate more expansively, though still 'in such a way as in no degree to fall short of a translator's duty to convey the meaning.'[64]

Let us now turn to the text of his translation to consider if the execution of the task bears out the translator's intentions. True to the statement that he would not produce a Roman tragedy, but follow the stylistic peculiarities of the original, Erasmus refrained from borrowing heavily from the Latin poets. There are some reminiscences of Virgil and Horace, a few parallels with Seneca, and one or two rare words taken from Prudentius,[65] but on the whole the translation is Erasmus' own creation,[66] or rather recreation, of Euripides' language.

The promised accuracy and fidelity to the original are fully realized in the *Hecuba*, which is close to the Greek text even in quantitative terms: 1378 Latin lines for 1295 Greek ones. Indeed, Erasmus steered a careful course between literal and servile translation: there are few omissions and relatively few expansions. The latter are rarely the result of whim, of a subjective delight in *copia*, or an inability to devise a translation close to the Greek wording. They usually reflect Erasmus' consideration for Latin idiom and represent his effort to avoid obscurity.

The following examples will illustrate the various means employed by Erasmus to achieve clarity: adaption, circumlocution, and expansion. Small liberties are indicative of Erasmus' finely tuned ear. In line 96 (Eur 87), for instance, θείαν Ἑλένου ψυχάν (the divine soul of Helenus) is rendered into Latin by an apposition in the ablative, *divina Helenum mente*; in line 786 (Eur 748) the Greek phrase εἰς ταὐτὸν ἥκεις (you join me) is replaced by the corresponding Latin idiom *mecum facis*. In lines 378–81 (Eur 345) Erasmus shows a good feeling for Latin composition as well as for the mythological dimension of the Greek phrase θάρσει, πέφευγας τὸν ἐμὸν ἱκέσιον Δία (take heart, in my case you are safe from the suppliants' god, Zeus) which is translated expansively as

Animo bono sis iubeo, meque nuntia
scito quod ad me pertinebit, te fore
in tuto et effugisse, si quos supplices
curat favens aequusque respicit, Iovem.

The circumlocution *animo bono sis* (I ask you to be of good
cheer) is adopted for idiomatic reasons; the double translation of
πέφευγας (you have escaped) by *te fore in tuto et effugisse* (that you
will be safe and have escaped), and the expression *meque nuntia
scito* (know, for I announce it) which is merely implied in the
Greek direct command, are added flourish; the phrase *quod ad me
pertinebit* (as far as I am concerned) renders adequately the
succinct ἐμόν, which is not simply possessive but, as Erasmus
perceived, restrictive; the clause *si quos supplices curat favens
aequusque respicit* (if he has any care for suppliants and regards
them with favour and fairness) is added to explain the function of
Zeus expressed by the epithet ἱκέσιος (protector of suppliants).

In other cases stylistic or metrical reasons may have been the
main consideration prompting Erasmus to adopt a circuitous
translation. In lines 34–5 (Eur 32), αἰωρούμενος (suspended) is
translated twice: once by *supernis sedibus* (in their heavenly
abodes) and again by *superaque in aura* (in the upper air). In lines
1011–12, the repetition *nec licet confidere, confidere inquam non licet*
(cannot trust, must not trust, I say), though not exactly corresponding to the Greek structure, has the same emphatic effect as
the fourfold negation οὐκ... οὐδέν... οὔτ'... οὔτ' in Euripides 956–7.

In lines 273–5 (Eur 248) a succinct πολλῶν λόγων εὑρήμαθ',
ὥστε μὴ θανεῖν (devising many speeches to avoid my death) is
expanded to accommodate all nuances of εὑρήματα:

Quo me necis subducerem periculo
omneis vafer tum comminiscebar dolos,
cunctasque pariter persuadendi vias.

The Erasmian version means: 'to escape the danger of death,
cunningly I devised all kinds of tricks together with all methods of
persuasion.'

The translation of lines 886–7 (Eur 846–7), which was revised
in 1518, affords an interesting example of the gradual transition
from a literal to a free translation. The original version runs

Mirum est ut omnes res cadant mortalibus,
moderantur ipsa et fata leges ac regunt

Wonderful it is how all things come to pass for mortals, and laws govern and guide the very fates.

This corresponds to the Greek in meaning as well as in structure:

Δεινόν γε, θνητοῖς ὡς ἅπαντα συμπίτνει
καὶ τὰς ἀνάγκας οἱ νόμοι διώρισαν

The Latin verses were replaced in the 1518 edition by

Mirum est profecto ut incidant mortalibus
praefixa certis cuncta fatis legibus,

a reasonably accurate rendition of the Greek meaning, and surely more elegant and appealing than the wording of the first edition, but a step removed from the original.

As projected by Erasmus in his preface (Ep 198), instances of free translation are both more numerous and more far-reaching in his *Iphigenia* than in the *Hecuba*. Two examples from the former play will illustrate how Erasmus, on granting himself greater freedom, achieved a poetic flavour which may have been difficult to attain through a literal translation. The first example is the passage in lines 2199–2209 (Eur 1528–31).

Da victorem Agamemnonem
victrice cum caterva
pulcherrimum triumphum
in Graeciam referre
laeta vincientem
inclytae tibi tempora
victoriae corona
laude parta nomini
quod usque vivat et quod
nullis senescat umquam
intercidatve seculis

Grant to the victor Agamemnon and his victorious troop a marvellous triumph to carry back to Greece, weaving around your glad temples a garland of splendid glory, fame won for your name, that it may live forever and never wane or die in centuries to come.

The corresponding Greek lines are

'Αγαμέμνονά τε λόγχαις
'Ελλάδι κλεινότατον στέφανον
δὸς ἀμφὶ κάρα θ'ἑὸν
κλέος ἀείμνηστον ἀμφιθεῖναι

Grant that Agamemnon may wreathe his head with a
garland of undying fame, a glorious crown for the spearmen
of Hellas.

In this passage Erasmus not only supplies several epithets of
his own (*victorem, victrice, pulcherrimam, laeta*), which are suitable
in context but have no direct equivalent in the Greek, but also
develops the meaning of Euripides' line 1530 to the point of
removing any parallel with the original. Moreover, he expands
the adjective ἀείμνηστον (remembered for ever) into the tripartite
clause of lines 2207–9.

Lines 1467–75 (Eur 1055–8) show similar characteristics:

> Deinde per aequora candiduli
> leveque per spatium sabuli
> aequoreo sata turba sene
> nexa sororibus e decies
> quinque, agitatque rotatque choros
> orbibus innumeris
> molliculo pede replicitis
> connubium levibus
> concelebrans choreis

Then by the sea, by the smooth expanse of glistening sand,
the numerous children born to the old man of the sea, a band
of ten times five sisters, dances and twirls in countless
circles, entwining their supple legs, celebrating the wedding with lighthearted dance.

The corresponding lines in Euripides are:

> Παρὰ δὲ λευκοφαῆ ψάμαθον
> εἰλισσόμεναι κύλια
> πεντήκοντα κόραι γάμους
> Νηρέως ἐχόρευσαν

Then along the glistening sand, forming a circle, the fifty
daughters of Nereus danced the wedding dance.

Again Erasmus supplied a number of epithets: *innumeris, molliculo, levibus;* he expanded the verb ἐχόρευσαν (they danced) into two synonymous expressions, *agitat choros* and *concelebrans choreis;* he added some phrases that have no parallel in the original, *leveque per spatium, molliculo pede;* and in the poetic tradition replaced the numeral 'fifty' by the circuitous 'ten times five' and the name of Nereus by the circumlocution *senex aequoreus* (old man of the sea). These phrases may not correspond to the Greek, but they certainly have a natural connection with the contents and heighten the effect of the pictures presented in the original composition.

In both passages Erasmus succeeded in crafting melodious lyrics, though at the price of diverging significantly from the original. The lines cited are extreme examples of the method of expansion, but amplification on a more modest scale is a common device in Erasmus' *Iphigenia* and one that helped to swell the number of lines to 2346, 717 more than Euripides' 1629.

We may now turn to the question of Erasmus' understanding of Euripides' difficult syntax. Of the two plays, the *Hecuba* is the more conscientious translation, with only one or two obvious mistakes in the final version and a very small number of unresolved difficulties or obscure renditions. The text of the *Iphigenia*, perhaps in proportion to its greater length, contains more serious lapses and awkward constructions. The following passages will serve as examples.

Confusion reigns in lines 942–5 (Eur 691–3):

> Quin hisce rebus sponte me potius mea
> insuper et istam parituram existima,
> ita ut nihil monitore te fuerit opus
> cum rite mihi sit elocanda filia

Therefore rather think in this matter that I will obey on my own account, and she too, so that I had no need of your counsel when I have to lead forth my daughter, according to custom.

Euripides' lines run:

> οὐχ ὧδ᾽ ἀσύνετός εἰμι· πείσεσθαι δέ
> κ᾽αὐτὴν δόκει τάδ᾽, ὥστε μή σε νουθετεῖν,
> ὅταν σὺν ὑμεναίοισιν ἐξάγω κόρην

I am not so insensitive. Consider that I will suffer the same
grief when I lead out the maiden with wedding song – so I
do not chide you ...

In this passage – as Waszink points out in his note *ad locum* –
Erasmus has difficulties with πείσεσθαι, the future infinitive of
πάσχειν (to suffer), which he translates as *parituram* (about to
obey, the meaning of πείθω in the middle or passive voice),
referring αὐτήν in line 692 to Iphigenia. The confusion spreads to
the next line where Erasmus takes σε to be the subject of the
infinitive, although with a correct interpretation of the first part
the context suggests a sympathetic 'so that I do not chide you'
rather than Erasmus' arrogant 'so that I have no need of your
counsel.'

In the 1524 edition Erasmus replaced lines 942–3 with one line,
quin ista et ultro me suasuram puta (therefore think that I shall
counsel this myself), which puts another misinterpretation in the
place of the first one: 'counsel,' ie 'persuade,' is the meaning of
πείθω in the active voice.

In another passage Erasmus' translation is perhaps not entirely
wrong, but at any rate misleading. *Colloquar diu / Troia reversus* in
lines 2343–2 does not yield the complete import of the Greek
words in Euripides 1625–6: χρόνιά γε τ'ἀμά σοι προσφθέγματα /
Τροίηθεν ἔσται (it will be a long time until I speak to you again, on
my return from Troy). The Latin lines could easily be understood
to mean: 'On my return from Troy we shall have a long
conversation.'

Factual misinterpretations occur at lines 953 and 811. In the
first case Euripides (line 699) speaks of 'Oenone's lord' (Οἰνώνης
πρόμον). Erasmus, mistaking Oenone, an archaic name for the
island Aegina, for the name of the well-known nymph, translated: *Oenones patrem* (Oenone's father). In the second case (line
611) Erasmus rendered φερνάς (dowry) as *comites dotaleis* (dower-
slaves), which is not borne out by the Greek. Waszink in his
commentary *ad locum* suggests that the dowry consisted of a
number of objects to be carried from the wagon into the palace by
male attendants. Such divergences and misinterpretations will
seem venial, however, if we consider that Erasmus composed the
translation 'without anyone giving me explanations, without the
aid of any commentaries,'[67] relying on his own knowledge of
history and mythology.

Having pointed out some of the defects in Erasmus' translation it is only fair to give examples also of his impressive skills. The following passages will demonstrate Erasmus' ability to stay close to the Greek original without sacrificing natural diction in Latin.

> Vae liberis meis
> vae patribus ac solo
> quod fumo mihi concidit
> Marteque captum et exustum
> ab Argivis. At ipsa in
> tellure vocabor externa
> serva, Asiam fugiens
> Europae famulantem,
> mutans morte faces thalami   (*Hecuba* lines 516–24)

The corresponding Greek lines (Eur 475–83) run:

> ὤμοι τεκέων ἐμῶν
> ὤμοι πατέρων χθονός θ'
> ἃ καπνῷ κατερείπεται
> τυφομένα δορίκτητος
> Ἀργείων; ἐγὼ δ'ἐν ξεί –
> νᾳ χθονὶ δὴ κέκλημαι
> δούλα λιποῦσ' Ἀσίαν
> Εὐρώπας θεράπναν
> ἀλλάξασ' Ἅιδα θαλάμους

If we analyse Erasmus' poetical devices and isolate the parts that produce this harmonious whole, we find the doleful cries ὤμοι, ὤμοι which introduce Euripides' dirge paralleled by Erasmus' *vae, vae* at the beginning of lines 516–17; in the following two lines the Greek is rendered word for word, and in the last three lines the position of keywords is preserved, with each Latin line beginning in a manner corresponding to the Greek: *serva* translating δούλα, *Europae* Εὐρώπας, and *mutans* ἀλλάξας.

A second passage manifesting Erasmus' superb skills as a translator comes from *Iphigenia* lines 1826–33 (Eur 1283–90):

> Proh, proh, tectae nivibus rupes
> atque Idaei Phrygiae montes,
> in quos olim Priamus tenerum
> pater infantem exposuit matre

procul amotum, uti morte periret;
Paridem, quem quondam urbis Phrygiae
Idaeum plebes Idaeum
dixit, dixit

Euripides' lines read:

ἰώ, ἰώ.
νιφόβολον Φρυγῶν νάπος Ἴδας τ'
ὄρεα, Πρίαμος ὅθι ποτὲ βρέφος ἁπαλὸν ἔβαλε
ματρὸς ἀποπρὸ νοσφίσας
ἐπὶ μόρῳ θανατόεντι
Πάριν, ὃς Ἰδαῖος
Ἰδαῖος ἐλέγετ' ἐλέγετ' ἐν Φρυγῶν πόλει.

Again the dirges begin with parallel expressions of grief, *proh,
proh* translating ἰώ, ἰώ; the Greek composite adjective νιφόβολον
(snow-covered) needed a circumlocution, *tectae nivibus rupes*
(crags covered with snow); the word ματρός, in the initial
position in Greek, is given an equally prominent position in Latin
at the end of line 1829; and the repetition of words in Euripides'
lines 1789–90 is preserved in Erasmus' *Idaeum ... Idaeum, dixit,
dixit.*

Both passages cited are virtuoso translations. Naturally flowing, animated, and melodious, they correspond line for line with
the Greek and closely parallel it in sentence structure and
imagery. The resulting verses convey the sense, force, and spirit
of the Greek, yet have the clarity and ease of an original
composition.

The merits of Erasmus' translation are evident to the reader,
but its fine qualities become even more apparent when his version
is placed beside a comparable piece of work. We have already
mentioned the existence of a translation by Filelfo and Erasmus'
familiarity with this work. It may therefore not be out of place to
put Erasmus' achievements into perspective by comparing the
two translations. To do so in a satisfactory manner it will be best to
quote the text of Filelfo's prologue to *Hecuba* and Erasmus'
corresponding lines in full. Filelfo's version runs as follows:[68]

Adsum relictis promptuariis latebris
portisque tenebrarum, colitur ubi deum
a regia procul Erebi, Cisseide
Pollidorus Hecuba natus ac Priamo patre;

qui urbem periculum cum teneret Argolici　　　　5
Martis ruinam veritus ad Thracis hospitam
Polymestoris me clanculum misit domum.
Is Cherrhonesiam optimam glebam serens
populum ferocem vi regit; mecum simul
multum dat auri pater ut esset filiis　　　　10
quo viverent, satis superstitibus suis.
Atqui Priamidum quoniam eram natu minimus
me misit extra genitor; arma nam iuveni
hastamque ferre non potis eram brachio.
Dum Troia rectis moenibus, dum turribus　　　　15
infracta staret, dum meus frater fere
Hector secundis utitur belli viribus
paternus hospes me quasi quem surculum
alebat augens miserum; at ubi patria periit
Hectorque frater et patris lares penitus　　　　20
cecidere, Pyrrhi et ipse procubuit manu
iugulatus impii pater ad aram deae,
occidit auri gratia me hospes miserum;
corpusque pelago tradidit, quo aurum domi
haberet ipse: iaceo nunc in littoribus,　　　　25
nunc in salo ponti sine sepulchro et flaetibus,
quam plurimis vorticibus actus fluctuum
nunc corpore relicto feror matrem ob Hecubam
iam tertium pendens diem, quantum mea
in Cherrhonesio solo ex Troia veniens　　　　30
adest misera parens; quietem Danai agunt
in littore omnes huius agri Threici
cum navibus simul suis; nam Peleo
satus parente super suo visus tumulo
omnis Achilles copias classis Danaae　　　　35
quae palmulas domum maritimas dirigunt
remoratur unus victimam suo dari
ac praemium Polyxenam tumulo petens
meam sororem, consecuturus quidem,
nec enim ab amicis non fert quem petit iugulum.　40
Fatum sororem cogit hocce die perimi,
cadavera duo filium tuebitur
mater duorum illius infauste ac meum;
namque ut sepulchrum rite contingat mihi,
servae offeram me pedibus in maris salo.　　　　45

Manes enim exoravi, ut in matris manus
cadam, ac sepeliar; quod itaque optavi mihi,
erit: anui matri eminus cedam meae.
Haec ex tabernaculo Agamemnonis venit
mei metu visi: o parens quae regia   50
genita domo servis; ut infoelix agis
quantum prius numquam; deus enim te bona
ex ante fortuna malis conficit varians.

Erasmus' translation runs as follows:[69]

Adsum profectus e profundis manibus
noctisque portis, caeca qua silentium
ab arce porro coelitum sita est domus,
Polydorus, Hecuba natus e Cisseide
Priamoque patre. Quem simul cepit timor,   5
ne Marte Graio Phrygia caderent moenia,
me furtim alendum Troico emisit solo
ad hospitam Polymestoris Thracis domum,
qui Cherronesi fertilem glebam colens
armis ferocem Martiis gentem regit.   10
Multumque mecum clanculum misit pater
aurum, urbis ut si concidissent moenia,
ne victu egerent liberi superstites.
Eram natu Priamidum novissimus,
atque hac foras potissimum me gratia   15
submisit, ut cui nec ferundae lanceae
et ad arma nondum tenera sufficeret manus.
Sed usque, donec recta stabant Pergama, et
nondum iacebant Ilii turres soli,
Hectorque frater Marte florebat meus,   20
bene apud tyrannum Thraca, patrium hospitem
crescens alebar plantulae in modum miser.
At ubi interivit Troia, simul et Hectoris
vita, ac penates concidere patrii,
deumque ad aras ipse procubuit sacras   25
mactante Achillis prole sanguinaria,
mox me paternus amicus auri gratia
miserum trucidat ac trucidatum salo
exponit, aurum ut ipse possideat sibi.
Nunc super harena littoris iaceo, hactenus   30
aestu per aequor huc et huc vectus vago

inhumatus, indefletus; at iam promico
charam ob parentem, corpore relicto meo.
Mihi supernis devaganti sedibus
superaque in aura, sol agitur hic tertius;   35
itidemque misera tertium mater diem
extorris amplis Ilii pomoeriis
in hac adest tellure Cherronesia.
Cunctique Danai littore hoc in Thracio
classem tenentes ociosi desident;   40
namque e sepulchro visus Aeacides suo
Argivum Achilles tenuit omnem exercitum
remum ad penates dirigentem ponticum.
Meam is sororem postulat Polyxenam
tumulo cupitum honorem et inferias suo   45
dari, ac feret: neque enim hoc sinent frustrarier
honore amici: deinde decretum iubet
fatale, caedi hac luce germanam meam.
Geminaeque prolis gemina mater funera
cernet, meumque et lachrumandae virginis;   50
nam quo sepulchri munus assequar mihi
ancillae in undis memet offeram ad pedes,
venia impetrata diis ab inferis, uti
tumulo potiar in matris incidens manus,
itaque (quod ad me) quicquid optavi, assequar.   55
At anu a parente paululum abscedam; haec quidem
iam regis e tentorio profert pedem
Agamemnonis, pavefacta de spectro mei.
O mater, huc, proh! Viva pervenisti uti
prognata cum sis regiis e stemmatis,   60
indigna ferres servitutis pondera,
tam afflicta nunc et misera, quam florens eras
quondam, ac beata. Te aliquis evertit deus
felicitatis pristinae invertens vices
bonaque anteacta paribus exaequans malis.   65

It should be stated from the outset that both versions are free of
serious mistakes and misinterpretations, but that Filelfo is the less
conscientious of the translators in that he does not always render
the full meaning of the Greek. Both men are, of course, placed
under the constraint of metrical requirements, but Filelfo chooses
to retrench, whereas Erasmus prefers to be expansive. For ex-

ample, Filelfo's phrase *promptuariis latebris* (the innermost recesses) in line 1 does not convey the full import of νεκρῶν κευθμῶνα (the innermost chamber of the dead); the translation of line 7 is also deficient, omitting the Greek phrase Τρωικῆς χθονός (the Trojan earth). In lines 9–10 the translation *mecum simul ... dat* skims over the content of σὺν ἐμοί ... ἐκπέμπει λάθρᾳ ... εἴ ποτ' Ἰλίου τείχη πέσοι instead of reiterating what is essentially a review of lines 5–7. In line 23 *hospes* is short an adjective; Euripides says ξένος πατρῷος (host on my father's side); in line 52 the phrase *quantum prius numquam* (as never before) only implies the converse of *infelix* (unhappy), whereas Euripides states the condition expressly: ὅσονπερ εὖ ποτ' ... (how happy once ...).

In each of these cases Erasmus provides an adequate rendition: *profundis manibus, multumque ... moenia, paternus amicus, quam florens ...* (lines 1, 11–12, 27, 62). Unlike Filelfo he solves the problem of scansion by amplifying the Greek text to create the appropriate metrical pattern. Thus he adds phrases and modifiers: *caeca ... ab arce* in lines 2–3, *huc et huc* in line 31, *supernis ... sedibus* in line 34, *amplis* in line 37, *indigna ... pondera* in line 61, and *ac beata* in line 63. The additions are suitable interpretations of the context, but have no literal basis in the Greek.

Similarities between the two translations are very limited. Both begin with the emphatic *adsum*; an inaccuracy in Filelfo's line 9 (Erasmus line 10) is remarkable in that it is shared by the two men and therefore likely adopted by Erasmus: both translate φίλιππον (fond of horses) as *ferocem* (savage); it also appears that the diminutive *clanculum* (Filelfo line 7, Erasmus line 11) was copied by the latter. At this point the parallels end. As might be expected from Erasmus' uncomplimentary remarks about Filelfo's version, he now presented an independent translation.

In composition and choice of words Erasmus' superiority is undeniable. He observes the poetic tradition by using alliteration (*Argivum Achilles, tyrannum Thraca, aestu per aequor, vectus vago, invertens vices*), the familiar patterns of noun and modifying adjective (a b A B and variations, less frequently A b a B), archaic forms (*prognata, frustrarier, lacrumandae*), and words rarely employed in prose (*coelites, Graius, germana, vices*). By comparison Filelfo's vocabulary and word patterns seem plain and unadorned. Moreover, his phrases have a prosaic emphasis on verbs. Expressions like *multum dat auri; me ... misit domum; me misit extra; quod ...*

optavi mihi, erit focus the reader's attention on the verb, a tendency which is generally avoided in Latin poetry. In addition, Filelfo's positioning of initial words and their correlation with the remaining line is often artless. He tends to begin verses somewhat abruptly: for example, with a demonstrative pronoun (*haec* in line 49, *is* in line 8, which is extremely rare in poetry) or an isolated noun (cf lines 17, 41), without attempting to pair it with the following word – the most frequent pattern in Latin poetry – or to place it within a clearly recognizable structural set. Erasmus, on the other hand, offers smooth transitions, frequently using connectives like *et, sed, at, nam,* and enclitic *-que* (lines 2, 11, 15, 20, 25, etc). Moreover, he generally balances his verses in the approved poetic fashion, interlocking beginning and end by formal or conceptual similarities: *Hector ... meus, remum ... ponticum, meam ... Polyxenam, tumulo ... suo, indigna ... pondera.*

A comparison between two couplets will illustrate the difference in effect between Erasmus' deliberate artifice and Filelfo's somewhat casual construction. In lines 49–50 (Filelfo 42–3) Erasmus employs parallel construction (*prolis/mater*) and repetition (*geminae ... gemina*), poetic vocabulary (*proles*), archaism (*lachrumandae*), and metonymy ('funeral' for 'corpses'; compare Filelfo's literal *cadavera*). Filelfo uses the poetic adjective *infaustus* and the contracted genitive *filium*; he too employs repetition (*duo, duorum*), but he destroys its effect by placing the words in different lines and fitting them with different case endings. Moreover, his word order is unattractive, especially in the second line, which has a jumbled aspect.

Lines 15–17 (Filelfo 13–14) exemplify the two men's attention to fidelity. Filelfo is content to produce an accurate and scanning version of Euripides' lines

> ὑπεξέπεμψεν· οὔτε γὰρ φέρειν ὅπλα
> οὔτ᾽ ἔγχος οἷός τ᾽ ἦν νέῳ βραχίονι.

Erasmus is concerned with rendering the contents in the exalted style proper to the genre. He diverges from the Greek with calculated results. His *foras submisit* (secretly sent forth) is not only more elegant than Filelfo's *extra misit* (sent out), it also takes into consideration the meaning of the Greek prefix ὑπ-, which implies secrecy. Similarly, Erasmus' phrases *cui nec lanceae ferundae* (who could not carry spears) and *ad arma nondum sufficeret* (not yet strong enough for arms) have a more suitably dramatic tone than Filelfo's plain construction *potis esse* (to be able) with the infinitive. Finally, *tenera manus* (tender arms) is poetically more effective than Filelfo's literal *iuvenis bracchium* (young man's arm). The various devices employed by Erasmus are representative of his approach in general. He takes liberties, but he does so for the sake of stylistic improvement. This justification cannot always be advanced on Filelfo's behalf. One suspects that his free translations stem from a lack of resourcefulness rather than an active purpose. Consider for instance his line 40, in which he does not preserve the future tense of the original, although this is obviously an important element in a prediction. Moreover, by using the word *iugulum* (slaughter) he continues the line of thought introduced in the preceding verses, but fails to render the meaning of ἀδώρητος (giftless). In line 50 *mei metu visi* (fearful of my apparition) is both contrived and deficient. There is no attempt to parallel the Greek phrase φάντασμα δειμαίνουσ' ἐμόν (fearing my ghost – Eur 54). In each case Erasmus' translation is more felicitous, though less economical with words. His lines 46–7 preserve the future tense and incorporate the meaning of ἀδώρητος (giftless) in the verb *frustrarier* (to be deprived). In line 58 *spectro* (spectre) is preferable to Filelfo's *visi* because it contains the appropriate notion of a ghostly appearance.

This is not to say, however, that Filelfo failed to give a demonstration of his famous rhetorical skills. He offers proof of his dexterity in lines 15–17. The verses have a suitable plaintive character and appropriate epic tone. Lines 50–1, though presenting a somewhat retrenched version of Euripides' lines 55–6 (ὦ μῆτερ ἥτις ἐκ τυραννικῶν δόμων / δούλειον ἦμαρ εἶδες), can hold their own against the rival lines 59–61. Filelfo's concise translation contains all the essential elements of the Greek phrase; Erasmus' version, on the other hand, seems unnecessarily inflated.

In many cases, however, Erasmus' expanded translations are satisfying because he compensates for taking liberties by offering good poetry. Line 31, for instance (adrift on the tide, carried this way and that through the ocean), goes beyond the Greek (Eur 29) πολλοῖς διαύλοις κυμάτων φορούμενος (adrift on the rise and fall of many a wave), but it is no doubt an attractive line of poetry with its alliteration *vectus vago* and the disjunctive *huc et huc* which conveys the motion of the tide.

In some cases Erasmus succeeds extremely well in reproducing the Greek structure: Euripides' symmetrical ἄκλαυστος, ἄταφος (tearless, tombless – Eur 30) is nicely paralleled by Erasmus' *inhumatus, indefletus* (line 32). Filelfo, by contrast, offers an uninspired *sine sepulchro et flaetibus* (without grave and tears – line 26). Erasmus' *sol agitur tertius* (it was daylight for the third time) in line 35 introduces a suitable parallel image to Euripides' τρι ταῖον ... φέγγος (daylight for the third time – Eur 32), whereas Filelfo's prosaic *tertium ... diem* (third day) in line 29 sounds stale.

In these cases the reader must applaud Erasmus' skills – in the examples previously cited he will tolerate the free translation on the grounds that the end justifies the means. And he will be the more inclined to award the victory in this competition to Erasmus as the section discussed represents the sum of Filelfo's efforts, while it constitutes only a small part of Erasmus' enterprise, that of translating a complete play. We may therefore accept his verdict that the Italian humanist's translation left something to be desired[70] and conclude that he responded successfully to the challenge it presented.

THREE

A Friendly Competition:
More's and Erasmus' Translations
from Lucian

꙰

Erasmus' second visit to England in 1505/6, which he undertook on another invitation by Lord Mountjoy 'seconded by the entire scholarly community,'[1] proved a fertile period for his work as a translator. Not only did he produce a polished version of the *Hecuba* and a draft version of the *Iphigenia*, he also embarked on a series of translations from Lucian. the prolific author of essays and dialogues who flourished at the turn of the second century AD.[2]

Lucian's works, lost after the fall of Rome and unknown to the medieval West, were reintroduced to Italy in the first quarter of the fifteenth century. They gained instant popularity with Renaissance readers, who admired the author's rhetorical skills, quick wit, and biting irony, as well as the great variety of his subjects, which appealed to every taste. The editio princeps of Lucian's works was published in Florence in 1496, and by 1500 a considerable number of Latin translations were in circulation. Rudolf Agricola was among the early translators, but it was only after 1503, the year in which the Aldine edition appeared, that Lucian's works became widely available and popular north of the Alps.[3]

Erasmus was familiar with the author as early as 1499, when he cited his *Vera Historia* in a letter to Lord Mountjoy.[4] In his first catalogue of works he recalled an early attempt to translate one of Lucian's works, the mock-tragedy *Podagra*, a project which he abandoned, however, discouraged by the difficulty of rendering the numerous compound epithets into Latin.[5] In England he made a second, successful attempt at translating Lucian, this time joining forces with Thomas More. We cannot say with certainty which of the friends suggested the idea of collaborating on a translation and which of them proposed the subject matter. Most likely the two men developed a taste for Lucian's writings independently, and on discovering their preference made a joint decision to translate some of his essays and dialogues.[6]

The collaborators were well matched. Both Erasmus and More had begun their Greek studies a few years earlier. Like Cato the Censor, whose example Erasmus invoked,[7] they started late in life and achieved proficiency through industry and determination. Moreover, both men had literary avocations, but stood at the beginning of their publishing careers and were eager to give further proof of their abilities. To produce material suitable for publication may well have been on their minds when they embarked on the translations, though it was perhaps not the primary objective of their undertaking. Other practical considerations – the translations served as handy literary presents for Erasmus' English friends – may have been an afterthought.[8] Most likely, it was the desire to share an agreeable experience that first suggested the idea of a joint project. Moreover, pleasure could be combined with utility, for translating Lucian was not only an enjoyable pastime, but also a profitable exercise, an opportunity to practise linguistic skills.

Erasmus, who regarded Lucian as an excellent model of style, combining the virtues of 'invention, clarity, smoothness, and variation,' had already recommended his writings to students of Greek by including him in the canon of classical authors given in De ratione studii.[9] This endorsement of Lucian for school purposes was, however, not universally accepted. Some teachers shied away from presenting to their charges an author whose scepticism and irreverence were notorious. Indeed, the choice of author was an embarrassment to More in his later career and offered Erasmus' adversaries a handle for criticism.[10] Erasmus, however, continued to defend Lucian, applauding his diatribes against superstition, hypocrisy, and learned pretence, and praising his shrewd wit and well-aimed satire in portraying men's follies. He insisted that his writings offered an effective cure for the ills besieging his contemporaries. In the dedicatory prefaces to several of the translations Erasmus therefore pointed out that Lucian could not only raise 'a civilized laugh,' but also provoke thought and encourage moral judgment.[11] In Erasmus' opinion there was among Lucian's dialogues none 'more useful or pleasant' than *Timon*; none more appealing than *Gallus*, that 'floweret' from the garden of the Muses which not only pleased 'by its novelty and its rich colouring, beautiful shape, and fragrant scent' but also benefited the reader because it secreted 'a juice of sovereign potency for health.' *Pseudomantis*, too, had this twofold advantage: it could be read 'with a certain amount of profit, but also with a vast degree of pleasure.'[12]

The result of More's and Erasmus' enterprise were four translations by the former, five by the latter. They both tried their hand at Lucian's *Tyrannicida* and composed a retort to it. Their combined works were published by Bade in Paris (November 1506) under the title *Luciani opuscula*.

In the collection of Erasmus' translations the dedication of *Toxaris* bears the earliest date; it was presented as a New Year's gift to the bishop of Winchester, Richard Foxe, on 1 January 1506.[13] *Tyrannicida* with its corresponding declamation was dedicated to Richard Whitford, a mutual friend of More and Erasmus;[14] *Timon* to Thomas Ruthall, then chancellor of Cambridge University;[15] *Gallus* to Christopher Urswick, at the time warden of King's Hall, Cambridge;[16] and *De mercede conductis* to Jean Desmarais, orator at the University of Louvain, in whose house Erasmus had lived in 1504.[17] With the exception of Ep 187,[18] the dedicatory letters date from the spring or summer of 1506. Some of them were composed in England, others in Paris, where Erasmus supervised the printing of the translations.[19]

One of the translations completed by Erasmus in 1506 had an unusual publishing history: the text of the *Longaevi* was missing for some time and resurfaced only in 1513, when it was published by Erasmus' former servant-pupil, Germain Dreux, with somewhat ambiguous credits. In his first catalogue of works Erasmus recalled that he had dictated the translation to Dreux in Paris and alleged that the young man had absconded with the manuscript. Dreux, who never claimed to be the author of the translation, insisted, however, that he had found it among Lord Mountjoy's papers when he was employed as the latter's secretary. And there the matter rested.[20]

In the fall of 1506 Erasmus left Paris for Italy, accompanying the sons of the physician Boerio and acting as their tutor for one year. The journey was the realization of a long-standing desire of Erasmus' to visit the centre of Renaissance learning. Some ten years earlier he had expected to travel to Italy in the company of

Antoon of Bergen, but when the bishop's prospects for a cardinalate waned, the journey was cancelled.[21] Erasmus, for his part, did not abandon hopes of crossing the Alps. In 1498/9 he was investigating the possibility of studying in Bologna,[22] but when he was unable to make the necessary financial arrangements, he was obliged to defer his plans once more. It was not until 1506 that an opportunity presented itself to realize his dream.

The first stop on Erasmus' journey was Turin, where he was granted the degree of a doctor of theology; next, he moved on to Bologna where he was to supervise the studies of his young charges. On his arrival he found the city preparing for siege and was obliged to return temporarily to Florence, where he composed another set of translations from Lucian, either for the benefit of his students or simply to occupy his time profitably 'rather than do nothing.'[23] The second instalment of translations included *Dialogi mortuorum* ix, xi, xiii, xxi, xxiv–xxvi, *Dialogi deorum* xii, xix, xxi, xxiv, *Dialogi nautarum* i, *Hercules, Eunuchus, De sacrificiis,* and *Convivium.* The whole collection, which was dedicated to Jérôme Busleyden, the well-known patron of arts,[24] was dispatched to Paris posthaste, but did not reach Bade in time to be included in the *Luciani opuscula.*[25]

The journey to Italy introduced Erasmus to a new circle of humanists. Settling in Bologna, he formed a lasting friendship with Paolo Bombace, professor of Latin and Greek at the university, and the first of several contacts Erasmus made with classical scholars.[26] A fuller opportunity to engage in a fruitful dialogue with fellow scholars presented itself to Erasmus during his prolonged stay in Aldo Manuzio's household.

Erasmus had approached the famous Venice printer, asking him to publish a revised edition of the *Adagiorum Collectanea* and the Euripides translations.[27] His proposal was accepted, and after his contract with the Boerio brothers ended Erasmus moved to Venice to see the new editions through the press. He was received into the Aldine household and, during the following months, came into contact with such eminent scholars as the young prodigy Girolamo Aleandro and the native Greeks Musurus, Lascaris, and Demetrius Ducas. As a member of this learned society Erasmus not only profited from the experience of his colleagues, but also gained access to Greek manuscripts which he used to enrich the new edition of his proverbs, now on the stocks.[28]

Venice provided Erasmus with a suitable setting for his research in Greek literature. Greek studies had been established in the city under the auspices of Ermolao Barbaro and Giorgio Valla. Aldo Manuzio was pursuing an ambitious publishing program and had assembled a distinguished group of scholarly collaborators to aid him in the selection, preparation, and editing of Greek texts. Sharing quarters with these learned men from January to September of 1508, Erasmus was no doubt able to improve his knowledge of Greek and was perhaps even bound by the constitution of the Aldine academy, which required its members to speak Greek during their sessions.[29] While Erasmus satirized the physical arrangements of the Aldine household in the colloquy *Opulentia sordida*, he also paid tribute to Aldo's enterprise in the adage *Festina lente* (2.1.1), mentioning in particular the active support he had received from Lascaris and Musurus. The latter, who taught Greek in nearby Padua, impressed Erasmus with his profound learning and his upright character. During his subsequent stay in Padua, between September and December of 1508, Erasmus heard, and no doubt profited by, the Cretan scholar's lectures. In fact, Musurus may have been his single most important source of information, providing much of the material used for the enriched edition of the *Adages*.

For some time now Erasmus had felt dissatisfaction with the *Adagiorum Collectanea* in their original form: 'They now begin to seem to me thin and poor, when I have at last read the Greek authors through.' In the preface to the enlarged edition of 1508 Erasmus again noted that the original collection had been made 'without much care, and also with hardly any Greek books to refer to.'[30] For the present edition Erasmus had consulted a large number of Greek sources. Moreover – and this is of topical interest to us – he set out to supply translations for his quotations. He adopted this policy for the benefit of his readers, although there was no precedent for the practice in classical literature and although he felt that the translations encumbered the text. Explaining his decision in the preface, he wrote: 'I have made allowance for the times in which we live. If only a knowledge of Greek literature might be so widely diffused that my tedious task in translating could deservedly be censured as superfluous! But for some reason we are inclined to be a little slothful in our approach to an activity as beneficial as this, and we are quicker to welcome any faint shadow of learning than that without which scholarship cannot exist at all, and upon which alone the integrity of all its branches depends.'[31]

Erasmus went to considerable lengths to provide this new 'reader's service,' which he carried on in subsequent editions. Sampling the first five hundred adages in their final form,[32] we find that he faithfully translated all but the most obvious phrases; that is, he allowed book titles to stand in the original form,[33] trusted the reader to recognize recurring proverbial expressions without further help,[34] and left untouched Greek terms occurring within quotations from Cicero.[35] He also assumed that the reader was familiar with and able to identify in Greek fount such loan-words as εἴδωλα, ἀρχέτυπον, ἐπιεικής (images, model, fair) and such technical terms from the spheres of grammar and rhetoric as παροιμία, εἰρωνικῶς, συμβολικῶς, πρότασις, ἐπίτασις, καταστροφή (proverb, ironically, metaphorically, protasis, epitasis, denouement).[36]

Because his quotations from Greek literature were numerous, Erasmus had set himself a cumbersome task. He discharged his duties conscientiously, but with an understandable lack of enthusiasm, producing for the most part prosaic and utilitarian versions. Since his purpose was not to demonstrate his skills as a translator but to instruct the reader, he allowed himself a fair amount of freedom, often expanding on the Greek text to clarify the point of the quotation. For example, in explaining the proverb 'The bull goes into the woods' he translated σύννομος (sharing the pasture) as *communibus cum vaccis pascuis uti* (using the pastures together with cows); discussing the proverbial 'God from the machine' he translated ἐξ μηχανῆς (from the machine) as *quasi deo quopiam tragico qui repente solet ostendi* (like some god in a tragedy who appears suddenly, as is the custom).[37] In a small number of cases Erasmus was content to paraphrase prose passages, reviewing only the main points; in translating poetry, however, he often resorted to a loose and expansive version of the Greek.[38] He tried to preserve the metre of the original, but warned his readers: 'I have ... made use of a licence employed by the authors from whom I borrowed the quotations, as for example an anapaest in the even-numbered feet of an Aristophanic trimeter, a tapering effect in the Homeric hexameter, a lengthening of a final syllable in the first arsis of any foot, and anything else of the kind.'[39]

Erasmus' amplified and expanded translations are usually effective, but occasionally uninspired. For example, the lines

> ... noxa est, vicinus ut improbus, ingens,
> contra ita maxima commoditas, si commodus adsit.
> Deest honor huic, bona quem vicinia deficit ...[40]

are an artless translation of Hesiod's famous dictum

> Πῆμα κακὸς γείτων ὅσσον τ'ἀγαθὸς μέγ' ὄνειαρ,
> ἔμμορέ τοι τιμῆς, ὅς τ'ἔμμορε γείτονος ἐσθλοῦ

A bad neighbour is as great an evil as a good one is a blessing; he who is granted a good neighbour is granted value as well.

On the other hand, the well-known Homeric passage describing Hermes putting on his sandals and taking up his wand has Virgilian qualities in Erasmus' translation:

> Mox ubi iam pedibus talaria subdidit aurea
> pulchraque et ambrosiam spirantia, quae simul illum
> aera per liquidum, simul ampla per aequora vasta
> telluris venti flatu comitante, ferebant;
> tum virgam capit, hac demulcet lumina somno
> quorumcumque velit, somnum quoque pellit eadem.[41]

The translations of prose passages are generally more faithful and accurate, but occasionally Erasmus diverges from the Greek to strike a familiar note or to offer an expression that has a proverbial ring in Latin. Thus he translates Plato's νήπιον παθόντα γνῶναι (the fool learns by suffering) as ... stultus post accepta mala sapias, modelled after the common Latin form of the proverb, malo accepto stultus sapit.[42] Similarly, he offers a neat rhyme, quae nocent docent for ἐξ ὧν ἔπαθες, ἔμαθες (you learn from your sufferings).[43] In some cases Erasmus plays censor to the Greekless reader, discreetly suppressing the meanings of καπρᾶν and ἱππομανεῖν (to want the goat, to be mad for horses), which refers to bestiality, and refusing to translate an explicit passage from Aristophanes' Plutus, explaining that he would gladly provide this service 'if the lines were as proper as they are elegant.'[44]

On occasion Erasmus used another author's translation rather than composing his own. At 204c he quotes Aratus in the classical translation of Germanicus Caesar; at 79B he gives Argyropoulos' rendition of some lines from Empedocles 'because at first I despaired of devising a suitable translation.'[45] Empedocles' words are:

Γαίῃ μὲν γὰρ γαῖαν ὀπώπαμεν, ὕδατι δ᾽ὕδωρ,
αἰθέρι δ᾽αἰθέρα δῖον, ἀτὰρ πυρὶ πῦρ ἀΐδηλον,
στοργῇ δὲ στοργήν, νεῖκος δέ τε νείκει λυγρῷ

These Argyropoulos translated, not without skill:

Terram nam terra, lympha cognoscimus aquam,
aetheraque aethere, sane ignis dignoscitur igni,
sic et amore amor, ac tristi discordia lite.

At length Erasmus supplied his own translation, 'on the request of friends,' setting it beside Argyropoulos' lines and adding a critical review. He noted that Argyropoulos had 'rendered ὀπώπαμεν [we recognize] by two verbs, *cognoscimus* and *dignoscitur* [we recognize, it is discerned], and omitted two epithets, δῖον and ἀΐδηλον'; also, that he had twice 'spoiled the elegant effect of repetition' in the original by using different words for 'water' (*lympha, aquam*) and 'discord' (*discordia, lite*),[46] 'not to mention the awkward composition *terram nam*.' He also reproached Argyropoulos for adding the 'adverb *sane* of his own accord'.

Having analysed his precursor's translation in such critical fashion, Erasmus then proceeded to defend his own version, which runs:

Terra quidem terra sentitur, lymphaque lympha,
aetherque aethere purus, at igni noxius ignis,
dulcis amore amor, atque odio funesta simultas.

On his own translation Erasmus commented: 'I have added an epithet to *amor* [love], but one that the poet would have added himself if the metrical rules had allowed it, just as he adds to its opposite νείκει [strife] his own adjective λυγρῷ [grievous].' He concluded this comparison, which of course was favourable to his own translation, with the disclaimer: 'I am not saying this to criticize a man who has done great service to belles-lettres, but to develop the critical faculties of young men for whose benefit this is mainly written.' Despite this qualification, which is obviously designed to soften his criticism, the remarks must have impressed his readers as pedantic and narrow-minded, especially coming from a translator who generally took equal or greater liberties in his own versions.[47]

Unfortunately there are not only inaccuracies but also errors in Erasmus' translations; for example at 99B where ὥσπερ με γαλῆν κρέα κλέψασαν / τηροῦσιν ἔχοντ᾽ ὀβελίσκους is translated *nunc uti feli rapta carne / observant gestantem verua*, referring ἔχοντ᾽ (which elides the dual ending) to the wrong antecedent; at 26F where the verb is associated with the wrong subject to produce a senseless clause; and at 88A where the Greek text is emended unnecessarily to support a mistranslation.[48]

These lapses did not escape the critical reader's eye. Paolo Bombace reported to Erasmus from Padua that his old mentor Musurus had expressed a low opinion of the translations in the 1508 edition of the *Adages*.[49] This criticism did not discourage Erasmus, however, and he continued to provide translations for later, expanded and enlarged, editions, noting 'that many readers had felt the want of it.'[50] It seems therefore that the majority of his readers were less critical than Musurus – perhaps also less qualified to pass judgment – and depended on Erasmus' translations for a better understanding of the context.

After the printing of the *Adages* had been completed, Erasmus left Venice for Padua. By the close of the year 1508 his funds were running low, however, and he was obliged to take on a pupil, Alexander Stewart, the illegitimate son of James, king of Scotland.[51] Together they travelled on to Siena and Rome, but when Erasmus' obligations terminated and he received news of Henry VIII's accession to the throne along with invitations and promises of financial support from Warham and Mountjoy, he decided to return to England, leaving Rome in the summer of 1509.

On his arrival in London, Erasmus stayed first at Lord Mountjoy's house, then in More's household, where he shared quarters with Andrea Ammonio, the king's secretary. This congenial company may have induced Erasmus to take up translating Lucian once more,[52] though financial necessity commended it as well. At least one of the pieces composed at this time, the translation of *Icaromenippus*, was prepared in hopes of a reward;[53] *Saturnalia* was dedicated to Warham, a man whose generosity Erasmus had experienced before and from whom he was expecting much at the time; and *Astrologia* was written for Boerio, Erasmus' recent employer.[54] The new set of translations included, in addition to the three pieces just mentioned, *Cronosolon, Epistolae Saturnales, De luctu,* and *Abdicatus.* These Erasmus sent to Bade on 14 May 1512, but owing to circumstances that remain unclear they were not printed until June 1514.[55] A revised edition of the complete collection of translations, for which Erasmus himself provided the copy, was produced by Froben in 1516 and reprinted with further emendations in 1521 and 1534.

The translations were well received. Their popularity only waned when 'a knowledge of the Greek tongue began to be widely shared, as happened most successfully in our part of the world,' as Erasmus commented in his catalogue of works, adding in true scholarly fashion that he had hoped for, and indeed welcomed, this development.[56]

Let us now turn to the substance of Erasmus' translations and consider them from the craftsman's point of view, using for our examination a selection of compositions: *Timon* and *Tyrannicida* from the first instalment of translations; *Icaromenippus* from the second set; and *Longaevi,* the last piece to be published in the collection.

One of the difficulties to which Erasmus himself drew attention was the variety of compound adjectives and nouns occurring in Lucian. Erasmus dealt with them in more than one fashion. In a considerable number of cases, especially where the scenario suggested theatrical language, he chose to render them by an equivalent Latin compound, usually of his own coinage, but modelled on the practice of Roman poets.[57] Thus Jupiter's epithets ἐρίγδουπος, νεφεληγερέτα, βαρύβρομος, ὑψιβρεμέτης, ὑψιπέτης (loud-thundering, cloud-gathering, low-thundering, thundering-on-high, and flying-on-high) are translated by the equally sonorous *grandistrepis, nubicogis, gravifremus, altifremus,* and *altivolus.*[58] At the other end of the scale we find some almost disappointing simplifications: πολυθρύλητος (literally, 'much-spoken-of') translated as *nobilis* (famous); τὸ φιλόκαινον (literally, 'that which is innovation-loving') by the noun *contentio* (contentiousness); and πολυπραγμοσύνη (meddlesomeness), a complex term both in structure and in meaning, by the simple Latin word *curiositas.*[59] Occasionally Erasmus used the conservative approach of separating Greek compound words into their component parts, rendering them into Latin by a conjunction of verb and object, noun and objective genitive, or similar construction. Examples of this practice can be found in *Timon* where the phrases *cuncta necantis* (killing everything) and *ad facinora fervidus* (keen on deeds) translate πανδαμάτωρ and θερμουργός (all-destroying, impetuous creator), where *numquam non querulus* (always complaining) stands for μεμψίμοιρος (fault-finding) and *Gigantumque extinctor et Titanum victor* (exterminator of giants and victor over Titans) for Γιγαντολέτωρ καὶ Τιτανοκράτωρ (giant-killer and Titan-crusher).[60] Similarly we find, in the *Icaromenippus*, the expression *quae nullis notis deprehendi possent* (which cannot be discovered by any signs) for ἀτέκμαρτος (without a mark) and *arcem in edito sitam* (citadel set on high) for ἀκρόπολις (city-on-high).[61] In the *Longaevi* Μονόφθαλμος, title of king Antigonos the One-eyed, is rendered at one point literally as *unoculus*, at another point as *luscus*, which is more common in Latin but does not offer the etymological parallel.[62] The technical term ἱερογραμματεῖς, on the other hand, is latinized and subsequently explained: *id est, sacri scribae* (that is, sacred scribes).[63]

Latinization is a common device in Erasmus' translations, as we have seen.[64] In the *Timon* we find *zelotypus, sycophanta, prooemia* (jealous, denouncer, preludes), which were introduced into Latin in classical times, as well as *thynnus, stigmaticus*, and *cophinus*, (tunny, pointed, box), which belong to post-classical usage.[65] Some loan-words received Erasmus' special attention. Thus we find *misanthropus* with the added explanation *id est, hominum osor* (that is, a hater of men).[66] Δημοκρατία, usually employed in its latinized form, *democratia*,[67] is rendered by a paraphrase, *popularis administratio* (government by the people)[68] and συκοφαντεῖν (to be a slanderer), a common loan-word in the Renaissance and one that the reader could be expected to recognize in transliteration, is translated by a Latin phrase proper, *calumniis uti* (to employ slander).[69]

A remarkable feature in Erasmus' translations is his knack for rendering interjections and exclamations by an appropriate Latin idiom. In the *Tyrannicida* the interjection ὦ οὗτος, which is akin to our colloquial address 'man,' is represented by *quaeso te* (I'm asking you) or *vir egregie* (excellent sir).[70] In the *Icaromenippus* we find πῶς ἔφησθα (What did you say? How is that?) translated as *quid audio* (What do I hear?); πῶς λέγεις (What are you saying?) as *istud qui fieri potuit* (How could this be?); and νὴ τὴν Νύκτα (By

Night, indeed!) as *testis est mihi Nox ipsa* (Night herself is my witness!).[71] As in all of Erasmus' translations we find a good number of free versions, many chosen for idiomatic reasons; for example, ἀπορῶσι (literally, 'they are at an impasse') is translated as *haerent* (they are stuck); the concise Greek ὥσπερ εἰς ἀκροβολισμὸν (like a skirmish) requires an expansive phrase *iaculorum in morem ... ex edito loco devolantium* (in the manner of javelins ... hurtling down from above); and a similarly curt expression, πάντως ὁ κεραυνὸς ἦν (literally, 'all thunder and lightning he was'), appears in its Latin form as *perpetuo fulmen erat* (always a thunderbolt he was).[72] Another idiomatic phrase, ἀγχόνη γὰρ ἂν τὸ πρᾶγμα γένοιτο αὐτοῖς, is skilfully translated by an appropriate Latin construction, *nam illa res illos praefocaverit*, both meaning 'this put a stranglehold on them.'[73] Not all of these free renditions are felicitous, however: the succinct πρὸ τῆς κυματωγῆς (beyond the breakers) is translated in rather heavy-handed fashion as *ultra solum fluctibus opertum* (beyond the ground that is covered by the waves).[74]

In a number of cases Erasmus converts Greek participles into Latin relative clauses, an expedient solution when the Latin verb lacks the corresponding voice or tense. Thus ἀδικοῦντες (being unjust) becomes *qui flagitia committunt* (who commit acts of injustice); οἱ παρηβηκότες (those past the prime) *qui aetate defecti sunt* (who have lost their youth); αὐτοὺς ζηλοτυποῦντες (being their own rivals) *qui ipsi quidem sibi subtraherent* (who detract from their own worth).[75]

In typical Ciceronian fashion Erasmus introduces two Latin expressions for one Greek word, translating ἀσεβής (impious) as *impia nefariaque* (impious and nefarious); ἐπιτριβῆναι (to be crushed) as *dirumpi ... conficique* (to be crushed and overpowered); εὔζωνος (well-equipped) as *probe succincta atque expedita* (well-equipped and outfitted); χαλεπώτερος (rather difficult to deal with) as *acerbius etiam et atrociore* (rather harsh and unyielding).[76]

Erasmus' rhetorical skills manifest themselves especially in the great variety of expressions used in the *Longaevi* where examples of long life invariably terminate in the phrase 'died in the nth year.' Surpassing even the inventiveness of Lucian, Erasmus produced the following phrases for the verb 'to die': *diem obire, vitam finire, diem extremum obire, vitae diem obire, perire, interire, sublatum esse, supremum vitae diem obire*.[77] In the same essay another catchword, δίαιτα (diet), is represented in Latin by a wider range of expressions: *pura vitae ratio, vitae moderatio, victus temperies.*[78]

We have already observed that Erasmus sometimes acts as an interpreter, adding explanatory phrases for the reader's benefit. He did so in the *Longaevi* to clarify the meaning of *hierogrammates* and in the *Timon* to show the meaning of *misanthropus*. In the latter piece we also find a phrase added to explain the name ἐννεάκρουνος (with nine spouts) referring to a well near Athens; similarly, διφθέρα, a proverbial reference to something rare or obsolete, usually quoted in transliteration as *diphthera*, is here translated *pelleque hircina amictus* (clothed in goatskin).[79]

In some cases Erasmus allowed himself liberties without any obvious need for circumlocution. Εὐδαίμων (fortunate) could presumably be translated by a Latin adjective, but Erasmus preferred the alliterative *cui fortuna faverit* (whom fortune favoured). In another case he made φιάλη (cup) a 'golden cup' (*phialam auream*). Elsewhere he translated a simple Greek οὐ δυνηθέντος (unable) in a rather long-winded fashion as *si voluntati meae facultas defuisset* (if I had been willing, but unable).[80]

In a few instances Erasmus added his own nuance to the Greek text, converting καθεύδεις (you are sleeping) into a somewhat more boorish *stertis* (you are snoring); παρωσάμενοι τῆς τιμῆς (ousted from their place of honour) into a much gentler *abdicantes* (abdicating); ὡς πλησιάσαντας (as if they had approached) into a more forceful *ut qui tetigerint* (as if they had touched); and ἀναγκαῖα (necessary) into a paler *frugifer* (useful).[81]

In some cases Erasmus' divergence from the Greek must be the result of a misinterpretation, error, or variation in reading. At 490:1 *flumen quotidie exundans* (a river flooding every day) is an odd translation for ποταμὸς ἑκάστη σταγών (every drop a river). A misunderstanding is also at the root of the translation given at 498:4–5: *per contumeliam et arrogantiam illi manu iniecta talem reddent* (taking hold of him in their insolence and arrogance, they will make him such a man), where the Greek says 'giving him into the hands of Pride and Insolence' (Ὕβρει καὶ Τύφῳ ἐγχειρίσας). Another awkward translation occurs at 497:13, where a difficult Greek clause, ἢ ἐμὲ προέσθαι ὑπομείνειεν ἄν (rather than putting up with losing me) is rendered by *quam uti me compellatur reiicere* (rather than being forced to reject me).

Misinterpretations in the *Timon* account for the translation of πεδότριψ (wearing out chains) as *paedagogus* (teacher) and ἐπὶ ταύτην τὴν ἐσχατιάν (towards this outlying farm) as *ad extrema redactus consilia* (come to his wits's end).[82] This particular Greek phrase occurs twice more in the text, and in each case Erasmus offers a different translation, obviously because he was uncertain of its exact meaning. Thus he experimented with *extrema via* (end of the road) at 497:25 and finally struck the correct note with *semotum ... agrum* (remote farm) at 500:27–8.

A number of errors remained undetected, but others were emended in the edition of 1514. At 493:4–5, for example, the first edition had a wrong translation, *ab observantissimis molestissimisque paedagogis ali ad usuram et rationem* (to be brought up by the strictest and most bothersome teachers for a life of usury and counting money), whereas the text of 1514 reads correctly (but with omission of one Greek adjective): *a scelestissimis educari paedagogis, foenore et computo* (being brought up by the worst teachers, Usury and Profit).[83] Similarly the word Ἀνάκειον, originally translated as *lacunar* (ceiling) at 492:10, was correctly identified in the 1514 edition as the temple of Castor and Pollux. Ἐμβρόντητοι (dumbfounded), originally translated as *intonantes* (thundering) at 489:3 was corrected to read *attoniti* (thunder-struck). At 493:33 the tense was corrected, and at 495:28 the erroneous *licet ipse quoque eadem quandoque expertus in sese* (having perhaps had the same experience) was emended to read *experiens num sibi quoque similia liceant* (testing if he too was allowed similar things) for ἀποπειρώμενος εἰ καὶ αὐτῷ τὰ τοιαῦτα ἔξεστιν. Two omissions are caught, at 495:21–2 (*seque mutuum intuentes*) and at 496:34 (*ac versicoloribus amictus*), but two others, neither of them significant, remain at 500:37 (πρὸς αὐτούς) and 492:28 (ἄθλιοι).

In the *Tyrannicida*, too, a number of errors were corrected in later editions; for instance, at 507:13 *nolens*, missing in the 1506 version, was added in the 1514 edition; at 508:36 a missing sequence of rhetorical questions was restored.

The majority of emendations undertaken in later editions were, however, not corrections of mistakes, but stylistic changes. Words or phrases were replaced, reflecting Erasmus' inclination at the time of revision. Thus emendations in the *Timon* include suppositions like *bonitatem* for *benignitatem* at 492:4, *iactato* for *vibrato* at 490:35, *tetigerint* for *attigerint* at 497:17, but also changes of somewhat greater significance and more definite purpose; for example, at 498:32, where a Homeric line, originally translated in prose, is given metric form, or at 496:24–5, where a more poetic version is introduced for the original translation of a quotation from Theognis.[84] The replacement of a clumsy phrase, *obsequium dare*, in the 1506 edition of *Tyrannicida* by *obsecundare* in 1514 is a definite improvement, as is the parallel construction achieved by changing the conjunctions *et tamen – iam tum* to *iam tum – iam tum*.[85] On the other hand, the correct comparative *magis idoneum* (more suitable, translating ἑτοιμότερον) is in fact changed to the less accurate, though perhaps smoother, positive *paratum*.[86]

The *Longaevi*, which lack revision by the author, contain a disproportionately larger number of errors. Apart from several omissions,[87] two, albeit venial, misinterpretations occur because of Erasmus' unfamiliarity with the historical or geographical details involved: at 625:39–40 Erasmus speaks of a ruler, *Manon dictus Aromatarii filius* (Manon, called son of Aromatarius), while the Greek refers to the 'spice-bearing region of Omania' (Ὁμάνων τῆς ἀρωματοφόρον βασιλεύσας). At 627:13 the technical term διδάξας τὴν Πυτίνην (producing the play 'The Flask') is rendered by Erasmus as *pugilarem artem didicisset* (he learned the art of boxing). In the introductory paragraph, at 623:9–10 a sentence appears in truncated form. Lucian says: 'The gods ordered me, a man of letters, to present you with something from my workshop'; Erasmus produces a garbled version, speaking of gods ordering the author 'to send some literary offering to a man of letters.' Similarly awry is the translation of Lucian's clause 'observing your similarity to octogenarians in condition and fortune' as 'considering an imitation of the octogenarian's conditions and fortune' at 624:15–16.[88]

Drawing a comparison between the translations reviewed, whose composition spans a period of seven years, we note very little variation in Erasmus' level of competence or in his methods of translation. It seems that his skills were well developed when the first translation from Lucian was completed, and that the degree of fidelity and accuracy in subsequent versions depended mainly on the circumstances surrounding the composition, not on the author's linguistic progress. Certain methods and characteristics are well formed and present in all pieces: an energetic and creative effort to match Lucian's lively diction; a leaning toward *copia* expressed in the use of variation, repetition, and circumlocution; a didactic vein leading to the addition of explanatory phrases; and a desire, matched by dexterity, to transform Greek idioms into naturally flowing Latin phrases.

The forensic display speech, *Tyrannicida*, which was translated by both Erasmus and More, affords the reader an exceptional chance to gauge Erasmus' linguistic and methodological skills and to measure them against those of a worthy rival. We were able to draw a comparison between parallel versions on a previous occasion, setting Erasmus' prologue to *Hecuba* against Filelfo's translation, but in that case the competitors were from different eras and cultural backgrounds. Thomas More and Erasmus, on the other hand, are more closely matched rivals. They belong to the same generation of northern humanists for whom a knowledge of Greek came late and represented a difficult attainment. Moreover, the two men composed their respective translations in the spirit of a friendly competition, thus inviting the reader to act as an arbiter. A critical examination of the two versions, which were intended as a 'contest of wits,'[89] will therefore be more relevant than a comparison between the works of incidental rivals.

The two men's levels of proficiency in Greek and their skills in Latin composition are fairly balanced. Both present a clear, faithful, and idiomatically correct version of the original, but the reader quickly notices stylistic peculiarities setting the translators apart. Thomas More generally offers a plain and simple translation, following the original in structure and phrasing as far as Latin idiom permits; Erasmus likes to wax eloquent, to elaborate and expand on the original text. This tendency is obvious even in their respective choice of words, with Erasmus showing a notable preference for predicate phrases over simple verbs. Where More uses *inservire* (serve), *gaudere* (enjoy), *parere* (obey), *honorare* (honour), *iudicare* (judge), *mactare* (kill), *mori* (die), and *vivere* (live),[90] Erasmus expresses the same actions or conditions using a composite phrase: *operam commodare* (provide service), *voluptatem capere* (take pleasure), *morem gerere* (indulge his whim), *honorem decreare* (confer honour), *causas agere* (conduct lawsuits), *caedem peragere* (perpetrate a killing), *exire e vita* (depart from life), and *in vita morari* (remain in life).[91] Only the last choice can be justified in other than stylistic terms: the wider context of the passage does indeed suggest the idea of 'going on living,' a sense which is better served by Erasmus' composite predicate than by More's simple verb.

In many instances More gives a plain, almost bare rendition of the Greek, while Erasmus opts for an ornate and elaborate structure. This approach is frequently, but not always, effective. Successfully deployed, Erasmus' circuitous translation gives the text a rhetorical ring. For example, More's phrase *amplius aliquid ... expectabam* (I expected something more) may be a faithful translation, but Erasmus' expanded phrase *amplius quiddam ... me consecuturum arbitrabar* has the exalted tone proper to a declamation.[92] Similarly, *e diverso perpendenti quod publicam libertatem mea caede redempturus essem* (considering on the other hand that I would redeem the people's freedom by my death) has the necessary weighty character, while More's literal translation *propriam tamen caedem communi libertate compensans* (redeeming the public freedom by my own death) has the quiet tone of a statement.[93] In another passage More describes the mortally wounded son of the tyrant in clinical terms as *vix respirantem, lacerum, ac morte plenum* (barely breathing, mangled, and on the point of death), while Erasmus, using more vivid and emotional language, says: *semivivus, sanguinolentum, caede conspersum* (half-dead, blooded, and bespattered with gore).[94] In other cases Erasmus' expanded versions, though good Latin, seem unnecessarily removed from the original. Thus he translates τὰ φανερὰ τοῦ σώματος (the visible parts of the body) as *in his corporis partibus quae conspicuae magis magisque sunt oculis obviae* (in these parts of the body that are more conspicuous and more apt to meet the eye). Here More's simple and faithful translation presents a more satisfactory solution: *in parte corporis conspicua* (in the conspicuous part of the body).[95] Although Erasmus' delight in *copia* contributes to the rhetorical colour of the Latin composition, his translation seems capricious on occasion. Thus he remodels a straightforward transitive verb περιέστησα (I hemmed in), rendering it into Latin as a complex structure: *effeci ut ... circumsisterent* (I brought it about that they hemmed in).[96] In another case he paraphrases the verb ἠδίκει (he acted unjustly) and, choosing the expression *per vim faciebat* (he acted with violence), introduces a specific for a general notion.[97] In a third case he translates φιλότεκνος γὰρ ἐς ὑπερβολήν as *indulgens in filium supra quam credi queat erat* (he was more indulgent towards his son than one could credit)[98] which is not only cacophonous (*queat erat*), but also unnecessarily wordy. In each of the three cases More's plain and literal version appears adequate, and indeed preferable. He translates the above phrases as: *circumsepsi* (I hemmed in), *iniuste fecit* (he acted unjustly), and *in filium propensus supra modum fuit* (he was indulgent towards his son beyond measure).[99]

In his preference for the abundant style Erasmus also employs the familiar device of supplying two Latin terms for one Greek word: *rationem viamque* (mode and manner) for τοῦ τρόπου (mode); *confligendum ac dimicandum* (combat and fight) for ἐπιχειρήσεως (attack); *acerbius etiam atque atrociore ... genere* (harsh and more atrocious) for χαλεπώτερον (harsher).[100] In another mode of expansion he adds explanatory words or interprets the meaning of the Greek rather than restricting himself to the wording of the original. Thus he writes *me quidem imprudentem fecisse* (that I have done this unwittingly), which is the implied meaning of the Greek phrase ὡς ἐγὼ μὲν ἁπλῶς αὐτὸ ἔπραξα (that I have merely done it).[101] Elsewhere he expands on the Greek πάντα οὗτος κατώρθωσεν (he accomplished everything), saying *cuncta quae destinavit peregit* (he accomplished everything he had planned).[102] In a third case Erasmus interprets, or rather, gives a proper Latin turn to, the idiomatic τὰ διὰ μέσου (the intervening actions, literally 'those in the middle'), translating it explicitly as *quae vero ad id conducunt* (the things leading up to it).[103] In each of these cases More offers an adequate literal translation: *me videlicet id fecisse tantum* (indeed, that I have merely done the deed), *is omnia peregit* (he accomplished everything), *media autem omnia* (what happened in between).[104]

In a few cases Erasmus' elaborate versions seem effusive rather than rhetorical; for instance, when he translates οὐ δυνηθέντος (being unable) as *si voluntati meae facultas defuisset* (if I had been willing but unable). More translates the same participle in a straightforward manner as *cum ... ego non potuerim* (while I was unable).[105] Elsewhere Erasmus' expanded phrase seems laboured and affected. He writes: *non censes ea capere oportere quae iis debentur qui beneficio iuverunt?* (Don't you think that they who helped by their good deed ought to receive what is owed them?), whereas More says more economically and elegantly: *indignum benemeritis praemio ducas?* (Do you think him unworthy of the reward for his good deeds?).[106] In another case Erasmus offers a circuitous phrase for the Greek ἰσαρίθμους τοῖς ἀνῃρημένοις (of the same number as those slain), saying *praemia laturum quae numero aequarent eos qui essent interempti* (to receive in future rewards that equal in number those who were killed); More translates the compound adjective more skilfully as *praemia pro peremptorum numero suscepturum* (to receive in future rewards in proportion to the number killed).[107]

Whereas Erasmus tends to be long-winded to a fault, More is inclined towards the other extreme, offering contracted and succinct translations to the point of falling short of the meaning in Greek. Thus he translates νομίζων ἕξειν ἔκδικον with laconic brevity as *ultorem sperans* (hoping for an avenger); Erasmus is more successful in rendering the full impact of the Greek phrase, saying *qui crederem mihi superesse ultorem* (believing that I would leave an avenger).[108] In another case More's curt translation is deficient: he simplifies the phrase οὐδ' εὐκαταγώνιστον (not easily conquered), translating it as *neque facile* (not easy). Erasmus successfully captures the sense of the Greek compound adjective, saying *neque mediocrium virium opus* (the work of no small effort).[109] In a third passage More translates πεπονημένοις (achievements) rather sparingly as *factis* (deeds); Erasmus produces a fuller and more satisfying translation which conveys not only 'action' but also 'effort': *quae virtute confecta sunt* (valorous deeds).[110] More's literal translations can be rather blunt, and on occasion jarring: placing *non* at the beginning of a series of emphatic questions, More preserves the Greek sentence structure in almost servile fashion; Erasmus' classical phrasing, beginning the questions with *nonne*, is preferable.[111] Similarly, More's phrase *securitatem denuntians* (announcing safety) is a barely adequate rendition of θαρρεῖν ἤδη προκηρύττων; Erasmus' translation *bono iam ut animo sint edicens* (telling them to be of good cheer), which supplies the proper Latin idiom to convey the idea contained in the Greek phrase, is smoother to the ear of a Latin reader than More's literal translation.[112]

Of the two friends, More is generally the more accurate translator. There are one or two omissions, but no misinterpretations in his version. Erasmus' translation, on the other hand, contains the usual quota of errors evidencing his working speed and his self-confessed reluctance to proofread. He translates τοσαῦτα (so many) as *tantis* (so great); τοὺς ἐπιβουλεύοντας φοβῶν (terrifying the conspirators) as *insidias formidabat* (he feared conspiracies); τοὺς τυραννουμένους, which in this context has a passive meaning, 'tyrannized,' as *tyrannidem affectantes* (aspiring to tyranny).[113] All of these phrases are translated correctly by More, who writes *tot, insidiatores terrebat,* and *subditos.*[114] In one case Erasmus misinterprets a whole clause, writing *tantum ista ac statuisses praeclarum facinus futurum fuisse videatur* (just to have intended it would have seemed a famous deed), whereas the Greek means 'just to have intended it, even if it had not been successful' (μόνον καὶ τοῦ βουλεύσασθαι ταῦτα, εἰ καὶ μὴ χρηστὸν ἀποβεβήκει). More translates the relevant part of the clause correctly: *etiam si nihil inde boni provenisset* (even if no good had come of it).[115]

In the overall assessment of the translators' merits, the question arises whether they consciously developed the idiosyncracies pointed out in our analysis, using them for the purpose of investing their speaker with character, or employed these devices unwittingly according to each man's natural inclination. To invest the speaker with character is indeed a desirable aim in an original forensic speech. The author of a translation may, however, be expected to reproduce only the ethos and pathos of the original. Our speech is that of a claimant who demands the prize money set out for tyrannicide. Lucian's style is deceptively plain, the rhetorical element of his speech lying in the sophistic mode of reasoning, in the skilful use, or rather abuse, of well-known methods of argumentation. Thomas More, like Lucian, depicts a stubborn but level-headed man who insists on his rights, relying mostly on the persuasiveness of well-rehearsed arguments with an inherent emotional bias; Erasmus has created a verbose and pathetic orator who harangues his audience and assaults their ears with a din of words. Since some of the devices employed by Erasmus are already familiar to the reader and recur in a less obtrusive form throughout his translations, we may conclude that he issued the claimant's plea in a form congenial to his own temperament and that he voted for an emotional appeal rather than plain statements. Erasmus' gushy orator may be a more interesting figure and certainly makes for lively reading, but his character is not rooted in the Greek text, which portrays subtler courtroom manners and a more sedate forensic style. The amusing element of Lucian's epideixis lies in the improbability of the case. In fact, the very earnestness of the speaker contributes to the humour of the situation. Erasmus' buffo version with its comic exaggeration gives the court performance the character of a charade, while More's plain translation preserves some of Lucian's deadpan humour, as he applies grave arguments to a ludicrous business. Both versions demonstrate their authors' rhetorical skills. As for their appeal to Latin readers, the choice between Erasmus' blustering hero and More's shrewd demagogue remains a matter of personal preference.

FOUR

The Cambridge Years:
Plutarch's *Moralia*

※

On the accession of Henry VIII, Erasmus' English friends had urged him to seek the patronage of their new king. Warham promised his personal support, Lord Mountjoy gave a glowing account of the young monarch's generosity: 'Heaven smiles, earth rejoices; all is milk and honey and nectar. Tightfistedness is well and truly banished. Generosity scatters wealth with unstinting hand.'[1] Beguiled by such words, Erasmus left Italy for England. Soon, however, he had cause to regret the move and blamed himself for not recognizing Mountjoy's promises for what they were – flowery rhetoric.[2]

When Erasmus arrived in England in the summer of 1509, More offered him hospitality and Warham remained a reliable patron, but royal support was slow in forthcoming, and soon Erasmus found himself in financial straits. In September of 1511 he moved to Cambridge to take up a teaching position at the university. He lectured on the grammar of Chrysoloras, then switched to Theodore Gaza's grammar, hoping thereby to draw a larger crowd of students.[3] He also undertook to teach theology – 'for the sake of doing some service to learning,' as he told Ammonio, for the pay offered him was unattractive.[4] His pecuniary situation, a recurrent topic in his letters to Ammonio and Colet, became a matter of serious concern to him. The complaints were seasoned with Erasmian wit, but the laughs were sardonic. He joked about his 'Christian poverty,' his sedulous imitation of the philosopher Diogenes, the ill-starred fate which forced him to go 'a-begging publicly in England.'[5] Royal support was now only a distant hope, and Erasmus found himself obliged to take money from his students, accept the generosity of his friends, 'squeeze every penny' from his patrons, and keep away from London for fear of being dunned.[6]

Despite worries about his livelihood, Erasmus remained dedicated to his scholarly work. Theological studies dominated his interests. He prepared himself diligently for his lectures on Jerome, he translated the Mass of St Chrysostom, and he continued collating manuscripts of the New Testament.[7] He also embarked on a translation of St Basil's commentary on Isaiah, sending a sample to John Fisher in hopes of receiving a 'little something by way of emolument for my labours.'[8] The bishop's reaction was discouraging, however. He sent Erasmus only a small gift and let it be known that no more could be expected from him. To add insult to injury, Erasmus heard rumours that Fisher suspected him of 'polishing up a previous version, and not translating from the Greek.'[9]

Although Erasmus devoted most of his attention to theological subjects, he did not completely neglect the classics. It was during the Cambridge years that Erasmus prepared the set of Lucian translations already discussed[10] and began work on Plutarch's *Moralia*.[11] The first century AD philosopher and biographer was a devout and scholarly man. His writings, which were numerous, included rhetorical works, treatises on popular ethics, dialogues on philosophy and religion, antiquarian research, and biographies written in an anecdotal style. His writings were first collected in the thirteenth century.[12] Byzantine scholars introduced Plutarch's works to Italy where his biographies especially enjoyed great popularity. A complete Latin version of the *Vitae* was produced by Campano in 1470, and prior to it, a large number of individual *Lives* had been translated into Latin by such notable scholars as Filelfo, Guarino, and Barbaro. The editio princeps of the *Vitae*, published in Florence in 1517, was soon followed by an Aldine edition (Venice 1519). Of the moral essays, on the other hand, only selected pieces had been translated: *De liberis educandis*, by Guarino in 1411, and *Quod principi deceat ...*, by Rinucci da Castiglione in 1423.[13] The editio princeps of the complete *Moralia*, supervised by Demetrius Ducas, was published by Aldo in 1509.

During his stay in Aldo's house Erasmus had assisted Demetrius Ducas in the preparation of this edition.[14] He was therefore familiar with the text of the Aldina and most likely based his Latin version on it.[15] In the autumn of 1512 he reported to Pieter Gillis that he had 'translated several works of Plutarch' which he intended to send on to Bade.[16] He had, however, expressed certain reservations about the Paris printer: he was slow to publish his translations from Lucian; he could not 'muster enough Greek' for the *Adages*; the Euripides had been full of mistakes.[17] In the end the translations from Plutarch were published by Froben in August 1514.

It remains unclear to what extent Erasmus took an active part in this switch of publishers, whether he had given clear instructions to, or merely acquiesced in the actions of, his agent Franz Birckmann, who took the manuscript of Basel and offered it to Froben.[18] At any rate the year 1514 marks Erasmus' first business transaction with the Basel printer who was to become his principal publisher for the next two decades.

In the late summer of 1514 Erasmus left England, persuaded partly by fear of the plague and partly by his worsening financial situation. After stops in St Omer, Ghent, and Strasbourg, where he was given a distinguished reception by the *sodalitas literaria*, he travelled on to Basel, where he stayed, with interruptions, until May 1516. Erasmus described the scholarly collaborators of the Froben press in enthusiastic terms: 'Beatus Rhenanus, whose unassuming wisdom and keen literary judgment are a great pleasure to me, nor is there anything I enjoy more than his society every day; Gerard Lyster, a physician of no common skill and a good knowledge of Latin, Greek, and Hebrew besides, and a young man born to be my friend: the learned Bruno Amerbach, who also has the three tongues.' His stay in Basel also gave him an opportunity to meet members of the university, in particular Ludwig Baer, 'a man still in the prime of life, but so well-read, of such high character and such wisdom, that I reckon he must bring no common distinction to his native Germany,' and the poet laureate Henricus Glareanus, in whom Erasmus recognized 'a young man of high promise.'[19]

During his stay in Basel the translations from Plutarch were published. The collection consisted of eight pieces: 'How to distinguish a flatterer from a friend,' 'How one can profit from one's enemies,' 'About the preservation of health,' 'That a prince needs knowledge,' 'That it is most necessary for the philosopher to converse with princes,' 'Whether the ills of the souls are more serious than the ills of the body,' 'Whether the saying Λάθε βιώσας is correct,' and 'About the desire for riches.'

The first essay was dedicated to Henry VIII; the second and

third were New Year's presents for John Yonge and Wolsey respectively.[20] The other pieces, which were short – for the most part not exceeding three printed pages – remained without dedications.

Erasmus' hope for a reward from his patrons was, at least for the moment, disappointed. Ill health kept him from presenting his manuscript to Wolsey at the opportune time (that is, during the New Year's season); the king was occupied with weightier matters (England was at war with France); and John Yonge was in camp with the royal army. Erasmus was therefore obliged to present the translations again after their publication, which at least in Henry's case yielded the desired attention.[21]

More than a decade later Erasmus produced two further translations. Two of them he dedicated to the Hungarian diplomat and businessman Alexius Thurzo, the third to a young friend, Francis Dilft, who had stayed in his house in 1524/5 and was at the time holding a canonry at Antwerp. The three translations were published by Froben in 1525 and 1526 respectively.[22]

In the prefaces to his earlier versions Erasmus explained that he had chosen Plutarch as his subject because he was the most learned among classical authors[23] and because he offered a great wealth of information. At the same time he noted that both the style and the subject matter of Plutarch's writings presented difficulties to all but the most attentive and informed reader. It was Plutarch's custom to string pieces of information together and present them without offering explanations or interpretations, to quote abstruse matter from a variety of ancient sources, and to weave these quotations into the text until it seemed 'a patchwork, or rather, a mosaic fashioned of exquisitely arranged patterns.'[24] In many instances the Renaissance reader was left in the dark as to the exact meaning of a quotation because he was unfamiliar with its context and was prevented from discovering its meaning or confirming his interpretation by the fact that the source was no longer extant.[25] Moreover, Plutarch was in the habit of going from one topic to the next, abruptly and unexpectedly, taxing his readers' powers of concentration. His style, too, was complex, involved, and obscure in a 'Boeotian' way, demanding an alert and resourceful mind.[26]

Because of these peculiarities, it was not surprising that the text of Plutarch's *Moralia* had been corrupted in many places. 'He of all authors deserves to be read, he more than any other is impossible to read,' Erasmus ruefully noted.[27] Thorny textual problems confronted the translator, 'monstrous faults at well-nigh every line' impeded his progress.[28] Erasmus had found himself in a similar position before, being obliged to correct and emend as well as translate a text,[29] but his success in dealing with Plutarch was varied: he was able to eliminate some of the problems, yet 'skipped over' others, as he admitted in the preface to the Froben edition of 1525.[30]

In recommending Plutarch to the reader Erasmus first described him as a source of information. In later years he praised him as a source of inspiration as well. Even in the preface to his earlier translations he noted that Plutarch's writings had an ethical constituent, that his precepts were applicable to life. Thus he recommended the essay 'On preserving good health' to John Yonge as being 'more philosophical' than the purely scientific writings of Galen and Paul of Aegina;[31] and he described the essay 'How to tell a flatterer from a friend' as 'useful' and providing an effective technique for distinguishing true friends from impostors.[32] In his prefaces to later translations Erasmus elaborated on this moral element: 'Socrates brought philosophy from heaven down to earth; Plutarch introduced it into the bedrooms, private quarters, and inner chambers of the individual ... He teaches in his books matters that anyone at any time can right away apply to his practical life.';[33] Erasmus valued and recommended Plutarch's writings for their edifying character. In his catalogue of works he called Plutarch an uplifting writer who could impress moral guidelines on his readers and whose works were suitable 'to mould a man's character.'[34]

Although there can be no doubt that Erasmus' main reason for translating Plutarch was his respect for the author's integrity and learning and a consequent desire to disseminate his works, the preface to the 1525 edition indicates certain secondary motives, at least for the later set of translations. In the dedicatory letter to Thurzo[35] Erasmus declared that he had embarked on his work seeking peace of mind. Decrying the religious controversies which embroiled theologians everywhere and made their scholarly works the object of contention and malicious attacks, Erasmus described Plutarch as a haven, a refuge from the storms of a troubled age. He had turned for inspiration to the writings of a classical author manifesting an almost Christian piety and presenting a position of unquestionalbe morality: 'In such regions I wander the more willingly, as I see the affairs of Christendom reaching such a pitch of frenzy that it is not safe to speak of Christ, whether in a good or bad sense, for *Under every stone a scorpion lurks!*'[36] Let us now consider how successful Erasmus was as a translator of Plutarch, sampling first one of the early pieces, 'How one can profit from one's enemies.'[37] The essay is of particular interest because it spawned rivalry between Erasmus and the French humanist Christophe Longueil. Longueil had been working on a translation of the treatise when he was forestalled by the publication of Erasmus' version.[38] It is not surprising, therefore, that he reviewed his competitor's work in a less than charitable spirit. After all Erasmus had spoiled his chances of publication and rendered his labours futile. The criticism he offered in a letter to Ruzé[39] (to whom he dedicated the unpublished manuscript) is, however, polite, and the points he raises are to some extent justified. He was prepared to yield the crown to his competitor as far as style was concerned, but – he said – his own lack of flair was more than outweighed by Erasmus' lack of fidelity (pp 553–4). He did not advocate rendering the text into Latin word for word, but neither could he approve of putting stylistic considerations before accuracy. Erasmus had 'abandoned the task of the translator and slipped into paraphrasing the text' (p 556). Longueil also noted that Erasmus' translation contained mistakes which he attributed to the author's carelessness as much as to textual difficulties (ibid). A closer look at Erasmus' translation will substantiate at least some of Longueil's criticism. No doubt, Erasmus paid more attention to rhetorical appeal than to an accurate rendition of the Greek text.

The Ciceronian device of using two synonymous expressions for one single Greek phrase, which we have already encountered in earlier translations, is also represented in this piece of work. Three examples of this practice will illustrate the point: *se ... armant ac muniunt* (they arm and fortify themselves – lines 27–8; omitted by Longueil) translates ὁπλίζοντες αὑτούς (arming themselves); *excitat et movet* (he shakes up and moves – line 71; Longueil: *movet* – line 119) stands for κινεῖ (he moves); and *bellos et laudatos* (good and praiseworthy – line 102; Longueil: *generosos* – line 173) conveys εὐδοκιμοῦντας (noble) in the Greek text. The difference between Erasmus' rhetorical and expansive version and Longueil's concise rendition is best illustrated by their respective translations of ἄνδρα ... ἐν λόγοις εὐδόκιμον, ἐν πράξεσι καθαρόν, ἐν διαίτῃ κόσμιον (a man ... reputable in speech, clean in action, orderly in his life). Erasmus has *virum ... admirandum in dicendo, in rebus gerendis sincerum et incorruptum, in temperantia victus sobrium ac moderatum* (a man ... admirable in speech, sincere and honest in conducting matters, sober and moderate in the temperate manner of his life – lines 105–6). Longueil's version is more to the point and parallels the Greek construction: *virum ... verbo probrum, fato purum, victu honestum* (a man ... reputable in speech, pure in action, honest in life – lines 177–8).

Erasmus' tendency towards expansive translations appears to be more pronounced here than in his earlier versions. In some instances a phrase is added for balance; for example, at line 25 where *non solum* (not only) offsets a phrase beginning with *verum etiam* (but also), whereas Longueil contents himself with an accurate, but rather lopsided, *didicit illos interficere, mox et ab eis iuvari* (he has learned to kill them, and soon to be helped by them – lines 40–1). At lines 41–2 Erasmus supplies *non valet in istum modum* (in this respect it is not valuable) to introduce the contrasting *sed lucem et calorem ministrat* (but it supplies light and heat; Longueil: *at idem ignis lumen praebet et calorem* – line 65).

In other instances Erasmus' additions are explanatory; for instance, at lines 60–1, where the phrase *ansam captans* (seizing a handle) is complemented somewhat gratuitously by *calumniae* (for slander). Longueil translates only what he finds in the Greek text, λαβὴν ζητῶν: *ansam quaerens* (seeking a handle – line 102). Similarly at lines 74–5 Erasmus complements a reference to people who live soberly by the subjective remark 'for fear of illness' (*suspicione morbi*). On the other hand, we find useful explanations at line 89, where the 'craftsmen of Dionysius' (τοὺς περὶ τὸν Διόνυσον) are identified as singers (*hoc est, cantores*; similarly Longueil: *Dionysiacos ludiones*, Dionysian actors – line 143); at line 145, where *nemesis* (transliterated) is translated by *hoc est, reprehensionem* (that is, wrath; Longueil: *contumeliae vindictam* – lines 242–3); and at line 217, where the source of a quotation is given as *Homercum illud* (that saying of Homer's).

In choosing a suitable term to translate Greek words that lack an exact parallel in Latin, Erasmus gives an uneven display of his talents. With some versatility he translates πολιτικός as *urbanus* (urbane – line 99), elsewhere as *civilis* (political – line 20), and more expansively as *civilis et in administranda republica versans* (a citizen engaged in the administration of the state – line 15). All three phrases are appropriate and skilful translations. Longueil never quite matches Erasmus' resourcefulness. He uses *scitus, civilis,* and *in republica versans,* respectively (lines 170, 26, 19). On the other hand, Erasmus renders ἄγρια ζῷα (wild animals) in rather desultory manner as *animantes* (animals – lines 23–4; similarly Longueil: *animalia* – line 37), although a term with coextensive meaning (*fera*) exists in Latin. In another case the imaginative, but rather fanciful, translation of ἄδιψος (preventing thirst) as *fugasitis* (literally, 'putting thirst to flight'), which is found in the manuscript, is corrected in the printed version to read *adipson,* an uninspired transliteration of the Greek term (line 224). Longueil voted for a more comprehensive rendition: *ad arcendam sitim* (to prevent thirst – line 378).

When Longueil complained about Erasmus' inaccuracy, he was criticizing his liberal approach rather than questioning his competence as a translator. Omissions in Erasmus' translation are rare,⁴⁰ and so are outright errors. In fact, one mistake was introduced in the revised edition of 1516, remained through two more editions, and was finally caught in 1520.⁴¹ Other mistakes, evidencing Erasmus' unfamiliarity with the Greek words λισσός (smooth), πυτία (coagulant), and ἀνυπεύθυνος (unaccountable), remained, changing a 'precipitous rock' into a 'rock of Lissus' (*Lissi scopulum* – line 229), the coagulant into 'milk' (*lac* – line 27), and silence 'for which one cannot be called to account' into a 'harmless silence' (*innoxium* – line 223). Longueil did not do much better. He recognized πυτία (translated by *coagulum* in line 42), but not λισσός, which he translated as a proper adjective (*Lissada petram* – line 384), and oddly enough, he also has *innoxium* (line 377) for ἀνυπεύθυνος. In one instance, however, Erasmus misconstrued a whole phrase. Translating Plutarch's αἰτίαν ἔσχε πλησιάζειν⁴² (he incurred the charge of being intimate), Erasmus stumbled twice, each time choosing the inappropriate one of two possible meanings and ending up with an incongruous phrase: *adeundi ... causa haec fuit* (the reason for his approaching was ... – lines 18–9). Longueil improved somewhat on this version. He left his options open, cautiously translating πλησιάζειν as *privatim conveniendi identidem colendi* (meeting privately as well as currying favour – line 308). Like Erasmus he translated αἰτία as 'reason' (*causa* – line 309), but intimated the legal meaning by the words *male audit* (he met with ill repute – line 307).

An interesting turn occurs in Erasmus' translation at lines 146ff where he plays the censor – a role in which we shall find him more often in subsequent translations. A king's homosexual tendencies, described by the Greek adjective παιδομανής (mad after boys), are discreetly glossed over and his vice referred to in general terms as 'a rather shameful kind of lust' (*foediori libidinis generi*). Longueil has no scruples translating παιδομανής by *paedicator* (one who is fond of boys – line 245).

Considering Longueil's review of Erasmus' translation in light of the evidence presented, we find that his criticism was not unjustified. All the same it appears that the keen-eyed critic who was so quick to discover and point out Erasmus' shortcomings was himself by no means successful in avoiding all the pitfalls of translating from the Greek. Although he could lay claim to a greater degree of fidelity to the original, adhering more closely to the structure of the Greek, the compliments he paid to Erasmus' stylistic prowess were more than polite phrases. In that respect Erasmus' version was truly superior to that of his competitor.

Let us now turn to another of Erasmus' translations, the essay 'On the wrong kind of shame.'[43] In this last piece to be published in Erasmus' Plutarch collection, we note a new development: the retention of occasional Greek terms in Greek fount rather than in their latinized form. This practice would imply that the readership of 1526 could be expected to have either an elementary knowledge of Greek or at least an interest in the original term. In one instance the retention of the Greek word is suggested by the context, a discussion of the etymology of δυσωπία (shame). Erasmus explains that this term is 'composed of ώπή (mien) and δυσ-, a prefix which indicates difficulty' (lines 22–3). The same term recurs at line 17, again in Greek fount, and at line 10, in its latinized form. A little further on, at line 19, κατήφειαν is retained in its Greek form. The term lacks an exact Latin equivalent, but as Erasmus explains in an addendum, 'it could be rendered into Latin by *pronitas* or *putiditas* [a downcast state or being in the dumps].'[44] In another passage he has cogent reasons for using Greek, finding it impossible to render a pun into Latin. He therefore explains the point, retaining the original Greek terms: 'He has in his eyes, not κόρας, but πόρνας, that is, not "pupils" but "lovers," a pun on the ambiguous Greek word κόρη which can mean both "girl" and "pupil of the eye"' (lines 24–5).

In addition to native Greek words we find a number of loan-words; for example at line 328, *soloecismus* and *barbarismus* (solecism, barbarism), both naturalized in classical antiquity. There are a number of expanded translations, prompted by idiomatic or stylistic considerations. We find Erasmus substituting two Latin terms for one Greek word at line 8: *germina quaedam ac flores* (shoots and blossoms) for ἐξανθήματα (outgrowths); adding a personal note at line 147: *laudes adulantium* (praises of flatterers) for ἐπαίνους (praises); or elaborating on the meaning of the Greek at lines 215–16, where the expression ἀγνωμόνως δυσωποῦσιν (unreasonable petitioners) is paraphrased by the phrase *qui improbe molesti sunt petendo quod aequum non est* (those who are unduly bothersome, making unfair demands).

In addition we find a somewhat larger number of misinterpretations than in earlier versions. These are either factual mistakes, misunderstandings, or questionable free translations. A misconstruction at line 130, for instance, stems from Erasmus' unfamiliarity with the poet Lasus of Hermione,[45] but the translation *interruptum sermonem urge et absolve* (press on with the interrupted speech and finish it) in line 134 for διακόψας ἐπείγου καὶ πέραινε τὸ προκείμενον (interrupt his speech now and make haste to complete what is at hand) must be an error. Another misinterpretation occurs at line 220 where Erasmus reads ἑταίρους (friends) for ἑτέρους (the others) and translates the Greek phrase, which undoubtedly runs τοὺς ἑτέρους διατραπέντες (turning away from the others), incongruously as *subversis amicis* (his friends having been corrupted). We also find a number of rather independent translations: for example, *cum iam imminet gloriae* (when he is close to glory – line 346) for ἐπίδοξον ὄντα κρατήσειν (when he is likely to win).

Looking over the two translations, one published in 1514, the other more than a decade later in 1526, the reader is struck by the stationary level of Erasmus' skills. He seems to have learned all he needed in the first few years of his studies; thereafter the accuracy of his translations reflects his state of mind more than his competence. One suspects that at least some of the uninspired translations and misinterpretations in the second piece were due to the distractions, preoccupations, and fatigue of a beleaguered mind. The desultory, literal, and therefore senseless translation of several corrupt passages adds to this impression and betrays a lack of concentration.[46] On the other hand, the methods, familiar from Erasmus' earliest translations – repetition, explanatory additions, the versatile and creative rendition of idioms – are all represented, if not accentuated, in the Plutarch versions. If any element distinguishes the later translations from his earlier works, it is Erasmus' growing awareness of the reader's needs, an awareness marked by a transition from the faithful reproduction of words to a full interpretation of their meaning, from a desire to offer proof of competence to a concern for the reader's understanding of the text.

In examining Erasmus' motives for publishing translations from Plutarch we have noted his admiration for the author's learning and philosophical image, and his desire to escape for a while the sound and fury of theological disputes by applying his mind to a non-controversial subject. To these observations must be added the fact that Erasmus was preparing an enlarged edition of the *Adages* (published in 1515) and was for this purpose rereading a number of classical authors, among them Plutarch. In a way the translations are therefore a by-product of his research, as was another work completed at this time, the *Parabolae*, a collection of similes and metaphors.

The *Parabolae* were Erasmus' 'special gift for a special friend,' Pieter Gillis of Antwerp.[47] They were designed as an adjunct to the *Copia* and published by Schürer in Strassburg in 1514. Proving extremely popular, they were soon launched by other printing houses, successively and in competition with one another. A revised edition was published by Martens (Louvain 1515), further corrections by the author were incorporated in an edition by Bade (Paris 1516), and a final version containing additional changes was produced by Froben (Basel 1522).[48] Erasmus had collected the material for his *Parabolae* mostly from Seneca, Pliny, and Plutarch.[49] The passages taken from the latter fall within the scope of our examination since they involved not only selection, but also translation.

In his arrangement Erasmus followed the sequence of the text given in the Aldine edition. His criteria of selection were broad. He shunned neither casual nor commonplace metaphors and included the most trivial and the most general *parabolae* alike. Moreover, he was undisturbed by repetition and made no attempt to group subject-related similes together. The resulting text was not simply a translation of selected passages from Plutarch and other classical authors. In transferring passages from the *Moralia* to his collection, Erasmus often abridged, simplified, or reinterpreted his original. Moreover, he added nuances of his own or even created new parallels from clues provided in Plutarch's essays. The following examples will illustrate his approach to the source material.

Whenever a comparison in Plutarch is drawn out and elaborated in detail, Erasmus reduces it to the essentials, often substituting general terms for specific ones. Thus he says: 'women with the cravings of pregnancy ... stuff themselves with unwholesome food,' while Plutarch says 'with salt-pickles'; or, '[a drug] renders valuable services,' while Plutarch specifies 'is purgative, stimulative, or tissue-building'; or, 'Vestal virgins have a fixed programme: first, time for learning, then for practice, and third for teaching. It was the same for priests of Diana.' Here Plutarch lists the individual steps for priests of Diana as well.[50] A more significant change is introduced in a passage in which Plutarch explains that a Greek magistrate cannot use his discretionary powers without regard for 'higher authority,' a reference to their Roman overlords. Erasmus ignores this allusion to specific political conditions, using instead a nobler and more generally applicable thought: the man who holds office must exercise his power 'so as not to go beyond what *the law* prescribes.'[51] Trimming source material in this manner, Erasmus may well claim for himself 'such praise as is due to brevity and convenience.'[52]

Plutarch's text is rich in comparisons, so much so that he often accumulates parallels, using a number of them to illustrate one aphorism. In such cases Erasmus tends to choose only one, presumably the most powerful and appropriate image. For example, to illustrate the aphorism that a brilliant and rapid career does not necessarily attract envy, Plutarch cites the case of a new performer delighting an audience tired of seeing the same old acts. Next, he likens a brilliant career to a fire that blazes up quickly at the start and therefore does not cause smoke. Erasmus uses only the second part of the parallel, which is a vivid and imaginative comparison; he passes over the first part, which seems less relevant, exemplifying fickleness rather than acceptance without envy.[53] In several cases Erasmus suppresses part of a comparison because it contains a proverb – that is, a type of comparison which he reserved for his *Adages*. At other times his choice reflects Plutarch's emphasis. Where the Greek author has linked two comparisons, but added more weight to one of them, or developed it to a larger extent, Erasmus follows suit and chooses the more elaborate parallel. In one passage, for instance, Plutarch compares an overly critical friend to a schoolmaster, but immediately discards this image and launches into a more detailed comparison to a physician who continuously prescribes powerful drugs. Erasmus follows Plutarch's lead, ignores the succinct reference to the schoolteacher altogether, and records only the comparison between friend and physician.[54]

In the examples given so far we have seen Erasmus introducing changes for the convenience of the reader. He maintains the sense of Plutarch's parallel, but presents it in a more succinct form. Sometimes, however, we find that he reinterprets a simile or shifts its emphasis. Some of these changes may be deliberate and reflect Erasmian preferences; a few, however, are more likely the result of misinterpretations.

An error must certainly be assumed whenever Erasmus, diverging from Plutarch, presents the reader with a version that is either absurd or less meaningful than the original. An example of the first kind is Erasmus' rendition of a passage in which Alexander the Great is said to have preserved the strength of his favourite horse by riding another steed into battle and mounting Bucephalos at the very last moment. Erasmus misconstrues this episode and depicts Bucephalos as being carried into battle by other horses. In another passage he speaks of a man putting a gadfly into a bull's ear. The correct meaning is, of course, that the gadfly lodges of its own accord in the bull's ear.[55]

Other changes, too, are unfortunate and serve only to obscure or weaken Plutarch's comparison; for example, when Erasmus writes: 'The master of a ship works through the voice and orders of other men: but he who would be master of a polity must have knowledge of his own so that he needs no other to speak for him.' As it stands, the point of comparison is obscure: does it mean that a ship's captain can dispense with knowledge? Plutarch, however, is clear on this point: both ship captain and politician must possess the requisite knowledge, but the captain may use his mates as 'mouthpieces' while the politician must do his own talking, that is, must be wise *and* eloquent.[56]

In another case Erasmus misses Plutarch's point altogether. He likens a flatterer to a bad painting: both imitate the faults of their object. In the form stated by Erasmus the comparison repeats thoughts expressed in much the same terms shortly before. Plutarch, however, does not repeat himself. He introduces a new angle, saying that an extravagant painting apes reality with gaudy colours; just so the flatterer greatly exaggerates *his* services.[57]

In these instances Erasmus' changes are for the worse, and it may be assumed that they were introduced in error. Other reinterpretations change the point of view or give a different nuance from Plutarch's simile without, however, impairing the overall sense. That is to say, they differ from the original, but can stand on their own. These changes, too, may be unintentional and the result of rapid and careless reading, but one cannot exclude the possibility that they reflect Erasmus' attitudes and opinions and that Plutarch's moral was purposely altered by him. After all, Erasmus had no qualms about censoring the Greek text when translating it; how much more would he be inclined to take liberties when offering a paraphrase.

Slight differences in interpretation can be found in the following passages: 'Eloquence does not suffice to govern a people unless reason be there too to govern what is said.' These are Erasmus' words. Plutarch, however, is not referring to the speaker's intellect, but to his character. He contends that only an honourable man has the authority and credibility to suggest a plan of action.[58] Erasmus also diverges from Plutarch when he says: 'He who tries to take the multitude without sufficient power is thrown down from the seat of government.' He does not make clear that the power of which Plutarch speaks is πείθω, persuasiveness.[59] Elsewhere Plutarch states in a neutral fashion that there are two paths leading up to political success, one 'quick and brilliant, but not without danger; the other pedestrian and slow, but safe.' Erasmus expresses his preference, saying 'when wealth and glory are our aim, we should contrive to achieve them late but safely.'[60] In another passage Plutarch likens flatterers to water because it assumes the shape of the vessel into which it is poured, just as the flatterer assumes the manners and interests of his friend. Erasmus uses a different image, referring to the water's colour which changes according to the ground over which it flows.[61] One substantial change which is not readily explained as the result of superficial reading is the interpretation of a passage in which the flatterer is said to encourage his friend's faults by criticizing ἀναντία (their opposites) – that is, the corresponding virtues. This is illustrated by Plutarch in a number of examples. The flatterer calls frugality 'rusticity,' contentedness 'lack of vigour,' and an interest in politics 'meddlesomeness.' By disparaging these virtues he abets his friend's profligacy, unscrupulous actions, and indolence. In view of the examples provided by Plutarch it is difficult to see how Erasmus could miss the point and construe the passage to mean: 'The flatterer praises the faults *of others*.'[62] It is more likely that he introduced this nuance intentionally, thinking it more appropriate or more representative of life.

In the following examples Erasmus does not change Plutarch's meaning, but shifts its emphasis. Plutarch comments on the relationship between old politicians and their young protégés. He notes that the success of a protégé enhances the image of his patron. He gives several examples to make his point, then mentions one exception: Agesilaus, who cast aside his mentor Lysander. Erasmus fastens on this one negative example and generalizes it: 'Men rise from obscurity through acquaintance with the great and then strangle those by whom they have been promoted.'[63] Again it is difficult to imagine that Erasmus overlooked five positive examples only to notice the odd one out. It is more likely that he discounted them and preferred the pessimistic view, perhaps in accordance with his own experiences.

Although Erasmus usually finds his parallels ready-made in Plutarch, he does on occasion take other figures of speech from the Greek text, converting them into *parabolae*. In one case Plutarch describes the typical actions of a flatterer: he covers up his friend's faults rather than correcting them. For example, if a friend makes a poor speech, the flatterer does not criticize its contents or the speaker's enunciation, but counsels him to avoid drinking cold water lest he develop a sore throat. Erasmus turns this example into a comparison, saying: 'The man who complains of his friend over some trifle, and in weightier matters holds his tongue, acts ... like an incompetent speaker who answers none of the points at issue and says he has lost his voice or cannot read his notes.'[64] In another passage, Plutarch exclaims: 'A shadow can better perform this task!' He disparages the flatterer's useless practice of imitating his friend at every turn. Erasmus phrases this as a comparison: 'Your shadow, whatever you may do, responds and is always there; like that the flatterer follows you wherever you may turn.'[65]

In a few isolated cases Erasmus devises his own parallels, prompted by a clue in his classical source. For example, Plutarch gives a series of examples in which flatterers adjust to the caprices of their masters, one day philosophizing with them, another day joining them in their revels. He concludes the passage with a reference to turncoats who behave 'as though they had undergone a transformation in Circe's house.' Erasmus ignores Plutarch's examples and general trend of thought, fastening on the image of Circe and devising his own parallel which has no connection with flatterers and their manoeuvres: 'Circe's potions change men suddenly into wild beasts; likewise the passions suddenly make a man different.'[65]

Elsewhere Erasmus records Plutarch's comparison between the unleashing of reproaches and the release of a pent-up stream of water, but then goes on to introduce a new parallel: 'Just as rheum when it has accumulated gradually comes out into the open and overcomes a man at the very moment when it is itself overcome by the process of nature, so some men dare not warn their powerful friends until they have come to grief ...'[67] This interpretation is suggested by the Greek word ῥέον (stream, flow) which can mean 'discharge' in medical usage.

The examples cited afford us a glimpse of Erasmus' working methods and at the same time throw an interesting light on his general approach to classical sources. It is obvious from his practices that he did not regard Greek authors as sacrosanct, that he was not overawed by their venerable age and the tradition they represented, and that his respect for them did not prevent him from exercising his critical faculties or developing an independent train of thoughts.

To collect material from an existing source or to present it in the form of a digest may not seem like a challenging task for a serious scholar of Erasmus' standing, and he realized that some of his readers might question the merit of his undertaking, saying 'this man has a pretty knack of making his work sound important, as though it were really difficult to produce parallels when they lie to hand everywhere.' For such critics Erasmus had a ready answer: in the first place the editor of a digest or compilation deserved praise for good selection and arrangement, for 'there is credit also to be won from the skilful mounting of a jewel on a sceptre or in a ring.'[68] Even in his translations Erasmus had dared to present the text on his own terms – to expand, interpret, and censor his source; in the *Parabolae* he took advantage of the greater freedom granted the editor of a compilation, choosing his own setting, imposing his own point of view, and adapting the material to a new context. Confident of having been successful in this task, Erasmus invited the reader's applause. The success of the publication bore out his expectations and showed that the audience appreciated his efforts to present them with a rich store of parallels in a novel and thought-provoking context.

FIVE

Philology, the Handmaiden of Theology: The Translation and Annotation of the New Testament

꽃

Our study of Erasmus' translations has been limited to the classics, but any examination of his methods and techniques would be deficient if it neglected his most significant contribution to philology: the translation of the New Testament. One might say that Erasmus' biblical scholarship is not extraneous, but peripheral to our topic, for by his own admission his translations from the classics were only a means to an end. It was in the New Testament that his accumulated experience was put to the test. The result of his labour, which represents the culmination of his Greek studies and the definitive test of his achievements, is therefore the perfect foil against which to check our observations concerning his translations from secular texts.

So far we had to deduce Erasmus' principles of translation from his practices, but in the *Annotations* to the New Testament and in the prefatory material accompanying the various editions we have his *ipsissima verba* on the subject, for his apparatus not only constitutes an instrument of exegesis but also represents an exposition of his methods of translation, allowing us a glimpse into the author's workshop, a view behind the scenes.[1]

Erasmus began work on the New Testament during his second visit to England in 1505/6. The undertaking was connected with his Greek studies and his belief in the importance of consulting primary sources, but also with his turning away from the scholastic method of exegesis to a philologically oriented approach, and more specifically, with his discovery of Valla's annotations on the New Testament, which confirmed the direction of his thoughts.[2] By 1514 he had completed not only his translation of the Greek text but also annotations on the entire

New Testament. The first edition, published in Basel in 1516, contained, however, not his original translation, which he was inclined to pass over in silence, but a slightly modified, somewhat more conservative version. It was only in the second edition (Basel 1519) that Erasmus returned to his earlier, more innovative version. The text and notes were revised for a third and fourth edition (Basel 1522, 1527) and finally received their definitive form in a fifth (Basel 1535). Extensive prefatory material explaining and justifying the author's purpose preceded the various editions of the New Testament: the *Paraclesis* or *Exhortation to study Christian philosophy*, the *Methodus*, which was later expanded into the *Ratio verae theologiae*, an *Epistle concerning the philosophy of the Gospel*, a list of solecisms, errors, obscure passages, and corruptions in the Vulgate, an *Apologia* of the author's principles of translation, and *Capita argumentorum contra quosdam morosos et ineruditos* (Arguments against certain petulant and uneducated people).[3]

The principle behind Erasmus' translations – the application of philological techniques to Scripture – as well as individual points of his translation and annotations aroused a great deal of controversy and involved him in numerous bitter disputes with theologians at home and abroad. This is, however, not the place to discuss in detail the genesis of Erasmus' biblical translation, the history of its publication, and the reaction of contemporary theologians; we are concerned only with those aspects of his work that shed light on his principles of translation and give depth to the observations we have made so far concerning his versions from the classics.

Any comparison between his work on the New Testament and his secular translations will, of course, take into consideration Erasmus' attitude towards biblical and classical sources, respectively. We have noted the air of superiority which he assumed in dealing with the classics. Far from being cowed by their standing in literary tradition, he pointed out their limited applicability to Christian philosophy. He declared that he would alter not only their form but also their contents, did not stop short of censorship, and often imposed his own literary taste on the wording of the original. Erasmus' approach to the Greek text of the New Testament and the Vulgate translation was necessarily different. He was motivated by a pious concern for restoring the word of God and brought to his work not only the refined taste of a humanist but also the simple faith of a Christian and the trained mind of a theologian.[4] His remarks in the *Annotations* are therefore of two kinds: some of his arguments concern variants in the text or deal with matters of interpretation; others refer to stylistic and grammatical points. It is the latter type of comment that concerns us here.

The fact that Erasmus ventured to present a new translation of the Bible implies criticism of the accepted version, and his comments in the *Annotations* verbalize this criticism. He did not spare the translator, 'whoever he was,'[5] candidly accusing him of inattention, clumsiness, and inconsistency.[6] Nevertheless he restrained himself in the first edition, 'fearing that some people would not suffer significant innovations; but when scholars and friends in high places spurred me on and gave me courage, I introduced them more freely, so as to make the whole New Testament speak in simple, yet proper, Latin. I excepted only certain words and idioms that I considered too entrenched to be changed.'[7] In many cases, therefore, Erasmus criticized the Vulgate, yet retained the traditional text, conceding that some things must willy-nilly be overlooked, since they were too ingrained to be changed without causing a great uproar.[8]

Some of Erasmus' remarks concerning biblical translation may be given a wider meaning and referred to translation in general; for example, his reflections on the author's limitations. It is the translator's task 'to bring out the meaning in the most suitable terms,' but there are inherent problems in the process of transferring the content of a phrase from one language to another. 'Let them not drag me into court if the text does not correspond to the original word for word,' Erasmus pleads with his readers, 'for, try as you may, it cannot be done.' Some aspects of the original text can never be fully realized in translation: 'Often the figure or significance of a Greek phrase cannot be rendered, because the charming effect of an idiom does not find its corresponding expression in the translation.'[9]

We recall that Erasmus voiced similar concerns in his prefaces to translations from the classics, that he affirmed the difficulty of making 'good Latin out of good Greek' and expressed misgivings about his ability to convey the stylistic qualities of the original, for the Latin language cannot reproduce even their shadow.' He was conscious of the conflicting demands imposed on the translator, who must faithfully reproduce both the factual meaning and the 'force and effect' of the Greek words.[10] On the other hand, the translator of secular works was not affected by religious scruples. He could set for himself wider margins and choose from a larger store of linguistic devices. In his earlier translations Erasmus voluntarily committed himself to a literal version, but in later years he professed a certain reluctance to acept the restraints such a commitment imposed on him and expressed an impatience with his obligations.[11] These misgivings did not extend to his work on the New Testament. As a translator of the Bible he exerted himself willingly and laboured diligently to produce an accurate and faithful translation. The task of conveying the meaning of Scripture – that is, of expressing God's message – was not a burden, but a sacred duty.

In reviewing the aims of the translator, Erasmus emphasized three elements: clarity, purity, and stylistic appeal. Only in the last point did his practices in the New Testament version differ significantly from those observed in his translations from the classics. Having chosen Greek authors who excelled in rhetoric or were professional rhetoricians, Erasmus strove to reproduce their style and consequently waxed eloquent, indulged his love of copia, and did not think it out of place to introduce Latin figures of speech to give his composition the quality and texture appropriate to its genre. The principle involved – the idea of preserving the tenor of the original – is operative in his biblical translation as well, but to speak to Christians in Christ's words meant to step down from the rostrum, to migrate from Cicero's urban splendour to the rustic abodes of the apostles. The rule Erasmus followed with respect to style was determined by his respect for their unadorned and ingenuous speech: 'In this work I have not striven for eloquence, but I have not avoided neatness where it lay to hand.'[12] He was committed to preserving the integrity of the Latin speech, provided there was no loss of simplicity.[13]

Yet Erasmus believed that an esthetic appeal could serve a pious purpose, that 'how it was said' was important. He recognized the effectiveness of rhetoric and the blandishments of style which allowed the mysteries of faith 'to flow into our hearts in a pleasant and powerful manner.'[14] He was often accused of wanting to improve God's word, when he was attempting to preserve a Greek figure of speech and to reproduce its effect. He expressed his pleasure when the Vulgate text offered an effective version and complimented its author for having 'translated this elegantly' or having 'rendered the sense well.'[15] Conversely, he criticized lapses in idiom and deplored their harsh effect.[16] He often drew stylistic devices in the Greek text to the reader's attention, pointing out 'the pleasant affinity' or 'the delightful play of words' which unfortunately could not be duplicated in Latin.[17] In one case, for instance, he noted that the translator of the Vulgate had 'ruined the beauty of *prosonomasia* and *enantiosis* by translating εἰσερχόμενον and ἐξερχόμενον as *ingreditur* and *procedit*, respectively.'[18] Elsewhere he expressed regret that 'the charm of the Greek figure which is contained in ποίμνη and ποιμήν is lost in translation.' The author of the Vulgate had used *ovum* and *pastor* whereas a different choice of words, *ovile* and *opilio*, would have duplicated the Greek figure and reproduced the sound effect.[19]

The *Annotations* also allow the reader to appreciate Erasmus' attention to choice of words and his interest in etymology. Concern for accuracy frequently prompted him to analyse the meaning, scope, and correct application of a Latin term. Thus he noted the difference between *nubere* (to marry, from a woman's point of view) and *in matrimonium ducere* (to marry, from a man's point of view); between *imputare* (to credit) and *reputare*, whose meaning in classical Latin is restricted to 'reckon'; between *confundere* (to disturb) and *pudefacere* (to embarrass); between *manducare* (to chew) and *edere* (to eat).[20] Similarly, he pointed out the historical development of a word's meaning, noting the classical and post-classical, the strict and popular connotations of *luscus, calumniari,* and *oeconomus*.[21] His interest in a word's exact meaning is also apparent from his observations on the etymology of compound Greek terms and the unfortunate necessity of translating them into Latin by means of periphrasis, as well as from his careful selection of Latin terms to convey the specific meaning of polysemous Greek words.[22] The same concerns surface in his translations of the classics. We have seen his versatility and resourcefulness in translating Greek words that have a broad range of meanings and his dissatisfaction with the limitations of the Latin language which did not permit the successful reproduction of compound words.[23]

Erasmus' remarks in the *Annotations* generally reflect the conscientious translator's attention to details that have an immediate bearing on the understanding and interpretation of a passage. In a few cases, however, his arguments lack substance. His criticism appears petty, his point subjective, and his remarks of doubtful significance. For example, one may question Erasmus' argument that *adiuvare* (to help, in a very general sense) is an inappropriate word to use for 'helping one who labours' and does not adequately convey the meaning of βοηθεῖν, which means 'to hear the anguished cries of a man in danger and to run to his assistance.'[24] The same petulant spirit moves Erasmus to criticize the Vulgate translation of παιδίον (boy) as *parvulus* (little one), an eccentric choice but one that is seconded by Caesar and Virgil.[25] Erasmus would have liked to see *puer* instead. His preference for a common over a rare word is understandable, but his explanation is as colourful and surprising as the Vulgate translation: 'Someone can be *parvulus* even if he is old, as for instance, the Pygmies ...' Erasmus' fears of misinterpretation are far-fetched, to say the least.[26]

Other corrections, too, appear wilful. For example, is the difference between *affectus* and *affectio* as significant as Erasmus would have us believe?[27] Tacitus' usage suggests that the meaning required here, 'love' or 'affection,' is conveyed by either term.[28] And how rigid is the distinction, made by Erasmus, between *invenire* (to find what one has been looking for) and *reperire* (to come upon by chance). Evidence from classical usage suggests that the two verbs were, to some degree, coextensive.[29]

Erasmus' quibbling prompted scurrilous replies from his opponents. After having changed *loquentes* (speaking) to *confabulantes* (conversing in a familiar tone), he found to his chagrin that someone had seized on the connection between *confabulari* and *fabula* (tale, fable) and accused him of having written 'that the gospels are nothing but old wives' tales.'[30] In this case, it seems, Erasmus was paid in his own coin. More serious was the resistance he encountered when he questioned the translation of passages which supported already embattled church dogma,[31] or when he changed the wording of John 1:1 from the traditional *in principio erat verbum* to *in principio erat sermo* (in the beginning was the word). Although his note carefully analysed the meaning of the related terms *verbum*, *vox*, *oratio*, and *sermo* (all referring to speech), and defended his choice in terms of theological tradition as well as of philological authority, he found himself obliged to meet the widespread criticism of conservative theologians in a lengthy apologia.[32]

His full treatment of synonyms makes Erasmus a precise and accurate translator at best, a pettifogger at worst. It is understandable that unkind critics said of his *Annotations*: 'They crawl on the ground and torment themselves over pitiful words and syllables.' Erasmus, however, defended his approach, saying 'he who compares, analyses, expounds, and interprets Holy Writ will himself realize that these small details are useful in no small degree.' The reader must suffer the inconvenience and apply his mind to details, considering that he was dealing, not with the inconsequential writings of secular authors, but with the word of God.[33]

Despite the fact that some of Erasmus' remarks in the *Annotations* are unpleasantly righteous, his point is usually well taken and the ingenuity he displays in backing his arguments cannot be denied. Sometimes he offers to the reader a wide choice of possible alternatives. For εὖ δοῦλε (Well done, slave) he suggests *bene/recte/euge/bene sane, serve*. Discussing the term ἀθῷος (innocent) he mentions as possible translations *iustus, innocens, insons, innoxius*. Elsewhere he explains that ταπεινός (lowly) may be rendered as *humilis, pauper, ignobilis, indocilis*, or *plebeius*.[34]

Although resourcefulness may be considered the translator's professional virtue, we cannot but admire Erasmus' fertility of mind. In his translations from the classics we have seen him use a similarly prodigal variety and kaleidoscopic range of synonyms to translate recurring terms in his text. In his biblical version he was, however, inclined to practise restraint. Concern for accuracy did not always allow him to indulge his love of words. He therefore restricted his demonstrations of word power to the *Annotations*, considering *copia* desirable only in a measure corresponding to the original. In this point Erasmus echoed Valla's criticism of the Vulgate, agreeing that its author had 'displayed variety to a surprising degree, when he should have avoided it.'[35] Erasmus demanded consistency: ideally a particular Greek word should be rendered by the same Latin word each time it occurred in the text, and the translation should vary only if there was a corresponding variation in the original. In Erasmus' opinion, the translator of the Vulgate had not observed the proper limits. He had displayed 'useless *copia*,' had shown a fondness for variation that was uncalled for.[36] 'For Heaven's sake,' he exclaimed in exasperation, 'what is the meaning of this avid love of variation, even to the point of muddling the sense?'[37] Erasmus did not fail to point out inconsistencies; for example, in his note on Mark 15:11: 'Just before, the translator said *summos sacerdotes*, now he translates it as *pontifices*; for in Greek it is the same word, ἀρχιερεῖς (high priests).'[38] Elsewhere Erasmus explained why he could not accept variation: he was objecting 'not because the interpreter translated it badly, but to keep a man from speculating in vain about the meaning of these words.'[39] Fear of possible misinterpretation or overinterpretation also caused Erasmus to take a stand against periphrasis. His definition of what constituted circumlocution was narrow. He rejected *sine misericordia* (without mercy) as a translation of ἀνελεήμονας (merciless) and demanded instead the cumbersome *immisericordes*, which parallels the structure of the Greek adjective. He called *non obedientes* (not obeying) for ἀπειθεῖς (disobedient) an 'unnecessary paraphrase,' suggesting instead *immorigeros, inobedientes*, or *intractabiles*, words which preserve the negative prefix.[40] With somewhat more justification he reproached the translator of the Vulgate for 'diverging from the Greek' by rendering ἀπεχώρησε (he departed) as *fugit* (he fled).[41]

We know, of course, that Erasmus made use of much greater liberty in his translations from the classics, that he soon surrendered his initial commitment to a literal translation and aimed at rendering a stylistically pleasing version of the meaning rather than producing a mirror image of the words in the Greek text. In his biblical translation he did not completely reject circumlocution, but curtailed the translator's freedom, considering the device a last resort, a move dictated by idiomatic considerations and commended by concerns for clarity.

When Erasmus used circumlocution in the New Testament, he was careful to defend his choice of words. For example, he insisted that μετενόησαν (they repented) 'could not be rendered as conveniently by *resipuissent*' as elsewhere; in another case he accepted two Latin words to convey the meaning of a Greek compound, seeing that there was no alternative; similarly, he excused the circuitous translation *sorte exiit* for ἔλαχεν because 'the translator, if I am not mistaken, aimed for greater clarity.'[42] He also accepted the Vulgate version *ab arbore fici* (from the fig tree) for ἀπὸ τῆς συκῆς, defending it on the grounds that 'the Latin word is ambiguous [that is, it can mean either the fruit or the tree], therefore the translator did well to render it by *periphrasis*.'[43] Erasmus' qualms about accepting this practice are based on the same fears as his rejection of *copia*: a circuitous translation invited more speculation than a literal one. His case in point was

Matthew 1:19, where παραδειγματίσαι (to disgrace, expose) was not translated literally as *exemplificare*, but more elegantly as *traducere*. This was misinterpreted by some as meaning 'to marry,' that is 'to convey' from one household to another, and produced 'a sea of never-ending questions.'[49]

When the ideals of clarity and accuracy were in conflict with one another, concern for clarity had to prevail. If a literal translation resulted in an ambiguous or obscure phrase, a departure from the original was necessary. In Erasmus' translations from the classics clarification was sometimes achieved by means of added comment. In fact, Erasmus used additions for a number of purposes, inserting them to interpret the meaning of Greek loan-words, to balance a Latin clause, or to satisfy the grammatical demands of the Latin language. However, in deciding whether or not the additions he found in the Vulgate were justified, he employed somewhat stricter criteria of evaluation. In one case he vetoed the addition of *est* (is) to complete a phrase, arguing that Greek ποῦ οὖν ἡ καύχησις (where then [is] boasting?) could be rendered literally as *ubi igitur gloriatio*, without detriment to style or Latin grammar.[45] In other cases he was more tolerant. Thus he retained the addition of *missi* in the phrase *missi a principibus* (sent by the leaders) where the Greek has only a prepositional phrase 'from the leaders.'[46] Although he termed this an addition *explicandi causa* (for the sake of explanation), he was probably also motivated by considerations of style, since in Latin usage prepositional phrases are normally supported by verbs and a discriminating reader might have found *a principibus* deficient. In another passage Erasmus himself suggested an addition to complete the sense of the verb: ἀπέστειλαν (they sent) was rendered as *miserunt*. Erasmus noted that the Latin verb needed an object and asked: 'Why has he not dared to add "messengers"?'[47] For similar reasons Erasmus retained *illis* in the phrase *illis commissa sunt* (they have been entrusted to them). In Greek the object is contained in the verb, a construction which cannot be duplicated in Latin without disregard for idiomatic expression.[48] On the other hand, Erasmus rejected the phrase *adoptionem filiorum dei* (adoption of the sons of God) for υἱοθεσίαν (adoption), noting that 'the translator has added some words for the purpose of explanation as he always does with this particular term.' Erasmus considered the explanation unnecessary, for 'who adopts his own sons?'[49] It is obvious from these examples that

Erasmus sought no simple answer to the question of explanatory and grammatical additions but that he examined and judged each passage on its own merits. Sometimes the translator was obliged to retrench his version from the Greek. This, too, was acknowledged by Erasmus. For example, commenting on the conjunction ὅτι (that) which 'the translator sometimes rightly omitted and here without reason added,' Erasmus ascribed this process to the translator's 'inconsistency rather than his inexperience or religious scruples ... for if he omitted it judiciously, why did he add it elsewhere?'[50] Similarly, the word αὐτός (himself) must occasionally be omitted for idiomatic reasons, and should have been in Luke 1:21, 'if the translator had wanted to speak Latin; yet he had no scruples omitting it elsewhere in similar constructions.'[51] In such matters it was necessary to use discretion. Both, additions and excisions, must be the result of critical examination and a reasoned decision and should not be made in a haphazard or wilful manner. We have seen that Erasmus had no compunction about expanding or contracting a secular text to clarify or improve the wording. This practice would not have been acceptable in dealing with Scripture. The word of God was not to be adulterated by explanatory remarks or abridged by paraphrasing. Erasmus therefore used the *Annotations* as a vehicle for comments on stylistic and semantic aspects and as a receptacle for the kind of remarks he had no scruples about inserting into the text of secular authors.

In his statements on the aims of the translator, Erasmus singled out clarity and purity as the most important criteria of judgement. He was satisfied that through his efforts the text of the New Testament was made 'clearer, purer, and more accurate.'[52] Listing the merits of his translation, he pointed out that he had emended what was faulty, made clear what was obscure, and explained what was confusing.[53] The fair-minded reader had to admit that his version was superior to the Vulgate: 'Consider: have I not expressed the meaning more faithfully, clearly, and effectively than the old translator?'[54]

The quest for correct diction was closely linked with the ideals of clarity and accuracy. 'Barbarous language,' Erasmus explained, 'admits of many variations and is difficult to understand because it diverges from natural speech. Nothing is clearer, nothing easier, than correct speech.' Erasmus' critics had objected to many of his changes, arguing that 'God was not offended by solecisms.'

Yes, answered Erasmus, but 'neither was he pleased.' To overlook solecisms was 'not civility, but iniquity.'[55]

In his versions from the classics, as indeed in all his compositions, Erasmus delighted his readers with the elegance and purity of his diction. He rarely deviated from classical standards.[56] His versions, in particular, were a triumph over the problem facing every translator: the difficulty of producing an idiomatically correct, yet faithful, version. We have seen Erasmus respond to this challenging task with creativity and resourcefulness. In his notes on the Vulgate he criticized the translator's literal renditions of Greek and Hebrew idiom not only because they offended Latin readers but also because they taxed their understanding. Long before the publication of the New Testament he had complained that 'the translators of Scripture, in their scrupulous manner of construing the text, offer such literal versions of Greek idioms that no one ignorant of that language could grasp even the primary, or, as our own theologians call it, literal, meaning.'[57] When he published his New Testament, Erasmus appended to his introduction a long list of instances in which, as he put it, 'the translator had forgotten that he was writing in Latin,' had 'attempted to imitate the Greek phrase, but with audacity rather than success,' and had 'used unheard-of words ... when he could have spoken Latin.'[58]

Erasmus himself introduced numerous corrections for idiomat- reasons, using the same justification over and over again: his changes would make the version *Latinius*, 'more Latin.'[59] For example, he found *quid nobis et tibi?* an unbearably literal translation for τί ἡμῖν καί σοι (what business do we have with you?). 'What, pray, does the translator want here with a Greek figure?' Erasmus asked; 'if he had wanted to speak Latin, he should have translated *quid tibi rei nobiscum est?*'[60] In this case the phrase in the Vulgate was merely jarring; elsewhere it was misleading as well. *Videbis eiicere*, for example, was an inept translation for διαβλέψεις ἐκβαλεῖν (you will have clear sight to throw out). The Latin infinitive could not convey this sense and Erasmus suggested instead *dispicies ut eiicias*.[61] Similarly, *cum consummasset praecipiens* could hardly be understood to mean 'when he had finished his instruction,' which is the meaning of ἐτέλεσε διατάσσων. Erasmus rightly criticized this translation as being a poor and literal rendition of a Greek figure.[62] For similar reasons he changed *quae in nobis completa sunt rerum* to *quae inter nos certissimae fidei sunt* (things which are most surely believed among us), exclaiming: 'I am asking you, who would understand the meaning of the evangelist from this translation [of πεπληροφορημένων ἐν ἡμῖν]?'[63] Erasmus' criticism of literal renditions also extended to translations of Hebrew idiom. For example, he rejected the expression *magis pluris,* a duplication of comparatives, which is peculiar to Hebrew but has no corresponding form in Greek or Latin.[64] In several cases he changed the wording of the Vulgate, commenting on one passage: 'I wish the translator had changed the Hebrew figure everywhere, just as he did here.'[65]

Erasmus also objected to the thoughtless retention of Greek vocabulary in its latinized form, 'as if Latin lacked terms.'[66] He proved that this was not the case by suggesting not one but four Latin terms for *thesaurize,* a loan-word frequently found in the Vulgate. 'Store up' could have been rendered into proper Latin as *reponite, recondite, colligite,* or *coacervate.* In another case Erasmus suggested, less felicitously, *simulator* for *hypocrita.*[67]

Erasmus' attention to synonyms, his narrow definition of periphrasis, his rejection of undue display of *copia*, and his demand for a literal, though idiomatically correct, version mark him as an uncompromising biblical translator. Rarely did regard for audience reaction lead him to diverge from his principles. In a very few instances he relented and curtailed his remarks, 'lest I be too troublesome to the reader' or make 'a business naturally without charm more tedious by my loquacity.'[68] Once he declared that it was not worth his while to quarrel about *barbarica vocabula.*[69] But such concessions are rare. More typical is his retort to a fictitious interlocutor: 'You will ask: what does it matter? It matters a great deal to the man who wishes to theorize on the basis of this passage.'[70] Occasional peevishness does not obscure the air of paternal authority which Erasmus projects in the *Annotations.* He had the readers' intellectual welfare at heart, and their enlightenment was not furthered by making allowances, but by relentlessly challenging their minds.

The philological comments embodied in the *Annotations* are enlightening to the reader who takes an interest in Erasmus' principles of translation because they describe the thought processes every conscientious translator pursues but is not normally called upon to verbalize. The fact that Erasmus took a different approach to secular and ecclesiastical sources respectively qualifies his remarks, but does not render them useless for a general study of his principles, for he firmly believed that the same qualifications – a sound philological background – were required from the biblical and from the secular translator. Indeed, he stated that 'the business of translating Holy Scripture is manifestly a grammarian's function' and that the grammarian contributed as much to the understanding of Holy Writ as the theologian.[71] Not only the translator of secular works but also the theologian needed a thorough grounding in the liberal arts, and especially in classical philology: 'It would be useful if young men destined for theology were carefully trained in the figures and tropes of grammar and rhetoric.'[72] Only a solid philological basis would allow them to appreciate the sources. Erasmus had once compared Greek sources to crystal clear rivers running with gold, and their Latin counterparts to muddy pools. He used much the same words to contrast biblical sources and *veteres theologi* (ie the Fathers) with their scholastic successors: 'there you will see a golden river, here some thin runlets, and those by no means clean or resembling their source.'[73] Erasmus condemned the arrogance of theologians who looked down on poetry as puerile, who despised rhetoric and all liberal arts 'although these very arts which they hold in contempt, have given us great theologians.'[74] Scripture, he noted, was full of poetical figures and parables whose translation required both a skilled philologist and a well-read interpreter.

While this summary review of the material accompanying Erasmus' translation of the New Testament reveals a more rigid set of rules than that governing his secular versions, we have also encountered a number of remarks that are applicable to both areas of his work and reflect his general views on principles and problems of translation. Certain common ideas emerge, forming a loosely defined system or approach to the task. It is true that Erasmus paid more attention to stylistic elements in his secular compositions, which were aimed at a humanistically oriented readership, than in his biblical translations, which were written mainly for theologians, but while the demand for rhetorical appeal affected the biblical translator less than the interpreter of secular works, other considerations were of importance to both. These included concerns for the use of correct idiom and clarity of expression, two goals which occasionally overshadowed the ideal of fidelity. Although Erasmus restricted the liberties of the biblical translator, he never curtailed his rights to the point of demanding a literal version at all costs, but accepted circumlocution where clarity and purity recommended it. Erasmus also showed a great interest in the scope and meaning of individual words, analysing the nuances conveyed by near-synonyms and making a careful choice among them, an inclination which is borne out in his secular translations.

In spite of the diversity of sources which Erasmus translated, the gulf separating the irreverent wit of Lucian or the rhetorical phrases of Isocrates from the simple precepts of the Bible, Erasmus did not see a fundamental difference in the translator's role. In each case a successful version demanded linguistic competence. Respect for scriptural sources required, however, that the novice should practise his skills on secular works and approach the more demanding task of interpreting the Bible only when he had acquired sufficient knowledge and experience. The perfunctory modesty which Erasmus had displayed in his prefaces to secular works, the diffidence he affected, would not have been appropriate in the translator of the Bible, whose responsibilities presupposed maturity and a confidence based on demonstrated ability. Accordingly, Erasmus stated his qualifications with a certain defiance and pride: 'If, according to Jerome, the best translator is the one who has best mastered both the language and the subject matter, I believe that I shall not be found inferior to the translator of the Vulgate in either field, if I may vaunt myself.'[75]

SIX

The Theologian's *Parerga*:
Isocrates, Galen, Xenophon

🕉

The year 1516, in which Erasmus' *magnum opus*, his translation and annotation of the New Testament, appeared, must be regarded as a dividing line in his career as translator. Since conceiving the enterprise ten years earlier, Erasmus had gradually channelled all his efforts towards its execution. The skill and knowledge acquired in the course of his Greek studies were to be concentrated and gathered into one to realize the task which he came to consider the chief aim in his life. The translations composed after 1516 therefore appear to be deprived of their immediate purpose and necessarily diminished in importance. Erasmus' often-professed motive for translating the classics – the testing of his skills on safe ground – had lost its driving force, but another purpose – the need to provide Latin readers with access to Greek literature – retained its validity. And so the translations published in the aftermath of the great work served at least this purpose, and perhaps some less exalted ones: gratifying friends and patrons with literary gifts, utilizing the odds and ends of scholarly research, filling rare hours of leisure with a profitable and agreeable occupation. The translations composed during the last two decades of Erasmus' life – the second instalment of Plutarch, the versions from Isocrates, Galen, and Xenophon, and the collection of *Apophthegmata* – fitted this framework.

The translation of Isocrates' parainesis *Ad Nicoclem* was the first classical treatise to issue from Erasmus' workshop after the publication of the New Testament, appearing in print only a few months later, in June of 1516.[1] The exact circumstances surrounding its composition are not clear. In 1501 Erasmus had sent an unspecified Isocrates text to Bensrott.[2] The accompanying letter indicated that he was working on a commentary or other study aid at this time. It has been suggested that the text in question was Agricola's translation of the protreptic epistle *Ad Demonicum*, which Erasmus edited in 1517.[3] It is more likely, however, that he was referring to a Greek text, since he asked Bensrott to supply him with Greek books in turn. Erasmus cited Isocrates again in letters dating from the years 1504 and 1511 respectively, referring to the author's method of exhortation and showing a familiarity with his epideictic speech *In praise of Busiris*.[4]

Isocrates, a fourth-century-BC teacher of rhetoric, political essayist, and self-styled philosopher, wrote a large number of court speeches, orations on the political future of Greece, and epideictic pieces in the sophistic tradition. In antiquity he was considered one of the foremost stylists and attracted a large number of distinguished students.[5] His works continued to be cited throughout the Middle Ages and were among those brought to Italy by Chrysoloras at the turn of the fourteenth century. Two of his display speeches, *Euagoras* and *Nicocles*, were subsequently translated by Chrysoloras' pupil Guarino, and his works were studied in Vittorino's school at Mantua. The editio princeps of the orations was published in Milan (1493) by Demetrius Chalcondyles. The Aldine edition, which formed the basis of Erasmus' translation, appeared in 1513.[6]

Ad Nicoclem, or *About Statecraft*, was originally published by Erasmus as an adjunct to his *Institutio principis*, the Fürstenspiegel which he dedicated to Prince Charles on the occasion of being appointed his councillor.[7] The dedicatory letter (Ep 393) is dated March 1516, but there is evidence suggesting that both the *Institutio* and the translation from Isocrates were composed somewhat earlier when Erasmus had first indications of his impending appointment.[8] The presentation of this particular Isocratean work was historically significant: Charles' great-grandfather, Frederick III, had received the same literary gift fifty years earlier, on the occasion of his visit to Rome in 1468. The book, a translation by Bessarion's friend Martino Fileto, was printed in 1513 on the initiative of Jacob Spiegel, Maximilian's secretary and a correspondent of Erasmus.[9] As a newly appointed imperial councillor Erasmus repeated the gesture of presenting a Hapsburg prince with classical advice on the art of government, but gave it a new dimension by adding a modern companion piece: his own handbook on the education of a ruler.

Ad Nicoclem, a hortatory epistle addressed by Isocrates to his pupil, the young Cyprian king Nicocles, consists of a string of maxims to guide the young monarch in his personal and public life. Erasmus added his own aphorisms in rivalry with the classical author, but expected his readers to peruse them in a different spirit: 'For he [Isocrates] was a sophist, instructing some petty king or rather tyrant, and both were pagans; I am a theologian addressing a renowned and upright prince, Christians both of us.'[10]

The moral content of Isocrates' *parainesis* was more closely related to Erasmus' own philosophy and educational ideals than that of any other classical author he had translated so far. Despite Erasmus' emphasis on the difference in their respective approaches to ethics, readers saw only the similarities, so much so that later collectors of maxims had no scruples about combining and interweaving the two sets of aphorisms.[11] Indeed, Isocrates' precepts formed the ideal counterpart, parallel, and companion piece to Erasmus' own instructions. One may assume, therefore, that the humanist chose his classical model not only following a historical precedent but also conceiving Isocrates' epistle to be an appropriate background for presenting his own pedagogical ideals. On more than one occasion he recommended the Greek author on these grounds, pointing out his merits both in the dedicatory letter accompanying the translation and in his preface to the *Apophthegmata*, in which he gave Isocrates an honourable mention among writers offering useful counsel to princes.[12]

Turning to Erasmus' translation, we note the by now familiar devices of reduplication and division of composite words into their parts: οἰκειοτάτους (most familiar) is translated by a twinning of adjectives as *familiarissimos maximeque domesticos* (well-known and very familiar); τιμαί (honours) as *honores ... et praemia* (honours and rewards); the composite word ἀνουθέτητοι (unadmonished) by a combination of object and verb as *admonitore carent* (they lack a critical adviser); and δυσκαταμαθήτως according to its component parts as *perdifficile cognitu* (hard to learn).[13] In this manner Erasmus gives his translation the appropriate weight and convincing effect of a *parainesis*.

We may also draw attention to a number of interesting and imaginative translations for Greek terms lacking a Latin equivalent: παρρησία (licence of speech) is variously rendered into Latin as *libere loquendi facultas* (opportunity to speak freely) and in an interpretative fashion as *admonendi libertas* (freedom to admonish); πανηγύρεις, the Greek word for Panhellenic games, is translated as *ludi publici* (public games); φιλάνθρωπος (philanthropic) as *civium* ... *amans* (fond of his citizens);[14] καιρός (the appropriate moment) in one case succinctly as *tempus* ([right] time), in another more fully as *ipsum rerum punctum* (the exact point of things).[15] With a fine sense for the Latin idiom Erasmus translates ἀρχικὸς εἶναι (literally, 'being ruler-like') in a free, but appropriate, manner as *principis dignitatem ostendere* (to display a ruler's dignity).[16] A similarly expansive translation renders λόγοι πολιτικοί (political speeches) as *orationes civiles et de republica gubernanda praecipientes* (public speeches and precepts about the government of the state). Elsewhere ἐπιεικῶς πραττόντων (acting with propriety) is rendered into Latin with flair and a personal touch as *placidam et humanam agunt vitam* (they lead a peaceful and humane life).[17] In these cases Erasmus has invested a Greek phrase of general content with specific ideas, and infused it with a subjective nuance. This process is also evident in his translation of Isocrates' vague and all-inclusive expression τοὺς μέλλοντάς τι τῶν δεόντων ποιήσειν (those who will do what is proper). Linking proper behaviour more specifically with reward, Erasmus translates the phrase as *qui munus aliquod cum laude gesturi sunt* (who will do their duty to applause).[18] Such subtle changes mark Erasmus' tendency to put his personal imprint on the material before him.

As noted before, he sometimes exceeds the measure of a translation proper. Entering the realm of paraphase, he replaces a simple Greek command, ζῆλου (emulate), by a circuitous phrase, *felices et imitandos puta* (consider fortunate and worthy of imitation), or substitutes for a simple verb, ἐνδείκνυσο (show yourself), a considerably expanded expression, *populum testem admitte* (make the people your witness).[19] The last-mentioned examples demonstrate the trend in Erasmus' translations towards everfreer renditions and subjective interpretations. We find him once more in the role of a commentator rather than a translator when he explains ὀλιγαρχία (oligarchy) as 'states in which the power is vested in the few' (*res publicas in quibus penes paucos est rerum potestas*).[20] We also see him exercising his stylistic preferences, carefully balancing a Latin sentence by adding a phrase here and there; for example in the clause *non quae tu merebaris sed quae ipse praestare potui*, in which the first part, 'not according to your worth,' is added by Erasmus to balance the phrase 'but according to my power'; in the same passage he also writes *non solum non conteres, quod in illis solet usuvenire, verum etiam ... maiora reddes* (not only will you not wear them out, as is wont to happen with those, but you will make them greater). In this clause the reference 'as is wont to happen with those' is an Erasmian addition.[21]

As in his other translations, we find signs of a hasty execution: omissions and errors. The latter are particularly distressing, as they occur in passages whose meaning is not obscure, whose structure and vocabulary should not unduly tax the skills of an experienced translator. Yet Erasmus equivocates, stumbles, and skirts his responsibilities as translator, juggling the text to suit a facile interpretation. In one instance the translation he offers postulates a change in case endings. The Greek text runs: τίμα ταῖς μὲν ἀρχαῖς τῶν φίλων τοὺς οἰκειοτάτους, ταῖς δ'ἀληθείαις αὐταῖς τοὺς εὐνουστάτους (honour with office those who are your closest kin, but honour in truth your most loyal friends). Erasmus renders the passage in contracted form, joining the verb with three dative objects: *primos honores tribue coniunctissimis, verissimis, amicissimis* (give first honours to your closest, truest, and more friendly associates).[22] Elsewhere Isocrates says: δοκοῦντας καρτερικοὺς καὶ φιλοπόνους εἶναι τοὺς τῶν δεόντων τι ποιοῦντας (those who have regard for their duties are considered austere and fastidious). Erasmus misunderstood the sentence, investing the two adjectives, which are ambivalent, with the wrong meaning. Καρτερικός can mean both 'self-disciplined' and 'austere'; φιλοπόνος can mean both 'industrious' and 'fastidious.' In each case Erasmus chose the positive instead of the required negative sense. To eliminate the difficulties arising from this unsuitable interpretation he resorted to emending the text and rather unscrupulously inserted a negative, translating: *eosque pro temperatis et industriis haberi qui nihil earum rerum agunt* (they are considered self-disciplined and industrious who do nothing of this sort).[23] In another case Erasmus introduces a contrast which has no basis in the Greek. He writes: *his quidem audiendis delectantur, caeterum cum ipsos labores et certamina spectant, molestia afficiuntur* (when they hear it they are delighted, when they see the actual struggle and contest they are distressed). The Greek, however, contains two parallel ideas depending on one verb (χαίρουσι, they delight in): ἀκούοντες μὲν γὰρ τῶν τοιούτων χαίρουσι, θεωροῦντες δὲ τοὺς ἀγῶνας καὶ τὰς ἁμίλλας (their ears are delighted by the story as are their eyes by the sight of the struggle and contest).[24] In yet another case Erasmus wrongly connects two sentences. Overlooking the word ἐργασίας in the sentence τὰς μὲν ἐργασίας αὐτοῖς καθίστη κερδαλέας (make industry profitable for them), he translates the phrase with reference to the preceding sentence, which deals with the country's laws: *fac ut earum observatio lucro sit civibus* (make observation [of the laws] profitable for the citizens).[25]

Somehow one finds such mistakes less excusable than those, noted on previous occasions, in which the Greek expressions lack clarity, were seriously corrupt, or referred to obscure facts and events, thereby presenting legitimate problems to a translator working without the aid of a commentary. In the cases noted here, Erasmus' errors appear to be the result of inattention and haste rather than of any real difficulties in the text. Erasmus himself was well aware of his weaknesses and deficiencies as a translator, but chose to take a nonchalant view of them. He openly admitted: 'That's the way I am, I can't change my nature. I pour out, rather than write, everything and find the labour of correction more bothersome than the labour of composition.'[26]

A decade elapsed between the publication of Isocrates' speech *Ad Nicoclem* and the next translation of a classical work. The intervening years mark a period in Erasmus' life that was filled with strife and controversy generated by the publication of his New Testament. Much of his time during these years was taken up with the defence of his work and with apologies answering the publications of his opponents.[27] At his own university he had to confront Jacques Masson, who attacked language studies, and Edward Lee, who published critical notes on his *Annotationes*. In France Erasmus' work was investigated by Noël Beda, the representative of the theological faculty of Paris, who had been instructed to report on suspect passages in his writings; and in Spain he faced Zúñiga, who had branded his views as blasphemous and heretical. The very foundations of Erasmus' research – the application of philological principles to biblical studies – was called into question. At the same time he was urged to take a stand on the dispute between Lutherans and conservative theologians, with both sides clamouring for his support and condemning his indecision. It was in these troubled times that Erasmus sought solace and peace in the undisputed wisdom of the classics:

Plutarch's remedies for the follies of mankind, Galen's exhortation to pursue the liberal arts, and Xenophon's portrait of the ideal prince.

We have already discussed Erasmus' translations from Plutarch's *Moralia*,[28] the last of which was published in 1526. In the same year Erasmus had commenced work on three tracts by Galen, the famous second-century-AD medical writer.[29] Galen, who began his career as an attendant to gladiators and rose rapidly to become personal physician to the Emperor Marcus Aurelius, was the author of philosophical as well as medical treatises which established him as one of the great scientific writers of antiquity. His influence abided throughout the Middle Ages. A favourite authority of medical schools, his works were translated in the fourteenth century by the Italian physician Peter of Abano, in the fifteenth century by Leonicenus and by the classicist Gaza, and in the early sixteenth century by the physicians Cop, Linacre, and Du Rueil, men who belonged to the circle of Erasmus' acquaintances.[30]

In 1525 the Aldine press was preparing the editio princeps of Galen's works. Erasmus kept informed about the project and expressed his eager interest in a letter to Francisco Asulano, who eventually presented him with the complete edition.[31] The first volume of the Aldina appeared with the colophon date of April 1525. We do not know when the first copy of this volume reached Erasmus, but by the spring of 1526 he had translated the first three items in it. He dedicated the versions to Antonin of Košice, a Hungarian physician who had rendered professional services to him in Basel and who belonged to the circle of humanists at King Louis' court.[32]

Erasmus' interest in Galen may have been aroused by a preoccupation with his own, rather precarious, health as well as by non-professional contact with members of the medical profession. He counted a number of physicians among his personal friends: Lyster, the corrector of his 1515 edition of the *Adages* who had also contributed some Greek verses to the prefatory material of his Plutarch translations; Cop, physician to the German nation at the University of Paris and later court physician, who was one of the scholars promoting his move to France; and Linacre, Henry viii's private physician, who had completed a series of translations from Galen between 1517 and 1524 and whose work Erasmus read with keen interest.[33]

Erasmus himself occasionally adopted the tone of a friendly physician, at one point advising his friend Gillis to 'beware of certain drugs,' to 'avoid all strong emotions, excessive joy, unrestrained laughter, too much walking, excessive study, anger especially.'[34] That he was considered by his friends somewhat of an expert in the science is evident from Henry Caduceator's request for a prescription 'if there appears to be some medicine to counteract this problem with my eyes' and Erasmus' answer to Schets' inquiry about treatment for another illness: 'Let him use a moderate diet, especially at dinner, let him beware of chills, especially of cold feet. He should not put pressure on his kidneys with a belt or garment. Let him eat light food, such as lamb or poultry. Let him abstain from hot and greasy food, such as fried stuff, strong wines, and too much bread, especially old bread. Also, he should urinate frequently ...'[35] Although Erasmus professed a lively interest in the science of medicine, he never sought professional knowledge and therefore chose among Galen's works three essays of a more general content: *Exhortatio ad artium liberalium studia* (An exhortation to study the liberal arts), *De optimo docendi genere* (The best kind of teaching); and *Quod optimus medicus idem sit et philosophus* (The best physician is also a philosopher).

The first treatise must have attracted Erasmus for its affinity with his own views on the superiority of education over other advantages, innate or acquired, such as strength, beauty, and wealth. The essay contains passages inspired by Galen's personal experience – for example, a lively tirade against the excesses of athletic training – but the topic 'What constitutes the highest good' was common stock and a standard theme discussed in rhetorical schools. Erasmus himself had included a model composition on the topic in his manual on letter-writing.[36] Moreover, he had composed a speech in praise of medicine which, like Galen's, purported to 'encourage, attract, and stimulate young men to conceive in their hearts admiration and love for the study of medicine.'[37]

Galen's second essay depicts the good physician as a philosopher and idealist, views akin to those expressed by Erasmus in his eulogy of medicine.[38] The essay 'On the best kind of teaching,' a refutation of sceptical doctrine, is, however, a surprising choice, since Erasmus often expressed his distaste for speculative philosophy and took no pleasure in the sort of quibbling that marks this piece.[39] Moreover, the Greek text of this particular essay presented unusual difficulties, being the most corrupt in a corrupt lot and requiring a considerable number of emendations and conjectures on the part of the translator.

Erasmus complained about the poorly collated text of the Aldine edition in the dedicatory epistle accompanying the translation as well as in letters to friends. He commented that he 'had never seen anything more corrupt' and that the edition was so full of mistakes that it required 'guesswork' on the part of the translator, and expressed his dissatisfaction with the printer who had shown more regard for his purse than for the quality of the text: 'What a serious sacrilege is committed for a few filthy gold pieces. For that money they could have hired a scholarly corrector.'[40]

Erasmus successfully emended a number of corrupt passages in the Aldine edition. Many of the corrections postulated by him were in fact adopted by later editors, and others which defied his skills remain a challenge also to modern philologists.[41]

In the translation we find the usual careful attention to Latin idiom and skilful manipulation of rhetorical devices, among them the use of superlatives and twinned expressions. For example, Erasmus translates Galen's ἀποβλήτοις and ἀληθές, positive adjectives, by the superlatives *contemptissimis* (most despicable) and *verissimum* (very true);[42] in a similar fashion he renders περὶ αὑτὸν ἔχων (keeping by his side) into Latin as *coniunctissimos habens* (keeping very close).[43] In several cases a simple Greek term is translated by two Latin words: λόγος (fame) is rendered as *nomen aut ... dignitatem* (fame or ... honour); ἠμελημένον (neglected) is translated as *neglectum et incuratum* (neglected and uncared for) and ἀθροίζειν (collect) appears in Latin as *colligunt et coacervunt* (collect and heap up).[44]

There is a notable tendency to add, amplify, and elaborate, for the purpose of embellishing a phrase, giving it balance, or explaining its import. Thus the phrase ἐν τοιαύταις περιστάσεσι πραγμάτων (surrounded by such troubles) is expanded into *in tantis negociis undique circumstantibus ac vallantibus* (surrounded and beset on all sides by such great troubles).[45] Balancing phrases are added in the following cases: *eosdem haud eodem in statu* (the same men, but not in the same position), where the second part is supplied by Erasmus; *quod aliis dicitur καταληπτόν* (the term 'apprehensible' which some people use), where the relative clause is added.[46] Elsewhere Erasmus complements Galen's list of carpenter's tools, adding an explanation of their use: *nec cubitum quo metiatur, nec xyston quo poliat, neque regulam ad quem dirigat, neque circinum quo circumdat* (neither an ell for measuring, nor a scraper for planing, nor a rule for drawing lines, nor a compass for drawing circles).[47]

With a certain flair he translates words lacking a coextensive term in Latin: φιλάνθρωπος (philanthropic) as *familiaris et amica humano generi* (a friend and patron to mankind), βάναυσος (manual) as *sedentarius*, a rare word (literally, 'sitting').[48] As in his other translations, Erasmus interprets technical terms to aid the reader's understanding. In one passage he explains δολιχός (Greek fount retained) as *in quo cursus ad viginti tria stadia porrigitur* (a course of twenty-three stadia) and *diaulum* (transliterated) as *in quo cursus ac recursus duplicat stadium* (two stadia back and forth).[49] In another passage he translates the philosophical terms *epoche* (transliterated), γνωστόν, and καταληπτόν (the last two retained in Greek fount) as *suspensam sententiam nihilque definientem* (suspended judgment, defining nothing), *cognoscibile* (perceptible), and *comprehensibile* (comprehensible).[50] Elsewhere he explains the loan-words *plasticen* and *tessera* as *ars fingendi* (the art of sculpturing) and *quattuor angulis nitens* (resting on four corners). Other loan-words, however, such as *nothus, basis,* and *oeconomus* (bastard, base, steward), which had been adopted in classical antiquity and were well-known to Renaissance readers, are retained without further explanation.[51]

In some cases Erasmus introduces a nuance not found in the Greek. In one passage Galen speaks of philosophy as 'the divine gift' of Apollo. Erasmus takes care to diminish the role of the Greek god, describing the art merely as a 'great gift' and stressing man's role in the discovery of philosophy: *sua sibi paravit industria* (he won it through his very own efforts). This accords with the views expressed in his *Praise of Medicine* where he relates that this science had once been considered an invention of the god Apollo and that Aesculapius had been given divine honours for his contributions to medicine. Erasmus conveys this information with a qualifying comment: 'I do not approve of these practices of the ancients [ascribing a divine origin to the arts]; I do however praise their intent and judgment ...'[52] In another passage Erasmus also shifts Galen's emphasis. Translating the simple noun διδάσκαλος (teacher) by a rather pompous clause, *qui docendi munus profitentur* (men who are engaged in the teaching profession), he seems to elevate the importance of the teacher's role.[53] Elsewhere he changes a neutral ἐπιστάς (approaching) into a stronger *insultans* (scoffing) and a quiet προχειρίζειν (adducing arguments) into the more aggresive *obicere* (cast into his teeth).[54] In each of these cases Erasmus has added a personal touch to the text, somewhat exceeding his mandate as a translator; in other cases he adopts a free version for stylistic reasons. We see the skilled linguist at work in a passage describing a ship battling violent storms. Carefully preserving the nuances of the original, Erasmus recaptures its epic tone in the words *procellis ac fluctibus obruta demergaturis in profundum* (overwhelmed by wind and waves about to plunge it into the deep), a description recalling Virgil's line *Incute vim ventis submersasque obrue puppis*.[55] Other examples evidencing Erasmus' creativity and imagination are his use of the neat phrase *ad terrorem arte factas imagines* (artfully made horror masks) to translate μορμολυκεῖα (hobgoblins), the idiom *ad calculos vocare* (to call to the counters, meaning 'to judge') to parallel ψηφίζειν (which means 'to judge,' also referring to the voting process); and *ante cognoscere* (literally, 'recognize in advance') to reproduce the etymology of προγινώσκειν (to make a diagnosis).[56] On the other hand, Erasmus translates δημαγωγός (demagogue) by a disappointingly colourless and deficient word, *orator* (orator), although an appropriately derogatory term exists in Latin (*rabula*).[57]

A few errors have also crept into the translations. Erasmus was obviously unfamiliar with the term ἐντείνας in the technical sense of writing an epic poem and translated it literally as writing a 'long poem' (*prolixo carmine*). In another case he garbled the meaning of the Greek sentence, saying that ' "apprehension" corresponds to "apprehensive impression" ' whereas the Greek has ' "apprehension" and "apprehensive impression", correspondingly.'[58] Another error occurs in the introductory paragraph of the *Exhortation* in which Galen contrasts the views of Hippocrates with those of his would-be followers. The Greek has two pairs of ὁ/μὲν; Erasmus lumps them together, attributing both sets of opinions to Hippocrates' disciples.[59] On one occasion he translates a gnomic aorist by a narrative tense, transforming a general statement into a historical one. Elsewhere he misconstrues an admittedly difficult passage completely: failing to recognize the disjunctive periods in Greek, he produces a meaningless sentence in Latin.[60]

Confronted with corrupt passages, Erasmus repeatedly offers literal translations, leaving the reader with obscure and puzzling statements, and in one case with a Latin sentence that does not run.[61] In another case he writes that the sophists 'discredit the theory that there is no natural power of judgment,' a defective clause which, as it stands, proclaims exactly the opposite of what is wanted; elsewhere he inexplicably translates πέπαυμαι λέγων (left off saying) by its opposite *coeperam dicere* (I started out saying).[62]

In one case, however, he makes a valiant effort to reconstruct the meaning of a corrupt passage as best he can. The Greek text, as established by its modern editor, Barigazzi, runs as follows:[63] ἀλλ᾽ ἑτέρου τινὸς· ἀπαιτήσεις μᾶλλον μὲν τοὺς τεχνίτας παρέχοντας τοῖς μαθηταῖς εὐθέως [ἀλλ᾽ ἑτέρου] τὸ λογίζεσθαι, τὸ καλούμενον ὑπὸ τῶν πολλῶν ψηφίζειν. This means: 'Something else is needed: craftsmen should be required to teach their disciples immediately to reason, or as the common people call it, "to reckon."' Erasmus translates this passage: *Sed alia quadam re fuerit opus, videlicet repetitione, ut artifices non statim artem praebent discipulis, sed aliud exigunt, nimirum considerationem eorum quae tradita sunt, quod a plerisque dicitur ad calculum vocare.* This means: 'Something else was needed, namely repetition; for craftsmen do not immediately convey their art to their disciples, they demand something else, namely a consideration of what had been transmitted, or as the common people call it, "a reckoning."'

Erasmus, who reads ἀπαιτήσεως for ἀπαιτήσεις, translates the word with some imagination as *repetitione* (a demanding back; in this context, a demanding of answers in reply to questions by the teacher); next, he conjectures a negative between μαθηταῖς and εὐθέως; finally, he gives a more specific meaning to λογίζεσθαι which suits the overall meaning he has infused into the sentence. In this manner he gives the passage a decidedly Erasmus note, treating it as a comment on pedagogical methods rather than a statement on the epistemological basis of teaching, as was no doubt Galen's intention.[64]

On the whole, Erasmus' version of this most difficult among the three essays he chose from Galen's works must be called a qualified success, in that it reflects the translator's linguistic talents but does not exhaust all the avenues open to the textual critic. The most effective among the three translations is, no doubt, the *Exhortatio*, an essay in which Erasmus' rhetorical skills are displayed to their best advantage. It is interesting to note, however, that the Froben edition of 1542 did not use Erasmus' version, as might be expected, but chose a contemporary piece by Ludovicus Bellisarius, a physician from Modena.[65] The preference shown by this choice invites a comparison between the two translators' versions.

Bellisarius shares with Erasmus a certain rhetorical flair, elegance, and purity of style. In fact, the two men's choice of words is so close that one is tempted to postulate a dependence. For several reasons, however, we are left to speculate on this point. A chronological relationship between the two translations cannot be established, since we have no biographical data for Bellisarius; his translation first appeared in the Giunta edition of Galen's *Opera omnia* (Venice 1541), but the date of its composition and first edition is unknown. Moreover, the similarities between the two versions occur mainly in the vocabulary. Sentence structure, composition, and interpretation of individual passages show considerable differences. For example, at 640:29 Erasmus reads ἐγκαλούντων αὐτήν (invoking her), translating *ipsius opem implorantes*; Bellisarius reads ἐγκαλούντων αὐτῇ (accusing her), translating *ipsamque accusantes*. At 642:12–13 Erasmus translates the Aldine text οὓς ἴσα καὶ τοὺς θεοὺς σέβομεν οἷον ὑπαρχοί τινες καὶ ὑπηρέται τοῦ θεοῦ (whom we revere like gods, being the followers and servants of the god), saying *quos par cum diis honore dignamus, tamquam assectatores ac ministros quosdam dei*, whereas Bellisarius seems to follow a variant, translating *quos omnes deus et sibi ministros elegit et apud se primos et quasi alteros Mercurios esse voluit quos nos aeque ac deos colimus* (all of whom the god chose as his servants and wished to be foremost in his presence, as if they were second Mercurii, and whom we revere like gods). Such divergences led Beaudouin, who analysed Bellisarius' translation, to the conclusion that he was following a manuscript tradition different from that of the Aldine edition.[66] It is conceivable, therefore, that Bellisarius composed his translation before its publication in 1526 and thus preceded Erasmus. The following examples will illustrate the similarities in vocabulary used.

ERASMUS:	BELLISARIUS:
... ut protinus in ea reluceat animi virtus. Est autem hilari vultu, oculis acribus. (641:4–5)	... sed in cuius forma animi virtutes protinus eluceant. Est enim hilari vultu, acribus oculis. (4E)
... ac fortasse miraberis alteri quidem Pactolum affluxu sui invehentem aurum, alteri vero marinos etiam pisces subservientes. (641:14–16)	... eosque fortasse miraberis, dum alteri Pactolum cernes auro fluentem, alteri marinos etiam pisces inservientes. (4E)
nam parietes omnes egregiis picturis ornatos esse, solum autem ex tesellis preciosis esse concinnatum, habens ex his deorum expressas imagines, vasa omnia pura ac nitentia, quin et stragulas et lectos pulchre magnoque artificio elaboratos esse (647:7–10)	Siquidem parietes omnes egregiis picturis ornatos inspiciam, pavimentum ex tesseris tam preciosis instructum, ut simulacra deorum ex sese expressa repraesentent, vasa omnia pura ac nitentia, lectum et eius fulcra miro artificio elaborata (6H)

Like Erasmus, Bellisarius tends to be expansive in order to clarify the context; for example, when Galen says very succinctly ὁ δ᾽ ἄνθρωπος οὔτε τινὸς τῶν παρ᾽ ἐκείνοις ἀμελέτητος (but man neglects none of those they have), and Erasmus repeats the antecedent and gives the point: *caeterum nec apud illa quicquam est artium quod homo non meditetur* (but man does not fail to consider any arts they possess), Bellisarius is even more explicit: *Homo autem ita ad artes aptus est ut si quae in alio animantium genere sunt, ne eas quidem immediatatas relinquat* (but man is so talented in the arts that, if any species of animal possesses an art, he does not leave it unconsidered).[67] In another passage Galen says ἀλλ᾽ ἴσως τῶν εἰρημένων μὲν οὐδενός, ἰσχύος δ᾽ ἀντιποιήσονται (but perhaps they will claim only strength and none of the aforesaid). Here Erasmus retains the concise form of the Greek, saying: *At fortassis nihil quidem ex omnibus his quae dicta sunt, sed robur sibi vindicabunt.* Bellisarius, however, translates more expansively: *Sed in caeteris fortasse de quibus modo disseruimus athletae cedent: quod verum reliquum est* ... (but perhaps the athletes will concede the points discussed before; as for the rest ...).[68]

Bellisarius composed fluent and harmonious phrases, but Erasmus was the one who coined the more memorable expressions. We have already noted Erasmus' poetic description of a ship buffeted by storms; Bellisarius' version runs: *in navi adeo tempestatibus iactata ut et fluctibus obruatur et submergi periclitetur* (in a ship so tossed by storms that it is overwhelmed by waves and in danger of being submerged). The clause is carefully balanced, to be sure, but it lacks the evocative qualities of Erasmus' translation, which, like its Greek counterpart, conjures up a line of epic poetry. Individual words such as μορμολυκεῖα or βάναυσος, which were creatively rendered by Erasmus, are translated by Bellisarius in a correct, but more predictable and pedestrian, manner as *larvas* and *mechanicos*.[69]

Both translators stumbled occasionally,[70] but on the whole produced a meaningful translation; both were inclined to elaborate on the Greek and to place concerns for stylistic appeal above considerations of accuracy. Erasmus, however, went one step further, changing not only the quantity but also the quality of Galen's words and adding a subjective note to the text.[71]

Weighing the respective merits of the translators, the sixteenth-century editor must have been hard pressed to decide between them, for the two authors excelled in the same field – the art of rhetoric – and shared the same weaknesses, a tendency to translate expansively and pass over details.

In 1529 the controversy between Rome and the reformers obliged Erasmus to leave Basel and seek refuge in Freiburg im Breisgau where Archduke Ferdinand had offered him hospitality and protection. Shortly before this move Anton Fugger had written to Erasmus inviting him to take up residence in Augsburg. Although both this offer and a second invitation were declined, the head of the famous banking and trading firm maintained a benevolent interest in Erasmus, who acknowledged his flattering attentions with a dedication of Xenophon's *Hiero*.[72]

The fifth-century-BC author who fought in the war against Persia and was later banished for his political view spent his years in exile writing history, biography, and works on specialized fields, such as economics. Though he was neither a historian nor a philosopher proper, his writings had a highly moralizing tone and contained strong anecdotal elements. The Italian humanists of the fifteenth century showed much interest in Xenophon's works. Guarino, Filelfo, and Bessarion had manuscripts of the *Hiero* in their libraries, and Bruni paraphrased the treatise in 1403.[73] The Aldine press produced Xenophon's *Opera omnia* in 1525, an edition which Erasmus ordered, perhaps that same year.[74] In the dedicatory letter accompanying the translation and dated 13 February 1530, Erasmus explained that he had begun work on the *Hiero* 'a few years ago,' but had not completed it because the text presented too many problems. Coming across the unfinished draft version, he had sat down and carried the task through to its completion 'without pausing for breath, making steady progress.'[75] The presentation copy was delivered to Anton Fugger in April and fetched a grateful reply.[76] The treatise was first printed by Froben (Basel 1530), and a revised edition was later added to Basil's *Duae Homiliae* (Freiburg 1532).

Presenting the work to Fugger, Erasmus explained that Xenophon was addressing himself to a 'tyrant' (*tyrannus*) in the archaic sense of the word, for the term had once been coextensive with 'king' or 'ruler.' He cautioned his patron and the general readership that not all notions of kingship contained in the book were relevant to their own times, but that a good many ideas were 'useful to know, even to princes in our age.'[77] It was the applicability of these ideas that was important, not their historical truth. Even if Xenophon's portrait of Hiero was inaccurate and the character of his hero fictionalized, the reader was bound to respect Xenophon as one of the wise men of antiquity 'whose authority gave their writings the force of precept.'[78] This instructive quality commended his writings to the reader and invested them with a certain dignity.

The translation of the *Hiero* is one of the more fluent and accurate versions among Erasmus' late productions.[79] We find no omissions to speak of, only one or two problematic passages, and several difficult sequences that are weathered with skill. There are, however, the usual number of additions, elaborations, and duplications that characterize Erasmus' other translations. Some of the additions serve the purpose of balancing the Latin sentence, as in two cases where a comparative standing on its own in Greek is offset by a relative clause in Latin: *deterius ... quam privatos homines* (worse ... than private men); *hi potius ... qui devorant* (those rather ... who devour).[80] Other additions express what is only implied in the Greek; for example, the phrase *adsentandi gratia laudent, non ex animo* (they would praise for the sake of flattery, not from their heart), in which the second part is added by Erasmus. In another passage he writes *quae cum odio metuque servili pugnant* (things that are at variance with hate and servile fear), whereas the Greek has only ἐκ τῶν ἐναντίων (at variance). In a third case Erasmus puts *ne quid tibi accidat quod nolint* (lest something happen to you that they do not want to happen), expressing the implication of the pregnant phrase μή τι πάθης (lest you suffer [some ill]).[81] In these cases a desire to preserve Latin idiom may have influenced Erasmus' choice of words; in other instances his additions only serve the purpose of expressing the Greek more fully. For example, Erasmus translates the adjective σοφός (wise) expansively as *viro tam erudito tantaque sapientia* (a man of such education and wisdom); in another case, *plebeios et artis imperitos* (common people, and unskilled in the arts) stands for the noun ἰδιωτῶν (unskilled people); elsewhere *contentio vincendique studium* (competitiveness and a desire to win) translates the verb φιλονεικεῖν (to be ambitious).[82] In one case the addition serves as an interpretation. Xenophon speaks of the desirable element in a marriage (τὸ ἀγαπητόν); Erasmus interprets the term and puts it into context, saying: *vigor caritatis quae inter eiusdem civitatis conjuges intercedit* (the power of love that exists between spouses of the same nationality).[83]

Occasionally Erasmus gives an unnecessarily drawn-out version, such as the convoluted clause *qui videbantur esse viri ea conditione ut maxime sua sorte debuerint esse contenti* (who seemed to be men in a position in which they should have been content with their lot), which stands for the elegant Greek τῶν δοκούντων ἱκανωτάτων (seeming worthy men).[84] In another case Erasmus offers an elaborate phrase, *sed dum nusquam non adest ac circumfertur, fit omnium iucundarum rerum corruptela* (but since it is always present and around, it becomes the corruptor of all pleasant things), for a somewhat less circumstantial, though complex, Greek ἀλλὰ καὶ πάντων τῶν ἡδέων συμπαρακολουθῶν λυμεὼν γίγνεται.[85]

In addition we find some rather free and unsuitable translations that must be the result of misinterpretation. The phrase *novi, inquit, te cum esses privatus* (I knew you when you were a private citizen) is rather unexpected for ἰδιώτην γεγενημένον (born a private citizen).[86] We must also assume a misunderstanding in another passage where Erasmus refers to the risk the rider takes if the horse is 'fearful and frightened, so that there is a danger of it causing some irremediable ill' (*expavescentem atque attonitum, unde periculum sit, ne quod malum det immedicabile*).[87] Xenophon, however, says: ὥσπερ γε καὶ ἵππος εἰ ἀγαθὸς μὲν εἴη, φοβερὸς δὲ μὴ ἀνήκεστόν τι ποιήσῃ (suppose that a good horse makes his master worry that he will do him some fatal mischief).

We have seen Erasmus abridging or changing a text he found morally offensive. His translation of the *Hiero* affords another such instance of censorship. As in the previously noted case,[88] Erasmus shrinks from attributing pederasty to a king who is being held up as a model. He therefore translates παιδικῶν (male lovers) as *puellarum* (girls) and changes the name of the king's favourite Δαϊλόχου τοῦ καλλίστου ἐπικαλουμένου (Dailochus, called 'most beautiful'), obviously considering a womanizing king preferable to a homosexual.[89]

As in Erasmus' other translations we observe his independence of the Greek text, his divergence for the sake of Latin idiom or a certain stylistic preference. Thus he changes the passive ἐξαπατᾶσθαι (to be deceived) into a verb of active meaning, *hallucinari* (to hallucinate), which puts the blame squarely on people who, in Erasmus' version, deceive themselves.[90] In another instance he nicely renders the Greek adjective [οὐκ]ἀνήκοοι (listening) by the Latin phrase *liberae sunt aures* (their ears are open), conveying the eagerness implied by the context.[91] In another case, however, he imposes a Latin concept where history does not warrant it, translating αἱ πόλεις (city states) as *res publica* (republic).[92]

The *Hiero* is a pleasing conclusion to Erasmus' respectable career as a translator. It contains few of the flaws that so often accompany his work, betraying the author's haste or carelessness, and displays the full range of his skills, his dexterity in conveying the full import of the Greek, and his attention to idiomatic correctness. Although the *Hiero* is Erasmus' last full-scale translation of a Greek classic, we cannot neglect another, later publication: the *Apophthegmata*, published in 1531, a work which takes his progression from literal translator to liberal interpreter to its logical conclusion: in this book Erasmus formally renounces the task of the translator and steps out as a commentator.

Erasmus presented the *Apophthegmata* to William Duke of Cleves, to whom he had previously dedicated *De pueris instituen-*

dis.[93] The book was printed by Froben (Basel 1531) and reprinted with slight alterations in 1532 and 1535. In the prefatory letter Erasmus pointed out that princes more than other men had an obligation to prepare themselves for their position, but being pressed to do so much in such a short time, they had a special need for study aids presenting important mattter, such as philosophy, political science, and strategy in compendiary form. It is interesting to note that Erasmus adopts in this letter a utilitarian position that stands in marked contrast to the famous Platonic vision of the philosopher-king. Dispensing with this idealistic view, Erasmus claims that a ruler cannot be expected to 'unravel the riddles and labyrinths of Socratic subtlety, irony, and induction,'[94] that Aristotle is of interest only to professional philosophers, and that even Cicero's philosophical writings are too specious to be of use to a ruler. A prince could not be expected to waste a lifetime philosophizing. History as well, although a useful discipline, was too large a field to be perused by a busy prince. It was obvious, therefore, that an author who pre-selected material and presented it in palatable form was rendering a desirable service to his king. In Erasmus' opinion Plutarch had been most successful in this task. He deserved special praise, not only for his selection of material, but also for his presentation which was 'concise, convincing, witty, and elegant.'[95]

The *Apophthegmata*, though largely a compilation of anecdotes taken from Plutarch's work of the same name, is generally counted among Erasmus' original works. Indeed, he himself claims as much, saying: 'I have somehow made this whole work my own because I present the Greek stories more clearly, inserting at times what I have found added in other authors, adding also much that is not in Plutarch's work, and playing the part of the scholiast, noting everywhere either the sense or the application of the anecdotes, though only in the cases that needed elucidation, and that briefly, so as not to diverge from the proper nature of an anecdote.'[96]

Erasmus was aware of existing translations of Plutarch's *Apophthegmata*, naming one by Francesco Filelfo and another by Raffaele Regio (Rhegius), with whom he was personally acquainted. He believed, however, that his work could make a further contribution to the field and was far from superfluous, not only because his precursors had made errors ('of course, they are both human'), but also because neither had gone beyond the task of translating, while he had chosen to act as interpreter as well.[97] Erasmus' preference for this role is significant. At various points in his career as translator he had expressed dissatisfaction with the task because of the restrictions it entailed. He conveyed this view to the reader in so many words,[98] but more importantly through his methods, the liberties he took, the censorship he invoked, the idiosyncratic interpretations he imposed on his classical texts. In the *Apophthegmata* he openly embraced the role he had covertly assumed before. He affirmed that he did not want to have his style cramped by the need to adhere and conform to a Greek text and its wording, but wanted to let his pen run on. Moreover, he wished to address himself to his own generation, write for his own times. Trajan, the recipient of Plutarch's literary offering, had been a learned and scholarly ruler and the readership of Plutarch's age had been knowledgeable about the historical background and significance of individual anecdotes; Erasmus was offering his literary gift to a fifteen-year-old, and, more generally, to the prince's coevals.[99] He believed that the youth of the addressee and the status of learning that could be assumed in a student audience warranted, and indeed necessitated, some sort of commentary and interpretation. Such considerations had prompted him to abandon the role of a translator in favour of the more effective and auxiliary role of a collector and commentator.

We know that Erasmus used the Aldine edition of Plutarch's *Apophthegmata*. He expressed his dissatisfaction with the quality of the text, which obliged him to emend corrupt passages and to establish the correct reading before going on to the task at hand. He therefore regretfully noted that 'the more laudable and celebrated an author is, the more his text is corrupted to make money.'[100] He also explained that he had planned originally to include only a small part of Plutarch's *Apophthegmata* in his collection, but as he warmed to the task, he was carried away and translated the bulk of his work.[101]

Although Erasmus had dedicated the *Apophthegmata* to William of Cleves, he was of course aiming at a larger audience. He pointed out that his collection of anecdotes combined entertainment with edification and was therefore particularly suitable for use in schools. In fact, he expressed the hope that this lightweight material would arouse the students' interest in more serious philosophical studies.[102] Erasmus concluded his dedication to the duke with a caveat: 'Remember that you are a Christian reading pagan anecdotes, therefore read them with discretion.'[103] The fact that Erasmus considered it advisable to add this qualifying remark reflects the ongoing debate on the merits of ethnic literature and the unallayed fears of conservative teachers who continued to treat pagan authors as potential corruptors of the young.

Analysing the first book of Erasmus' *Apophthegmata*, which contains the sayings of the Spartan kings, we find that Erasmus follows Plutarch's arrangement and presents his text in full, taking no more liberties here than we have noted in his formal translations, but adding a suitable commentary to each anecdote. Since Erasmus explained in his preface that he was not anxious about distinctions between aphorisms, jokes, insults, witty sayings, and *bons mots*, but 'carefully avoided confusing aphorisms with stratagems,'[104] one expects him to omit the latter as extraneous to his subject. His practice is, however, to include all material found in the Greek text and merely to add a critical remark indicating that a particular anecdote does not fit the category of apophthegm.[105] Some selection could also have been expected in cases where the same anecdote is attributed to different rulers. Here, too, Erasmus refrains from exercising an option. Following Plutarch's lead he repeats the anecdote, occasionally giving a cross reference, but generally recounting it without comment.[106]

The passages added by Erasmus to his quotations from the Greek text usually contain an exposition of Plutarch's meaning as well as supplementary information of the kind found in modern commentaries. He clarifies references to historical events or ethnic customs, explains technical terms, and translates key phrases. Thus we encounter comments on the role of the *princeps convivii*, the use of instruments in battle, the cult of Hercules, the function of ephors, the meaning of the Dorian terms *dicelicta* and *Leobotan*, and the difference between μάχεσθαι and ἀναμάχεσθαι.[107]

On occasion Erasmus adds material from a source other than Plutarch's *Apophthegmata*, enriching the text with passages taken from his *Lives*, quoting pertinent remarks from Horace, Virgil, or Homer, citing variants found in other authors such as Athenaeus, Cicero, or Probus Aemilius, quoting a line of poetry from a Roman comedy, or a *bon mot* ascribed to Socrates.[108]

In a few cases hasty reading has led Erasmus astray. At 209D Plutarch says that the power of making peace is vested in the state, not in the military leader: τῆς μὲν εἰρήνης ἔφη τὴν πόλιν εἶναι κυρίαν. Erasmus alters the thrust of Agesilaus' words, interpreting them to mean 'in peace the authority of the state prevails, ... not so in times of war.'[109] At 210A Plutarch says, rather obscurely, ὥστε μόνος ἀεὶ χρῆσθαι ταῖς ὥραις (that he alone used the seasons well). Erasmus, transferring to this passage information contained in another anecdote, conjectures the meaning to be: ut quattuor anni temporibus unicis tantum vestibus uteretur (that he used only one layer of clothes during the four seasons).[110] In the section relating the sayings of Agesilaus, he misinterprets ἐλευθέρους μὲν κακούς, δούλους δὲ ἀγαθούς ([the inhabitants] are bad freemen, but good slaves) to mean illos qui improbi essent, eos esse liberos; contra qui probi, eos esse servos (among them, those who were rascals were free, and by contrast, those who were good men were slaves). When the anecdote is repeated in Callicratidas' name, however, Erasmus translates correctly: liberi, inquit, mali sed servi boni (bad freemen, but good slaves, he said).[111] Elsewhere Erasmus obscures Plutarch's meaning by referring a pronoun to the wrong antecedent. Anaxandridas is reported to have said 'it was not by cultivating fields, but by cultivating ourselves, that we acquired those fields': οὐ τούτων ἐπιμελούμενοι, ἀλλ᾽ αὑτῶν, αὐτοὺς ἐκτησάμεθα. This is a reference to the Spartan practice of letting their slave, the Helots, cultivate the fields, while they themselves practised martial arts. Erasmus wrote: 'We have acquired Helots, not for their [the fields']) sake, but for our own sake.' He therefore arrived at an incorrect interpretation, explaining 'that is, he reproaches their stupidity, because they bring up servants for empty show, preferring to have them as companions and ministers of their pleasure, rather than employed in useful tasks.'[112]

In the preface to the Apophthegmata Erasmus explained that he had opted for a paraphrase and commentary rather than a translation because he did not want to be encumbered in his writing by considerations for the wording and content of the original. For the most part, however, he renders Plutarch's text into Latin fully and accurately. It appears therefore that he was not so much troubled by what was in the Greek as by what was left unstated. As translator he was obliged to suppress personal comment and to refrain from improving or expanding the existing text, although in practice he did not always observe these stipulations. The role he had adopted in writing the *Apophtheg-mata* conceded to him legitimately the rights he had, to some extent, assumed unofficially. He was not at liberty to interpret and explicate, to play the literary critic, to express his personal opinion, and to put the Greek text into perspective. He took the opportunity his new role afforded him to contrast Christians with heathens, to compare his own time with the grand age of Spartan supremacy.[113] He permitted himself to comment on a wide range of subjects of interest to him: contemporary marital relations, the competence of physicians, the importance of liberal arts, peda-gogical methods, childless couples, even the fashion of plucking hair.[114] The mores of princes were, however, the favourite target of his asides. He reproached them for choosing their teachers carelessly, for being warmongers, enriching themselves at the cost of their subjects, placing their whim above the law, and putting pleasure before duty.[115] Above all, the role he had assumed permitted him to pronounce judgment, to express his agreement with the sentiments voiced in the Greek texts or to show his disapproval of the acts and attitudes portrayed in individual anecdotes. Thus he punctuated one story with the indignant remark 'In this example there is nothing to emulate, nothing worthy of a Spartan!' and alternatively recorded his approval and wholehearted support, exclaiming 'Who will fail to admire such presence of mind!' or 'O truly manful spirit, disdaining all pleasure!'[116]

No doubt Erasmus enjoyed venting his own feelings on a particular subject, but his exhortations and admonitions were appropriate and provided a suitable frame for the work, since they underlined and developed the didactic element which Erasmus considered so important in books designed for a youthful audience.

SEVEN

Working for the Cause:
Study Aids and Exhortations

꣠

Erasmus had always been actively involved in the promotion of classical scholarship, giving his personal support to friends and correspondents, defending the New Learning in his publications, and offering practical guidance in his pedagogical writings. In this spirit he had first translated Gaza's Greek grammar,[1] hoping to make its contents more accessible to readers and thus to facilitate the study of Greek. The idea of translating the text probably stemmed from his own experience as a teacher at Cambridge. Basing his lectures on Gaza's *Institutiones grammaticae*,[2] he may have realized that his students found medium and message equally difficult to understand. They were encumbered by a double burden: the immediate task of learning Greek grammar and the incidental one of understanding the instructions, which were written in the very language they were about to learn. To allow students to concentrate on the primary goal of learning the rules of grammar, Erasmus found it expedient to eliminate incidental difficulties and translated Gaza's instructions into the international language of scholars.

Theodore Gaza of Salonika came to Italy in 1435 and taught Greek until his death in 1475. Erasmus admired his scholarship, praising his command of the Latin language and eulogizing his ability as a translator.[3] He was, in Erasmus' opinion, the most readable among authors of textbooks, presenting his subject, which was by nature tedious, in the best possible manner. An expert in his field, Gaza was 'equally judicious and reliable in giving the learner what he wants, his purpose from the outset being not to exhibit his own learning but to give his reader a chance to learn. In his first book it is truly astonishing how concise, how well-ordered, how clear a survey of grammar he gives us, as though he drew us a kind of picture of the whole.'[4] For himself Erasmus claimed such praise as was due to the translator who had 'increased the practical element' by providing headings and adding brief notes, 'so that the book can now be understood with a minimum of effort.'[5]

The translation of the first book, containing mostly paradigms, was printed by Martens (Louvain 1516) and, in a revised edition, by Froben a few months later. In 1517 Erasmus continued his work with a translation of the second book, concerned with the parts of speech, but the publication was held up for several reasons: the first book was selling badly; the intended patron, the physician Afinius, was holding back his gift; another potential patron, John Fisher, showed no interest.[6] In the end Erasmus dedicated the second book to the recipient of the first, the German humanist Johannes Caesarius. In the preface he ignored the publisher's marketing difficulties and insisted that there was a demand for the translation: 'I made the public a present of the first book, and they demand the second.'[7] He expressed the hope that Greek studies would soon advance to a stage which made his aid unnecessary and declared five years later that this stage had been reached, claiming his share of the success: 'I translated Gaza's grammar to attract more students to the study of Greek ... and was so successful that my work, such as it is, now seems useless'.[8] He declined an invitation by John Angelus to translate Gaza's *De mensibus*, a treatise on the Greek calendar,[9] but cooperated on another venture undertaken in the service of Greek studies: Froben's *Dictionarius graecus*.

According to prevailing practice in an age without copyright, the dictionary incorporated the work of earlier classicists, but gave credit only to the most recent compiler, Jacob Ceratinus.[10] Erasmus, who wrote the preface to the dictionary, acknowledged the work of the predecessors in a general way, then answered a fictitious interlocutor questioning his right to add a preface 'to other people's work': 'Ceratinus undertook the work on my instigation ... and in fact I too have added some entries ...' He pointed out that compiling a dictionary was a thankless task and undertaken by scholars only 'for the public good.'[11]

Erasmus' translations of Greek classics were his most signifi-cant contribution to Greek studies, but even when he was not actively engaged in the publication of classical texts he did his best to stimulate research. We have no evidence of any direct involvement by Erasmus in the edition or translation of a Greek text after 1531,[12] but his interest in Greek literature and his devotion to classical learning remained constant.

When Gryneus published his edition of Aristotle's *Opera omnia* in 1531, Erasmus added a preface, pointing out that the editio princeps, which had been published by the Aldine press in 1495–8, was sold out. The new edition therefore filled a need in the academic community. It was also welcome on the market, as Erasmus noted, because it was reasonably priced. After these preliminaries on the practical aspects of the publication, Erasmus proceeded to explain its scholarly merits. Gryneus' edition incorporated a number of emendations which were based on additionally consulted manuscripts and commentaries.[13]

Erasmus addressed his preface to Thomas More's son, John, recommending to him both the author, 'without doubt the most learned philosopher,' and the editor, 'a young man in all areas of philology of more than ordinary erudition.'[14] Gryneus, a fellow student and friend of Melanchthon, had been teaching Greek, first at Heidelberg, then from 1529 on in Basel, and was the editor of a number of classical texts, among them the works of Livy, Plutarch, Plato, and Ptolemy. On Erasmus' request he translated some passages from Chrysostom's homilies, and Erasmus repaid the favour by writing this preface for his edition of Aristotle's works.[15]

In the following year Erasmus was called upon once more to supply what amounted to an advertisement for the publisher. As he related to Boniface Amerbach, Froben's successors Episcopius and Herwagen had importuned him with requests to write a hortatory preface to their editions of Demosthenes and Ammianus.[16] He felt some misgivings about providing this sort of publicity and lending his good name to sell books and was determined to end this practice, indicating that in future he would no longer accede to such requests. In this case, however, he relented, yielded to the publisher's entreaties, and wrote a preface to the works of Demosthenes, addressing it to Johann Georg Paumgartner.[17] After acknowledging the Aldine editio princeps of 1504, he congratulated Herwagen on 'combining dignity with convenience' in his new edition.[18] He recommended Demosthenes as the foremost of Greek orators, but warned readers that his writings were not for beginning students of

Greek.[19] He also took the opportunity to encourage research, or at any rate recommend as a mental exercise a comparison of Demosthenes' and Cicero's respective merits as stylists and an examination of Demosthenes' influence on the Roman orator.[20]

In a letter to his friend Goclenius he also sought to direct scholars to write a commentary on Demosthenes, regretting that Rutger Rescius, who held the Greek chair at the Collegium Trilingue, had done so for the *Institutiones iuris civilis* rather than expend his time and efforts on a more worthwhile undertaking, and accusing Rescius of 'looking for profit and disgracing the college.'[21]

Some years earlier, in 1524, Melanchthon had encouraged Erasmus to translate Aeschines and Demosthenes, but Erasmus had demurred and reversed the request, saying: 'No one is alive today who could accomplish this more capably than you.'[22]

In 1533 Erasmus again provided a hortatory preface, this time to accompany the editio princeps of Ptolemy's *Geography*. He addressed it to Theobald Fettich, physician to Ludwig Elector Palatine, who had supplied the Froben firm with manuscripts for the edition.[23] Erasmus also pointed out several existing translations, the most recent of which was a version by Pirckheimer, completed in 1525.[24] Although he wrote enthusiastically about the subject of geography and its author, 'the first one to make this discipline a well established science,'[25] he expresed some reservations about Ptolemy's style, which was by virtue of his topic sober and devoid of rhetorical flair.[26]

In a letter to the French humanist Germain de Brie, Erasmus encouraged scholars in general to translate the classics. Among the authors he particularly recommended were Aristotle, Plato, Herodotus, Thucydides, and Plutarch.[27] Erasmus was careful to add that existing translations should not deter scholars from trying their hand at a particular work, for there was always room for improvement. He mentioned the successes of Linacre and Budé, as well as his own attempts to improve on the translations of his predecessors,[28] but tempered his advice with a note of caution: success invited envy. He related the unfortunate experience of Linacre, whom a courtier had accused of plagiarism and who consequently fell out of favour with the king.[29] Erasmus himself had encountered similar suspicions regarding his own work, but he suffered the recriminations, defied his detractors, and persevered in his undertaking.[30] He considered the task of translating Greek authors among the scholar's obligations to further the progress of classical studies. Concluding his remarks on the translators of past generations and their challengers, on the responsibilities of the new generation to improve and emend the work of their predecessors, he quoted the Homeric line ὄψιμον ὀψιτέλεστον ὅου κλέος οὐκ ἀπολεῖται: 'Late in coming, late to fulfil the promise: his fame shall never die.'[31]

Conclusion

꿐

To pass judgment on Erasmus the translator is to pass judgment on Erasmus the writer. In evaluating the effectiveness of his compositions we cannot rigorously separate stylistic dexterity from philological skill, for choice of words, period structure, and tenor of speech are as important to the success and popularity of a translation as accuracy and fidelity.

Several conditions combined to make Erasmus a successful translator. The breadth of his reading and the capacity of his memory – an important factor at a time when dictionaries, grammars, and commentaries were scarce – gave him the requisite skills to produce a faithful translation; his familiarity with all disciplines of learning provided him with the necessary background to interpret the meaning of the Greek text; his resourcefulness and zest for language allowed him to convey to the Latin reader the literary qualities of the original. Erasmus was able to popularize and revivify the classics because he satisfied the intellectual curiosity and the literary taste of his contemporaries, because he produced a competent, fluent, and readable version of Greek texts.

Productions from a scholar's study tend to 'smell of the lamp.' They are often contrived and self-conscious, betraying the author's struggle with textual difficulties and his efforts to adapt his own words to another man's thoughts. Erasmus' translations are unencumbered by such flaws: they have the quality of original, extemporaneous writings – perhaps because they were composed casually and rapidly, dashed off on the spur of the moment, as a form of recreation, to exercise the mind 'rather than do nothing,' as he once phrased it.[1] The speed of execution and the author's self-confessed reluctance to revise the text or verify his interpretation took its toll in errors and mistranslations, but also lent to his writings an agreeable freshness and fluency, a pleasant air of spontaneity.

The readability of Erasmus' translations lies in his preference for lively, direct, and concise expression, his flexibility in dealing with the idiomatic peculiarities of Greek, and his confidence in employing rhetorical devices in Latin. He paid close attention to purity of speech, departing from a literal version to satisfy the demands of Latin idiom, the rules of grammar, and the requirements of style. At all times he endeavoured to reproduce, or rather parallel, in Latin the images, figures, and structures used by the author of the original. Being sensitive to his reader's needs he was also at pains to achieve clarity in his translation. For this purpose he employed circumlocution, wherever necessary, to bring out the full meaning and implication of Greek text, expanded his version to explain or interpret technical terms or abstruse references, and even engaged in textual criticism, although somewhat reluctantly and not without protest.

In the *Ciceronianus* Erasmus acknowledged the paradigmatic value of the Latin classics, but deprecated their slavish and anxious imitation by Renaissance scholars. What he says about *imitatio* applies to a certain extent also to translation. Of course, the translator's task is more narrowly defined than the writer's, but Erasmus believed that translation, like *imitatio*, involved more than copying, that it demanded a measure of creativity and imagination. The good translator must be faithful to the spirit of the original, he must 'weigh the meaning, not count the words.'[2]

The degree of constraint suffered by a translator depends largely on his compatibility with the original author's pattern of thought and mode of expression. Erasmus sought out texts with a congenial point of view, writers whose opinions he could support and whose style he admired. Thus he could indulge his love of words and, in the name of preserving the tenor of the original, engage in the rhetorical practices of variation, amplification, and circumlocution. Variation, in particular, delighted him and he used it to good effect, indulging his 'vein of verbal fancy'[3] to give his readers the literary experience they might have gained from reading the original. His overall aim was to give the Greek author an authentic Latin voice, 'to furnish him with a Latin dress,' to let him speak as elegantly 'to Latin ears as he had spoken to Greek readers.'⁴ Erasmus selected the author to suit the translator: Lucian's wit and Euripides' poetry delighted him; he shared Galen's views on the value of liberal education; he appreciated the didactic and moralizing qualities of Plutarch, Isocrates, and Xenophon. He chose what appealed to himself and was instructive to his readers, so that the satisfaction he derived from his work and the advantage he hoped to gain for his readers facilitated his task.

Erasmus' style reflects the diversity of his models. He preferred florid diction, but wrote with epic breadth or concise wit, prosaic simplicity or poetic flourish, aplomb or unctuousness, as required in a particular context. Although he translated from a variety of sources, the manner in which he approached and handled typical problems of translation remained the same throughout his publications, which spanned almost three decades. His skills appear constant, as if the craftsman, like Athene, had sprung from Zeus' head fully grown. One does, however, note a shift in Erasmus' interpretation of the translator's role, a development which parallels his progression from apprentice to master. At first Erasmus felt a need to demonstrate his skills, asking for the reader's acceptance and approval; later he spoke with authority, like one providing a service, asking his readers to partake of his offering in the interest of their own intellectual welfare.

Consideration for the reader's needs as well as his own inclination led Erasmus further afield and drew him from the task of translating to that of compiling and modifying material from the classics for the instruction and edification of a contemporary audience. He advanced from the promise to render Greek into Latin word for word to scruples about the translator's role and a rejection of the restraints it imposed. Within his translations we find a corresponding development, an increase in the kind of liberties that spring from a didactic, almost patronizing, approach to the reader: explanatory additions, oblique versions that highlight, gloss over, or curtail the Greek text, elaborations and circumlocutions that elucidate its meaning. The rationale behind Erasmus' free translation was simple: this is what the author meant, he insisted, this is what he would say if he lived today, if he were a Christian, if he spoke Latin. Erasmus was acting as the Greek author's agent, speaking to the reader on his behalf. He felt confident in this role, either because he identified with the classical author's purpose and believed that their compatibility entitled him to some freedom in presenting his ideas, or conversely, because as a Christian he felt morally superior and justified in adapting the text to the ears of a contemporary readership. Most certainly he declined to follow his model slavishly. He was neither cowed by its greatness nor overwhelmed by its stature and venerable age, but always reserved for himself a measure of discretionary power over the text.

Despite the success of his compositions, Erasmus revealed fundamental misgivings about the task of translating. The process had its inherent limitations. No matter how faithful and accurate, a translation could never take the place of the original or fully compensate a Latin reader for his lack of Greek. Erasmus lamented the state of education that compelled him to provide translations. He regretted the need for this service and expressed the hope that his readers would soon be able to dispense with it. He rejoiced at the thought of his work becoming superfluous and welcomed the growing interest in Greek studies that would render his translations obsolete: 'How fortunate ... is our generation, in which we see Greek coming to life again everywhere. The neglect of Greek brought with it the universal decay of all sound learning and all elegant authors; we may hope that equally its revival will make them flourish too.'[5]

Notes

✣

For the abbreviations used, see the short-title list on page 175.

CHAPTER ONE

1 CWE 24, 317:20–1 (LB I 12C)
2 CWE 24, 318:3–4 (LB I 12D): 'we can use Greek words when we wish
   our meaning not to be understood by all and sundry.'
3 CWE Ep 149:22–4 (Allen lines 19–20)
4 See Bolgar *The Classical Heritage* 331. Compare Allen I.2:20–4 and
   Ep 3032:195–7: Education 'greatly flourished in Italy at a time
   when throughout our country horrid barbarism reigned and a
   deadly hatred of all good literature.'
5 *Compendium vitae* CWE 4, 404:42–405:43–4 (Allen I.48:36–7)
6 Hegius became headmaster at Deventer in 1483, the year of Erasmus' departure from the school. Together with his colleague Synthen, Hegius published a commentary on Alexander de Villa Dei's
   Doctrinale (Deventer 1488). For his poem on the Greek language
   see Hyma *The Youth of Erasmus* 110.
7 Cf *Compendium vitae* CWE 4, 405:44–7 (Allen I.48:37–40): 'At length
   his playmates, of whom the older ones were in Synthen's class, gave
   him his first taste of better teaching, and later he sometimes heard
   Hegius, but only on high days when he lectured to the whole school.'
8 Cf CWE Ep 28:18–20 (Allen lines 18–20), addressed to Cornelis Gerard
   in 1489 and replying to a request for poems: 'I have nothing more
   at hand to give to you, for whatever I had left was wrested from me
   by a friend of mine, and taken ... to Alexander Hegius the schoolmaster.' He praised Hegius in *Ad* 1.4.39, *Ciceronianus* LB I 1014B,
   Spongia LB X 1666A. His admiration for the teacher was acknowledged by J. Faber, who dedicated to Erasmus his edition of Hegius'
   Odae (Deventer 1503). Cf Ep 174.

9 Allen 1.55:80–1
10 *De pronuntiatione* ASD I-4, 32:590–1. The books mentioned were
   standard texts used in schools; cf *Compendium vitae* CWE 4, 404:41–2
   (Allen 1.48:35–6): 'They were forced to learn the paradigms, the
   textbooks being Eberhard and John of Garland.'
11 Garland's *Compendium grammaticae* ff 14^r, 45^r, 55^r; *Graecismus* 8.65,
   8.335
12 But his understanding of Greek was limited. Cf his explanation:
   'Why do the Greeks name the soul ψυχή? Because ψῦχος means
   "coolness" ...' (quoted by Hyma *The Youth of Erasmus* 110:16n).
13 ASD I-4, 41:923–6: *latrunculorum ludus, quem hodie scacorum vulgus
   appellat, sic ut hinc Graecae hinc Latinae litterae inter se concurrent*
   (the game of *latrunculi*, as people call the figures in a game of
   draughts nowadays, such that the Greek letters on one side match
   the Latin letters on the other)
14 Cf Reedijk *The Poems of D. Erasmus* (Leiden 1956) 135. The Greek
   appears in the Gouda manuscript of 1519, but there is no need to
   doubt (as Allen does, 1.592:9n) that it was written in Greek in
   the original draft, for CWE Ep 23:117–18 (Allen lines 111–13) refers to it: 'you gathered from the heading I wrote in Greek
   letters that my ode was addressed to Cornelis ...' This is the
   earliest reference we have to Erasmus' familiarity with Greek.
15 Allen 1.2.30; Ep 1110:1–7: 'Dear Sapidus, I perceive that there exists
   some wonderful force and ἐνέργεια of nature, for when I was a
   boy, good literature was banned from schools, there was no help to
   be had from books or teachers, no honour to be gained as an
   incentive for talented minds; in fact, when everyone everywhere
   deterred us from these studies and forced us into other things,
   some natural impulse – it could not have been judgment, for I was
   too young for that – carried me away to the temple of the Muses,
   like one possessed by spirits.' M.M. Phillips suggests, however,
   that there was a more tangible reason for Erasmus' interest in the
   classics: the memory of his father, who was a good philologist. Cf
   Phillips 'Erasmus and the Classics' 2–3. This idea is dismissed by
   Dibbelt 'Erasmus' griechische Studien' 55.
16 Like the school at Deventer, the one at s'Hertogenbosch was
   directed by the Brethren of the Common Life. Erasmus was sent
   there by his guardians, even though he considered himself
   'old enough for the university' (*Compendium vitae* CWE 4, 405:66,
   Allen 1.48:49–50: *satis maturus esset academiae*; compare CWE Ep
   447:103–5; Allen lines 95–8). He stayed at s'Hertogenbosch for
   two to three years. On this period in his life see Hyma 128ff.
17 CWE Ep 447:118–27 (Allen lines 111–17). The monastery at Steyn was
   an Augustinian house. Erasmus entered it ca 1487 and made his
   profession in 1488. See Hyma 145–66.

18 CWE Ep 296:58–60 (Allen lines 57–8)

19 Cf Allen I.2:31–3: 'Despite the threats of my teachers I secretly gathered what I could from books that came my way by chance.' Compare CWE Ep 447:380–1 (Allen lines 347–9): 'Within a few months they went right through the principal authors in these furtive and nocturnal sessions, to the great peril of his delicate health.'

20 Allen I.3:30–5

21 CWE Ep 296:57–8 (Allen line 56)

22 CWE Ep 149:11–13 (Allen lines 9–10), written in 1501. See also below 16–17. In 1492 Erasmus had become Latin secretary to the bishop of Cambrai, Hendrik van Bergen; in 1495 he obtained leave to study in Paris where he remained with interruptions until 1501.

23 Allen I.2:27–30

24 CWE Ep 30:5–10 (Allen lines 4–10), written from Steyn 1489; cf CWE Ep 8:11–13 (Allen lines 9–11), written from Steyn ca 1487, addressed to Servatius Roger in another bleak moment. Complaining of his loneliness, Erasmus wrote: 'the wakeful hours were an annoyance, my sleep restless, all my food tasteless, and the very study of literature, formerly my life's one consolation, became distasteful.'

25 CWE Ep 39:153–5 (Allen lines 139–42), written in 1494 when he was in the service of the bishop of Cambrai. Health problems had a similarly depressing effect on him; cf Epp 74 and 75, written from Paris in 1497. The critics of the New Learning continued to harass and discourage him. In 1520 he wrote 'I shall gradually withdraw from the arena [of bonae literae] unless the state of human affairs changes' (Allen Ep 1116:13–14); again in 1521: 'Their [his critics'] meanness is such that I almost regret my nightly labours' (Allen Ep 1242:37–8).

26 CWE Ep 20:62–4 (Allen lines 62–4) quoting CWE Ep 19:12–13 (Allen lines 12–13).

27 CWE Ep 529:43–4 (Allen lines 37–8). This letter is addressed to the bishop of Paris, Etienne Poncher, and may therefore be perfunctory in its praise, but see also the enthusiastic description in Ep 61, quoted below 8. Contrast with this Erasmus' references to life at the Collège de Montaigu where he spent the first year of his stay in Paris: 'There in the Collège de Montaigu, as a result of rotten eggs and infected lodgings, he contracted an illness, a morbid influence on a constitution until then quite free from taint' (Compendium vitae CWE 4, 408:116–18, Allen I.50:103–5).

28 CWE Ep 61:133–7 (Allen lines 124–9), composed by Erasmus on Heinrich Northoff's behalf

29 The letter is Ep 64. Greek occurs at Allen lines 12, 14,33, 68, 75,

and includes three proverbial phrases, an uncomplimentary reference to scholastic lectures at the university, and the loanword συκοφαντοῦμεν (we criticize), which is usually found in its latinized form.

30 CWE Ep 63:23–6 (Allen lines 21–4). For a scurrilous description of Grey's guardian see Ep 58 passim, eg CWE lines 57–61 (Allen lines 51–6): 'Never have the talents of the poets been capable of imagining a scourge so dire, so deadly, or so loathsome as not to be easily outdone by this monster. Can any Cerberus, Sphinx, Chimaera, Fury, or hobgoblin be properly compared with this pest whom the land of the Goth has recently spewed up on us?'

31 CWE Ep 66:17 (Allen line 16). Apparently Erasmus' manuscript was left in the hands of William Thale, who had it printed without the author's knowledge (Paris 1511), substituting his own name for Grey's, but leaving intact the word 'Leucophaeus,' obviously because he was unaware of its significance. When Erasmus published the book himself (Paris 1512), he dedicated it to Pierre Vitré, replacing the words 'my Leucophaeus' with 'my Pierre.'

32 Allen Ep 89:10

33 CWE Ep 93:88–9, 93–4 (Allen lines 76–9, 83–4). Erasmus' friend Jacob Batt was Adolph's tutor at the time.

34 Gaguin (1433–1501), scholar, diplomat, and foremost among French humanists, wrote on rhetorical, historical, and ecclesiastical subjects. In 1495 Erasmus addressed to him a poem, probably his first attempt to establish contact with Gaguin (carmen 38 Reedijk). For the use of his library see Epp 67, 121, 122.

35 Cf CWE Ep 46:31–49 (Allen lines 27–42), containing literary criticism of Erasmus' Antibarbari: 'look at those who make use of dialogue: they seldom employ continuous speeches, but often use short clauses and phrases. Among the Greeks the celebrated Plato will serve as a leading instance; among the Latin writers, Cicero and some others of later times ...' See also CWE Ep 531:452–5 (Allen lines 404–8) on the Adages: 'Robert Gaguin, who long ago (concealing what he thought himself under the mask of other men's opinion) reported that critics blamed me because that first collection of mine was so meagre, and I had included only a few items out of so wide a field ...'

36 ASD I-4, 102:974, CWE Ep 149:77–9 (Allen lines 66–7). Compare CWE Ep 138:43–7 (Allen lines 38–41): 'I must scrape together from each and every source a small sum of money ... to pay for the services of a Greek tutor.' See also CWE Ep 194:26–8 (Allen lines 22–4), where he speaks of a 'Greekling' eagerly awaiting a present.

37 Allen I.7:22–4; Allen Ep 3032:470–2

38 cwe 24, 667:11–13; compare *De recta pronuntiatione* asd I-4, 102: 985–6. To read Greek texts side by side with Latin translations was the most common method of learning Greek. See R. Sabbadini *Il metodo degli umanisti* 18–20.

39 Cf *De ratione studii*, 1511 edition, asd I-2, 114:2ff: 'Grammar therefore claims primacy of place and at the outset boys must be instructed in two languages – Greek, of course, and Latin ...' There is no reference to Greek instruction in *Conficiendarum epistolarum formula*, a pirated edition based on notes made by Erasmus in the Paris days and a forerunner of his *De epistolis conscribendis*, published in 1520. This authenticated version does contain a reference to Greek authors: 'The various letters of Greek authors will supply the readiest force of this kind ...' (asd I-2, 265:5ff). The 1512 edition of the *Copia* contains a passage on the use of Greek words in Latin compositions (cwe 24, 317:12ff: 'Not a little charm is added by the judicious mingling of Greek forms with the Latin ...'), but the greater part of the passage and most of its illustrative examples were added in the 1534 edition.

40 Cf the description in cwe Ep 118:20–9 (Allen lines 17–25): 'I find here a climate at once agreeable and extremely healthy, and such a quantity of intellectual refinement and scholarship, not of the usual pedantic and trivial kind either, but profound and learned and truly classical, in both Latin and Greek, that I have little longing left for Italy, except for the sake of visiting it. When I listen to Colet it seems to me that I am listening to Plato himself. Who would fail to be astonished at the universal scope of Grocyn's accomplishments? Could anything be more clever or profound or sophisticated than Linacre's mind? Did nature ever create anything kinder, sweeter, or more harmonious than the character of Thomas More?' On this circle of scholarly friends see A. Tilley 'Greek Studies in England' 221–4.

41 Quoted by Lupton *A Life of John Colet* 76. Later in life, Colet changed his position, no doubt under Erasmus' influence, and on receiving a copy of his New Testament in 1516 he wrote: 'I am sorry that I never learnt Greek, without some skill in which we can get nowhere' (cwe Ep 423:14–5, Allen lines 13–14). He directed that students of his school, St Paul's, be instructed 'in good literature, both laten and greke' (Lupton 168). For other positions on this debate see Grendler *Roman Inquisition and Venetian Press* 64–7.

42 cwe Ep 49:108–11 (Allen lines 94–5). Gaguin is cited at lines 69 (Allen line 57) and 107–10 (Allen lines 92–4): 'I am myself happy to be of my friend Gaguin's opinion in thinking that even ecclesiastical subjects can be treated brilliantly in vernacular works provided the style is pure.'

43 Cf CWE Epp 108:90–1 (Allen lines 80–1), 138:18–21 and 44–7
(Allen lines 15–18 and 45–7), 139:166–73 (Allen lines 143–9); he
published Valla's *Annotationes* in 1505 (the dedicatory letter is Ep
182). For Erasmus' approach to Greek at this time see Schwarz *Principles and Problems of Biblical Translation* especially 92–133.

44 CWE Ep 108:109–10 (Allen lines 96–7): 'Literature ceased to have
charms for me as soon as it ceased to be necessary to me.'

45 CWE Ep 149:25–7 (Allen lines 22–3); cf below 16–19.

46 CWE Ep 123:25–7 (Allen lines 22–4).

47 CWE Ep 124:72–4 (Allen lines 62–4).

48 CWE Ep 138:49–53 (Allen lines 44–7); compare Allen Ep 1167:36–8:
'I would obviously be lying if I denied my interest in polite literature; but my interest is such that I want to see polite literature
serving Christ's glory.'

49 CWE Ep 131:4–6 (Allen lines 2–4).

50 CWE Ep 131:8–11 (Allen lines 6–7); the Homer was intended for the
physician d'Angleberme; cf CWE Ep 132:91 (Allen lines 75–6).

51 CWE Ep 129:7–80 (Allen lines 66–8).

52 Greek words occur in Allen Epp 138:125, 139:75, 117.

53 CWE Ep 157:28–9 (Allen lines 23–4).

54 CWE Ep 157:46–52 (Allen lines 38–43).

55 CWE Ep 172:17–18 (Allen lines 13–14).

56 CWE Ep 131:11 (Allen line 8).

57 CWE Ep 158:10, 28–9 (Allen lines 6–7, 23–4); compare CWE Ep 160:5–10
(Allen lines 4–8).

58 CWE Ep 160:12–13 (Allen line 10).

59 Cf Proctor *The Printing of Greek in the Fifteenth Century* 141–4.
Greek occurs at Allen Ep 126:28, 74–5, and 112.

60 Greek appears in Epp 138–40, 143, 145–6, 149, 151–2, 157, 160–1,
177, 179, 180. For the type of words and phrases used and for
their purpose and effect see Rummel 'The Use of Greek in
Erasmus' Letters' 55–92.

61 CWE Ep 143:40–2 (Allen lines 36–7)

62 CWE Ep 172:13–15 (Allen lines 10–12)

63 CWE Ep 189:13–15 (Allen lines 12–14)

64 CWE Ep 203:3–4 (Allen lines 2–3); but cf Allen Ep 3032:506–10: 'I was
almost forty years old when I went to Italy, not to learn anything,
for that would have been too late, but to see the country. And I
brought more knowledge of the two languages to Italy than I took
away, although I confess that the sum total of my knowledge was
very small.' This sentiment is echoed by Beatus Rhenanus in his
biographical sketch, Allen I.59:110–11: 'Therefore he brought honour and learning to Italy, whereas the others used to bring it back
from there.'

65 The translations were published by Bade, Paris 1506. For details
see chapter 2 below.
66 Cf Epp 207, 209, and below 30.
67 Cf CWE Epp 3:38–9 (Allen lines 34–5): 'those branches of learning
which have given the greatest delight to us both'; *Copia* CWE 24,
317:20; *De ratione studii* ibid 669:5: 'a certain charm of subject-matter'
is ascribed to Lucian, Demosthenes, Herodotus, Aristophanes,
Homer, and Euripides. 'For Menander, to whom I would have given
even the first place, is not extant' (ibid lines 7–8); CWE Ep 39:156–7
(Allen lines 141): 'the poets' Pierian charm.'
68 CWE Epp 193:22–3 (Allen lines 21–2), 188:33 and 53 (Allen lines
28, 45), 199:14 (Allen line 10)
69 *Copia* CWE 24, 303:19, *De ratione studii* ibid 669:25–6
70 CWE Ep 199:12–14 (Allen line 9), Allen I.8:30–1, Ep 2273:25
71 CWE Ep 149:21–2 (Allen lines 17–19)
72 Ibid lines 54–5 (Allen lines 46–7)
73 Ibid line 70 (Allen lines 58–9)
74 CWE Ep 181:39 (Allen line 34)
75 Ibid lines 99–104 (Allen lines 89–93)
76 CWE Ep 182:133–9 (Allen lines 119–25)
77 Ibid lines 147–52 (Allen lines 132–5)
78 Ibid lines 205–8 (Allen lines 180–3); compare CWE Ep 149:51–4 (Allen
lines 43–6) and similarly in Allen Ep 1167:24–5: 'Leo ... realized
that the study of literature would illuminate, propagate, and con-
solidate Christian religion.'
79 CWE Ep 182:218–22 (Allen lines 192–5)
80 Antwerp 1519. Erasmus' answer was printed the same year: *Apologia reiiciens quorundam suspiciones ac rumores ...* (Antwerp 1519). The
text of the apologia is in LB IX 79–106.
81 LB IX 82A–B; Allen Ep 1183:35–40 contains a similar statement on the
role of philology, as promoted by Erasmus: 'My studious efforts
had no other purpose than to revive good literature which was
almost dead and buried in our parts; also to awaken a zeal for
Christian piety in a world that was attributing too much importance
to Judaic ceremonies; and finally, to recall to the source of divine
Scripture the study of scholastic theology which has degenerated
into minute discussion of pointless and insignificant questions.'
82 Allen Epp 948:92–3, 2468:77–9

CHAPTER TWO

1 For the Latin text see ASD I-1, 181–92 ed R.A.B. Mynors. All
subsequent notes to this text will be by page and line number. Erasmus thought that the last two pieces were spurious, but modern

scholars do not share his doubts. The Libanius translations appear to be the earliest product of Erasmus' Greek studies, with the possible exception of *Dicta sapientium* (published with *Catonis disticha*, Louvain 1514), a short list of aphorisms, some translated from a collection made 'by some Greekling,' others quoted from Ausonius' poems. There is only circumstantial evidence for the year of their composition: Ausonius is mentioned twice in letters dating from 1500/1 (Epp 126, 145), so is a 'hungry Greekling' (CWE Ep 149:78, Allen line 67).

2 A reaction set in, however, in the seventeenth century. Bentley described Libanius as 'a dreaming pedant, his elbow upon his desk,' and Gibbon called his speeches 'vain and idle compositions.' For these and other verdicts see A.F. Norman *Selected Works* (Cambridge 1969) I:xlvii–xlviii.

3 The manuscript survives at Trinity College, Cambridge ms R.9.26.
4 CWE Ep 177:8–9 (Allen lines 1–3)
5 Ibid line 72–3 (Allen lines 49–60)
6 Ibid lines 110–13 (Allen lines 92–4)
7 Cf ibid line 6 (Allen line 1): 'I have recently come into the possession of certain Greek declamations.'
8 Mynors in ASD 178 suggests that this was due to the fact that the translation made up only a slim volume and that Greek type was not yet widely available. For Erasmus' translations of Euripides, Lucian, and Plutarch see below chapters 3 and 4. These translations were published in the years 1506, 1512 and 1514 respectively.
9 191:26 and 36 (Γλαύκη); 186:11–12 for Greek ἀποστῆναί σε τῶν ἡμετέρων
10 189:2, 192:15, 28
11 186:18 (translating κλέπτων ψευδολογίᾳ τὴν πονηρίαν); 191:9 (where Erasmus misunderstood ἐν τέλει).
12 At 192:1 (translating τοῦτο εἰς ὑμᾶς ὁ πατὴρ ὠθεῖ δι᾽ἐμοῦ)
13 191:20 (translating ἐν χερσὶν ἦν τὸ δέρας τοῦ τρέμοντος)
14 For example, at 187:1, where the subject 'I and Ulysses' is missing; 187:2, where the sentence should begin with 'later on'; 187:26f, which says 'where he got his wife,' omitting 'and how.'
15 CWE Ep 177:10 (Allen line 4: *progymnasma*)
16 Ibid lines 118–19 (Allen lines 100–1)
17 185:18, 187:31f, 192:9, 185:9
18 189:14, 188:16, 190:9
19 185:9, 190:3, 189:17 and 185:16, 188:18, 185:6, 186:11, 188:6, 187:31
20 188:22, 192:31
21 186:25, 186:32, 188:22
22 186:24, 187:6, 190:19, 189:38
23 189:20, 190:34. These are instances criticized by Leclerc, in his

footnotes to the LB text, as introducing a wrong nuance. In fact, LB I col 556:6n warns the reader 'not to trust Erasmus in everything.'
24 See below 27 and note 31.
25 191:12, 190:27, 186:10; but cf Leclerc's censure LB I col 549:3n: 'Erasmus' intention of rendering the etymology of the verb ἀξιοῦν is a futile enterprise.'
26 186:4, 15, 21
27 185:14, 186:35
28 186:31, 187:17
29 188:24–5, 188:28–9
30 188:32, 190:6, 191:5
31 CWE Ep 177:114–17 (Allen lines 95–9); for Ruistre's reaction cf Ep 178:6–9 (Allen lines 4–8).
32 Jerome Ep 57.5.2, 5 (text and comm by G.J.M. Bartelink, Leiden 1980)
33 Cicero De optimo genere oratorum 5.14, quoted by Jerome Ep 57.5.3
34 Boethius In Isagogen Porphyrii PL 64 col 71; John Scotus Erigena, preface to Dionysius the Areopagite PL 122 col 1032. On the interdependence of their respective remarks see Schwarz 'The Meaning of fidus interpres in Medieval Translations.'
35 C. Salutati Epistolario ed F. Novati (Rome 1893) II:356; on the approach of Italian humanists to translation see A. De Petris 'La teorie umanistiche del tradurre e l'apologeticus di Giannozzo Manetti.'
36 See eg Cardinal Bessarion In illud ... 'si volo eum manere' ... (PG 161, col 626): '[The translator] must render the text word for word, especially in the case of Holy Writ ... except if the idiom of the receiver language does not allow the observance of this rule.'
37 See above note 33, also the examples given by De Petris in the article cited in note 35 above, esp pp 17–22, and Sabbadini Il metodo degli umanisti 23–7.
38 As early as 1489 Erasmus wrote an epitome of Valla's Elegantiae (published in a fuller version in 1529); in 1505 he published Valla's Annotationes; he mentions Bruni's translation of Aristotle (CWE Ep 456:118) and as early as 1503 professes a familiarity with his letters (cf CWE Ep 173:115).
39 L. Valla Opera omnia (Basel 1540, repr Turin 1962) II:139
40 L. Bruni De interpretatione recta ed H. Baron (Leipzig 1928) 87. Compare his definition of the ideal translator: 'He will enter into the author's mind, feelings, and intentions, and somehow transform [into Latin] his figure of speech, his thesis, his approach, and his tone, and will seek to express his whole fibre' (86).
41 Allen I.4:29–31. The text of the Euripides translations is in ASD I-1, 223–359, ed and comm by J.H. Waszink, to whose notes I am indebted for this section. See also his article 'Einige Betrachtungen über die

Euripidesübersetzungen' as well as Wilson 'Erasmus as a Translator of Euripides' and Schmitt 'Erasmus als Euripidesübersetzer.'

42 Allen Ep 3032:470–2, 517–20: 'I executed the work, indeed, not with proper care, but on afternoon walks, while the servants took their meal, and sometimes in bed, waiting to fall asleep again. And more than once, on a fluke, I completed a hundred lines in one dash.'

43 Cf above 14. Erasmus used the Aldine edition, cf Waszink in ASD 211.

44 Cf his remarks in Allen 1.4.32 ('Filelfo provoked me to this enterprise'); in CWE Ep 188:47–8 (Allen lines 40–1) he says, however, that he had embarked on the translation before he knew of Filelfo's. On other precursors (that is, authors of prose translations into Latin) see Waszinck ASD 204–6.

45 Cf Allen 1.4:34–6: 'I continued what I had begun because my host, Jean Desmarais, orator at the university and a man of singularly exact judgment, added his encouragement.'

46 Cf Calderini 'Intorno alla biblioteca e alla cultura greca del Filelfo'; Waszink 'Einige Betrachtungen über die Euripidesübersetzungen' 78–83. It appears, however, that malicious tongues accused Erasmus of having plagiarized Agricola's translation. Cf Allen Ep 3032:512–25: 'they spread the unjustified rumour that these were R. Agricola's works – I agree with them that he was a most learned man – and that I had stolen the manuscript and published it as my own. What can be more malicious?'

47 Cf Allen 1.5:21–30: 'Grocyn said with a sardonic grin: "Because that's the way you fellows are," implying that this is the sort of thing usually done by men of my type. This thorn stuck in my heart, unaccustomed as I was to such two-edged speech, and when I returned to Paris from where I was to set out for Italy, I gave the book to Bade to have it printed, adding *Iphigenia in Aulis* which I had translated in a more fluent and free manner during my stay in England. And whereas I had only presented one play to the archbishop, I dedicated both to him ... so great was my pride, although I lived in such tenuous circumstances.'

48 CWE Ep 207:33 (Allen line 29: *mendis scatent omnia*)

49 Cf ibid lines 43–50 (Allen lines 38–44): 'And I should have no hesitation in arranging for the printing at my own expense and risk had I not to leave Italy in a few months' time; ... now if you absolutely insist on my taking charge of a hundred or two hundred copies, though Mercury, the god of profit, is not as a rule particularly favourable towards me and it will be highly inconvenient to have this parcel conveyed, still I will not boggle even at this so long as you fix a fair price in advance.'

50 Cf Ep 209:11–27

51 CWE Ep 188:12–14 (Allen lines 9–11)
52 Cf CWE Ep 188:51–4 (Allen lines 44–7): 'For my part I was not deterred, either by these distinguished examples or by the work's many difficulties, but rather attracted by the more than honeyed sweetness of this poet's style – a sweetness conceded to him even by hostile critics.' Cf CWE Ep 208:8–9 (Allen line 5).
53 CWE Ep 208:29–31 (Allen lines 26–8)
54 CWE Ep 188:37–9 (Allen lines 31–3)
55 Ibid lines 60–3 (Allen lines 52–5)
56 Ibid lines 77–9 (Allen lines 68–70)
57 CWE Ep 209:32–5 (Allen lines 28–32)
58 CWE Ep 208:16–18 (Allen lines 13–15); cf CWE Ep 198:8–10 (Allen lines 5–9).
59 CWE Ep 208:25–7 (Allen lines 22–4)
60 CWE Ep 188:68–9 (Allen lines 60–1)
61 Ibid lines 64–6 (Allen lines 56–8)
62 Ibid lines 71–4 (Allen lines 63–5): 'I did not wish to announce that I was but paraphrasing, and so provide myself with the refuge wherein many translators excuse their ignorance and, like the cuttlefish, spread an inky obscurity round themselves to escape detection.'
63 CWE Ep 198:4–6 (Allen lines 3–4)
64 CWE Ep 208:14–15 (Allen lines 11–12)
65 *Hecuba* 243, 253, 529, *Iphigenia* 1733 (echoing Virgil); *Hecuba* 162, *Iphigenia* 255, 1261 (reminiscent of Horace); *Iphigenia* 475 (echoing Seneca); *Hecuba* 1109 (modelled after Prudentius) – cf Waszink's commentary ad locum.
66 Cf such creations as *Hecuba* 198: *provolitare*; 124, 487; *pontigradus*; 1117: *montigena*; 1120: *viricida*, etc. Compare Waszink's commentary and locum.
67 Allen Ep 3032:522–3: *nec ullius interpretatione, nec ullis commentariis sum adiutus.*
68 The text is taken from Calderini 310–11.
69 The text is taken from ASD I-1 223–5.
70 Cf Allen I.4:32–4: 'F. Filelfo who translated the first scene of this play in some funeral oration, not very successfully as it seemed to me then.' Compare CWE Ep 188:48–50 (Allen line 40–3): 'and Francesco Filelfo in one of his funeral orations translated ... the first scene of the *Hecuba*, but did so in such a fashion that I, usually bashful to a fault, was considerably encouraged by this great scholar's performance.'

CHAPTER THREE

1 CWE Ep 185:14 (Allen lines 12–13)
2 In this chapter the text is quoted according to ASD I-1 382–627,

ed Ch. Robinson. For an extremely helpful discussion of the genesis of the translations and their various editions see Thompson's introduction to the Yale edition of *The Complete Works of St Thomas More*, volume III. See also Delcourt 'Erasme traducteur de Lucien' and Heep *Die Colloquia familiaria des Erasmus und Lukian* 7–20.

3 Cf Robinson's introduction in ASD 363 and Thompson's introduction xxi–xxii.

4 CWE Ep 88:31 (Allen lines 27–8)

5 Cf Allen 1.6:36–7:4: 'I had begun to translate Lucian's *Podagra*, ... a wonderfully amusing work, but I gave up, discouraged mostly by the epithets of which the choruses are full. I had no hope of achieving in Latin that felicity in the use of compound words which we see in Greek diction. For if I had expressed these single terms by more than one word, the charm of the whole poetic composition would have been ruined.' For an approach to these problems by the Spanish humanist Andrés Laguna, see Zappala 'Andrés Laguna, Erasmus, and the Translation of Lucian's *Tragopodagra*.'

6 Cf Thompson's discussion of various theories, xxviii.

7 CWE Ep 149:13–14 (Allen lines 10–11)

8 'With such efforts we paid our respects to friends at various times, as is the custom in England' (Allen 1.8:7–8).

9 CWE 24, 669:3–6: 'The first [authors] to be imbibed should be those whose diction, apart from its refinement, will also encourage learners by a certain charm of subject-matter. In this category I would assign first place to Lucian ...'

10 Cf Thompson xxiii–iv; Robinson *Lucian and His Influence in Europe* 96–8; compare Erasmus' defence in LB IX 83C, answering J. Masson.

11 CWE Ep 293:23 (Allen lines 16–17)

12 CWE Epp 192:15 (Allen line 11), 193:26–8 (Allen lines 24–6), 199:12–14 (Allen line 15)

13 The dedicatory letter is Ep 187.

14 Ep 191, dated 1 May 1506

15 Ep 192, the last one written in England before Erasmus' departure for Paris in June 1506

16 Ep 193, dated from the castle of Hammes where Erasmus was visiting Lord Mountjoy ca June 1506

17 Ep 197, perhaps composed in Paris

18 Ie Ep 187, which is dated 1 Jan 1506

19 See above notes 15, 17.

20 For the text and background history see Thompson 'Erasmus' Translation of Lucian's *Longaevi*.' The discussion below 58–63 is indebted to Professor Thompson's commentary.

21 For these early aspirations see Renaudet *Erasme et l'Italie* 17–18, Halkin 'Erasme en Italie,' 40.

22 Cf CWE Epp 75:15 (Allen line 13), 82:19 (Allen line 17), 92:6–8 (Allen lines 6–7)
23 CWE Ep 204:40 (Allen lines 36–7)
24 The dedicatory letter is Ep 205, dated Bologna 17 Nov 1506.
25 The printing was completed, but the translations were added to some copies of the *Opuscula*. They were also printed separately (Martens: Louvain 1512).
26 Cf Renaudet *Erasme et l'Italie* 76.
27 See above 30.
28 On Erasmus' contact with Greek scholars in Aldo's house see Geanakoplos *Greek Scholars in Venice* 256ff and 'Erasmus and the Aldine Academy.'
29 Cf *De recta pronuntiatione* ASD I-4, 102.
30 CWE Ep 181:94–5 (Allen lines 85–6), 211:4 (Allen lines 2–3)
31 CWE Ep 211: 7–82 (Allen lines 62–8). He provided the translations reluctantly: 'I am quite aware that this is at variance with the practice of the ancients and contributes nothing to the attractiveness of the style' (lines 75–6, Allen lines 61–2).
32 Using the text of LB volume 2. The following references are to column and section.
33 Eg 14D, 17B, 21F, 28D, 30B
34 Eg 28D, 31C, 36A, 41D, all involving repetitions of the title of the proverb
35 Eg 41F, 59E, 127E
36 77B, 77C, 81C, 44A, 71F, 134B, 83F
37 44E, 53C
38 39C–D (explaining rather than translating Hesiod), 72F–73A (putting a quote from Aristotle into context), 118A (paraphrasing lines from Euripides' *Medea*). For expansive verse translations see eg 120B, 125C and F, 127B.
39 CWE Ep 211:89–93 (Allen lines 75–8)
40 40A, translating Hesiod's *Works and Days* 346–7
41 66E, translating Homer *Iliad* 24.340–4:

Αὐτίκ᾽ ἔπειθ᾽ ὑπὸ ποσσὶν ἐδήσατο καλὰ πέδιλα
ἀμβρόσια χρύσεια, τά μιν φέρον ἠμὲν ἐφ᾽ ὑγρὴν
ἠδ᾽ ἐπ᾽ ἀπείρονα γαῖαν ἅμα πνοιῆς ἀνέμοιο.
Εἵλετο δὲ ῥάβδον, τῇ τ᾽ ἀνδρῶν ὄμματα θέλγει
ὧν ἐθέλει, τοὺς δ᾽ αὖ τε καὶ ὑπνώοντας ἐγείρει.

Straightway he bound beneath his feet his beautiful sandals, immortal, golden, which were wont to bear him over the water of the sea and over the boundless land swift as the blasts of the wind. And he took the wand wherewith he lulls to sleep the eyes of whom he will, while others again he awakens alike out of slumber.
Compare with this the parallel passage in Virgil, *Aeneid* 4.239–44:

... et primum pedibus talaria nectit
aurea quae sublimem alis sive aequora supra
seu terram rapido pariter cum flamine portant.
Tum virgam capit, hac animas ille evocat Orco
pallentis, alia sub Tartara tristia mittit,
dat somnos adimitque et lumina morte resignat.

On Erasmus' translations of Homeric verses see M. Cytowska 'Erasme de Rotterdam, traducteur d'Homère.'

42 39A
43 39E
44 45E–F, 151B
45 Germanicus Caesar (15BC–19AD) was the adopted son of the Roman emperor Tiberius; Argyropoulos (c 1404–74) taught Greek in Italy. Reuchlin and Politian were among his pupils.
46 Erasmus conveniently forgets that in one instance he himself had to resort to the same means, using two different Latin words (odium and simultas) for νεῖκος, which is repeated in the Greek.
47 In some cases Erasmus uses exactly the same methods as those pinpointed in Argyropoulos' translation. Consider, for example, 120A–B, where Euripides' lines are: Πείθειν δῶρα καὶ θεοὺς λόγος. / Χρυσὸς δὲ κρείσσων μυρίων λόγων βροτοῖς. (They say that gifts persuade even the gods, and among men gold is worth more than a thousand words). Erasmus translates: Donis vel ipsos dictitant flecti deos, / certe inter homines mille dictis luteum / praepollet aureum prorsus ac praeponderat. Erasmus has added the epithet luteum (yellow) to the word 'gold' and has used two verbs, praepollet ... ac praeponderat (has more worth and weight), to translate κρείσσων (worth more).
48 At 26F Erasmus writes: in testulis quibusdam nutriunt, foventque animas brevi duraturas ... (they raise them in potsherds and cultivate their brief life ...). Plutarch's words are: ὥσπερ αἱ τοῦ Ἀδώνιδος κήπους ἐπ'ὀστράκοις ... θεραπεύουσαι γυναῖκες, ἐφημέρους ψυχὰς ἐν σαρκὶ τρυφερᾷ ... (ie a comparison: like women raising plants in potsherds, he cultivates ephemeral souls). At 88A Erasmus suggests that it would be an improvement 'if one read λῃστῶν, for λῃστήρια. This is, however, unnecessary. Strabo writes: τὸν παράπλουν τοῦ Κωρύκου πάντα λῃστήρια ὑπάρξαι (the waters along the coast of Corycus were everywhere the haunt of pirates; ie πάντα should be connected with παράπλουν).
   Erasmus frequently provides textual criticism. Usually his remarks are judicious and his suggestions have been adopted by modern editors. See, for example: 24C, 27D–E, 45B, 46C.
49 Cf CWE Ep 223:5–6 (Allen lines 4–6): 'his enemy Musurus spoke ill of his Adages and said that the passages of the Greek authors contained in them were ill-translated.'

50 CWE Ep 269:116 (Allen line 105)
51 Cf Renaudet *Erasme et l'Italie* 87–9, Halkin 42–3.
52 There is evidence that Ammonio shared More's and Erasmus' interest in Lucian. Cf Ep 245:37–40 (Allen lines 33–4) to Ammonio: 'I am quite delighted that you are Lucianizing (ὅτι λυκιανίζεις), and when I get back to London ... we will pursue Greek studies together (συνελληνίσομεν). 'In CWE Ep 246:2–4 (Allen lines 1–3) Erasmus sends Ammonio the text of *Icaromenippus*, asking him to have it copied out.
53 Cf CWE Ep 246:4–5 (Allen line 4) to Ammonio: 'I am preparing something by way of bait in readiness for New Year's Day ...'
54 The dedicatory epistle is Ep 261 (compare Ep 293). *Astrologia* was, however, printed without the dedication (Ep 267), perhaps because of a quarrel between Erasmus and Boerio; cf CWE Ep 267 headnote.
55 Cf Robinson's introduction 370–2, Thompson lviiff. See CWE Ep 264:25–6 (Allen lines 22–3).
56 Allen I.8:10–13
57 Eg, *nubicogis, grandistrepis, gravifremus* (see below note 58) are Erasmian words, but analogous to classical *nubifugus, grandiloquus, gravisonus*.
58 *Timon* 489:2, 6, 490:11; *Icar* 413:42
59 *Icar* 421:13, 419:11, *Tyr* 510:3, cf 417:28 (*curiosi*) – *curiosus* is, however, the classical translation for πολυπράγμων; cf Lewis-Short sv B2. For a similar range of techniques applied by A. Laguna in his translation of Lucian's *Podagra* see Zappala 428–9.
60 *Timon* 489:12, 17, 504:6–7, 490:13
61 411:32–3, 410:4
62 624:40, 625:2
63 623:23
64 Compare above 24, 54 and below 80.
65 492:34 (cf 493:31), 499:8, 21; 495:22, 494:8, 15
66 501:6
67 Eg *Tyr* 508:39
68 *Tyr* 508:22
69 *Tyr* 509:16, compare ibid line 23: *sycophanticum*
70 511:2, 24
71 410:15, 411:9, 418:5
72 *Tim* 489:4, 23, 25
73 501:14
74 504:33
75 489:19, 20–1, 493:12–13
76 491:2, 493:37–8, *Icar* 410:5; *Tyr* 509:20–1
77 625:5, 9, 11, 13, 21, 23, 26, 29, 31, 32, 39, 41
78 623:21, 23, 624:4
79 490:39 (*fons Athenis novem saliens venis*), 504:25, cf *Ad* 1.4.24 (you are

talking about a rather old diphthera): 'A *diphthera* was a relic from those old myths. They say that it was the hide of the goat that nursed Jove ...' (190E)

80 493:27, 416:6, 510:22–3
81 489:18, 490:9, 497:17–18, 490:7
82 493:14 (mistaking πεδότριψ or παιδότριψ for παιδοτρίβης); 490:29
83 Παμπονήροις παιδαγωγοῖς ἀνατρεφόμενον, τῷ Τόκῳ καὶ τῷ Λογισμῷ
84 At 498:32 the original line *Hunccine sermonem Iovi renuntio saevum et ferocem* was replaced by *Haec ego saeva Iovi refero atque immania dicta.* At 496:24–5 the original wording *sese in profundum immensumque pelagus praecipites dederint ac scopulis abruptis iliserint* was changed to *sese ... aereo e scopulo piscosi in aequoris alta praecipites abiecerint.*
85 507:17, 508:10
86 506:9–10
87 At 623:24 ('the Syrians' is omitted), 625:21 (ἀθυμήσας), 637:22 (ἱερώτατε Κυίντιλλε). On the accuracy of the translation see also Thompson's commentary ad locum.
88 At 624:15–16 Erasmus says: *ad imitandum vivacium hominum habitudinem ac fortunae benignitatem respiciens*; the Greek text runs: ἀπιδὼν καὶ σὺ τῶν μακροβίων ἀνδρῶν πρὸς τὸ ὅμοιον τῆς ἕξεως καὶ τῆς τύχης ἑτοιμότερον ... At 623:9–10 Erasmus says: *ut viro litterarum studioso litterarum aliquid mitterem.* The Greek runs: Τοὺς θεοὺς ἀνδρὶ περὶ παιδείαν ἔχοντι ταῦτα προστάσσοντας κελεύειν προσφέρειν σοι τῶν ἀπὸ τῆς τέχνης.
89 CWE Ep 191:20–1 (Allen lines (14–17): 'not to rival or to outdo such a skilful practitioner, but merely to wrestle, as it were, in this contest of wits with the most congenial of all my friends;
90 79:20, 81:7, 17, 85:23, 83:34, 85:25, 91:12, 6. The quotations refer to page and line of *The Complete Works of Thomas More,* vol III.
91 506:17, 507:5, 14, 509:10, 508:25, 509:13, 511:31, 26
92 79:26; 506:23 (translating ἐγὼ μὲν οὖν καὶ περιττότερον τι ... ὤμην γενήσεσθαι)
93 508:4–5, 83:9–10 (translating ἀλλαξόμενος δὲ ὅμως τὴν κοινὴν ἐλευθερίαν τῆς σφαγῆς τῆς ἐμῆς)
94 93:2; 512:19 (translating ὀλίγον ἐμπνέοντα, ἡμαγμένον, ἐμπεπλησμένον τοῦ φόνου)
95 512:12; 91:33–4
96 511:33
97 507:16
98 507:14
99 91:14, 81:19, 81:18
100 509:31, 507:39, 509:20–1
101 509:35

102 510:33
103 510:5
104 87:10, 89:10, 87:21
105 510:22–3; 87:38
106 509:34; 87:9 (translating οὐ τῶν ὁμοίων ἀξιώσεις τοῖς εὐεργέταις)
107 506:23–4; 79:27–8
108 93:16; 512:32
109 93:21–2; 512:37
110 85:38, 509:25
111 85:7–9; 508:36
112 83:31; 508:23
113 506:27; 23, 22–3
114 79:31, 81:27, 81:26
115 510:20–1; 87:36

CHAPTER FOUR

1 CWE Ep 215:16–18 (Allen lines 14–16) For Warham's promise see
   CWE Ep 214:4–5 (Allen lines 1–3): 'you will receive from me a hundred
   and fifty nobles, on condition only that you agree to spend the rest
   of your life in England ...'
2 In fact, it was written by Andrea Ammonio as Mountjoy's secretary; cf
   CWE Ep 283:86 and note. Compare CWE Epp 283:25 (Allen lines 20–1)
   and 333:36–52 (Allen lines 38–49): 'Mountains of gold and more than
   gold were promised in their letters by my friends ...'
3 Cf CWE Ep 233:10–12 (Allen lines 8–9): 'Up to this moment I have been
   lecturing on Chrysoloras' grammar, but the audience is small:
   perhaps more people will attend when I start on Theodore's.' Cf
   Thomson and Porter Erasmus and Cambridge 38–9, Tilley 'Greek
   Studies in England' 227–8. For Erasmus' translation of Gaza's
   grammar see below 127–8.
4 CWE Ep 233:12–14 (Allen lines 10–12)
5 Cf CWE Epp 225:9–11 (Allen line 8); 227:28 (Allen line 22), 237:59
   (Allen line 51).
6 Cf CWE Ep 282:55–7 (Allen lines 48–9): 'I have received just one
   [noble] from certain hearers of my lectures, and I took that under
   strong protest and with unwillingness.' Compare CWE Epp 270
   passim, 225:11 (Allen line 10), 248:39–41 (Allen lines 29–31): 'I should
   like to know whether my Maecenas has paid those twenty nobles to
   Bernard; this is what makes me tend to avoid London, as I hate
   nothing so much as being dunned.'
7 Cf CWE Epp 245:5 (Allen lines 4–5), 281:5–6 (Allen lines 3–5), 227:2
   (Allen line 1), 270:67 (Allen line 58).
8 CWE Ep 227:24 (Allen line 19)

9 CWE Ep 237:19 (Allen lines 15–16); cf CWE Ep 242:5–6 (Allen lines 4–5); 'I sent you the small present you had asked for.'

10 See above 57–69.

11 The text of his translations is in ASD IV-2, 117–322, ed and comm A. Koster, to whose notes the discussion in this chapter is indebted.

12 It is generally known as the Corpus Planudeum because it was thought to be the work of Maximus Planudes.

13 See Bolgar *The Classical Heritage* 435. For sixteenth-century translations see R. Aulotte *Amyot et Plutarque* 21–38. Erasmus attended Aleandro's lectures on the *Moralia* at Venice in 1507–8; cf Allen Ep 1195:50n quoting Aleandro's Ep 36 (Balan): 'quando io legea li Morali di Plutharcho graeci, et lui [Erasmus] non si dedignava interesse lectionibus meis quotidianis.'

14 Cf Geanokoplos *Greek Scholars in Venice* 229, Lowry *The World of Aldus Manutius* 240.

15 Cf Allen I.8:31 and note 27 below.

16 CWE Ep 264:27–8 (Allen lines 24–5)

17 Cf Epp 264:20–1 (Allen lines 17–18), 264:25 (Allen lines 22–3), 207:32–4 (Allen line 29).

18 Cf CWE Ep 283:189–93 (Allen lines 159–62): 'Also there are several books translated from Plutarch and Lucian which I had entrusted to him [Franz Birckmann] to give to Bade, to be added to the previous books he has in his possession; and I suspect he has given these also to the other man [Froben], and now he is asking me to send more of them. There is German honesty for you!'

19 CWE Ep 305:186–91, 204–6, 215 (Allen lines 181–7, 200–2, 210)

20 The dedicatory letters are Epp 268, 272, 284. Cf Ep 297.

21 Cf CWE 657:35–44 (Allen lines 33–41): 'I long ago translated from Greek into Latin Plutarch's treatise *How to distinguish flatterer from friend*, and dedicated it to your Majesty … Since, however, at that moment you were swept suddenly away into the storms of war … you had, I think, too little leisure for the products of the pen, for there was need to use the sword. And so I now submit the same work to your Highness, though already published …'

22 The dedicatory letters are Epp 1572 ('That anger must be controlled,' 'On meddlesomeness') and 1663 ('On false shame').

23 He repeatedly calls him *doctissimus* (most learned): CWE Epp 268:17 (Allen line 14), 272:48 (Allen line 42); cf 284:12–14 (Allen lines 8–11): 'even Greece herself, that fertile mother of great wits, never produced an author to surpass him for learning and charm.'

24 Allen Ep 1572:46–50: 'Plutarch's subtle style and the hidden meaning of quotations taken from the inner treasure chambers of all authors and disciplines gave me not a little trouble. His writings do not resemble continuous prose but a patchwork or rather a mosaic fashioned of exquisitely arranged patterns.'

25 Allen Ep 1572:50–5: 'Just as this was very easy for Plutarch who had a mind well supplied with all kind of literary gear, it is a very difficult task for the translator to discover his sources, especially since many authors from whose gardens he plucked his flowerets and he fashioned his garlands, are not extant.'

26 Allen Ep 1572:55–60: '[There is in his writings] something concise and abrupt, suddenly transporting the reader's mind to a different area; so that he demands not only a reader of all-round education, but also one who is attentive and watchful. Finally, Plutarch, to be sure, is Boeotian, but he keeps the "Boeotian ear" and "eye" far away from his writings.' The references to 'Boeotian' are allusions to two proverbs, *Ad* 2.3.9 ('Oblique and obscure phrases were called "Boeotian riddles"') and 3.2.48 (sv 'Boeotian ear': 'The stupidity of the Boeotians afforded a topic for many proverbs').

27 cwe Ep 268:18–19 (Allen lines 15–16), cf Allen 1.8:31–3: 'There was one inconvenience: Aldo printed this work following a manuscript which was corrupt in many places, nor were any ancient manuscripts within my reach.' Compare Allen Ep 1572:60–1: 'I shall pass over the mistakes of the scribes which, like brushwood, slowed our way.'

28 cwe Ep 268:20 (Allen lines 16–17).

29 See above 150 n 48.

30 Allen Ep 1572:62–3

31 cwe Ep 268:28 (Allen lines 22–3)

32 cwe Ep 272:48–50, 55 (Allen lines 42–4, 49)

33 Allen Ep 1572:65–6, 70–1

34 Allen 1.8:28–31: 'On his writings I exercised my skills the more willingly, as they are not only conducive to form language skills, but also to mould a man's character.' Cf Allen Ep 2431:90–1: 'none of the Greek authors is more uplifting and more worthy to be read.' Compare *Copia* cwe 24, 608:26–31:' an example from Plutarch could be introduced by saying that this writer was of all writers particularly worthy of respect in that he combined a thorough knowledge of philosophy with the eloquent style of a historian ...'

35 See above 74.

36 Allen Ep 1572:66–70

37 The translation of this essay was first published in 1514 and revised in 1516, 1518, 1519, and 1520. References are to the text in asd IV-2, 173–84, which has consecutively numbered lines.

38 The text of Longueil's translation can be found in Aulotte 'Une Rivalité d'humanistes.'

39 For the text of the letter see Aulotte's article, cited in the previous note. Subsequent references are to the page numbers of this article.

40 They occur at lines 93, 146ff (deliberate, see below 79), and 276. Cf Koster's commentary ad locum.

41 At lines 5–6. The manuscript and the 1514 edition read: *placidissimum*

vitae genus et a reipublicae negotiis semotum tibi delegisse. This was replaced by *placidissimam videlicet gerendae reipublicae rationem instituisse.* The original clause was restored in 1520.

42 αἰτία can mean either 'charge' or 'reason'; πλησιάζειν can mean either 'to be close' or 'to be intimate'

43 The text is in ASD IV-2, 309–22; lines are consecutively numbered.

44 *Pronitas* is postclassical and normally used in the metaphorical sense of 'inclination'; I cannot find *putiditas* documented elsewhere.

45 Erasmus writes: *sed imitare Xenophanem Lagi, quem cum Hermoneus meticulosum vocaret.* This is untranslatable, as Koster notes in his commentary ad locum.

46 Cf lines 8, 59–60, 77, 85, 122, etc. and Koster's commentary ad locum. At lines 121–2 Erasmus rendered corrupt Greek into senseless Latin (see Koster's comment ad locum: 'Erasmus hat das Griechische übersetzt, ohne sich den Inhalt zu vergegenwärtigen); at lines 362–3 he offers a similarly careless translation (Koster ad locum: 'Dieser unverständliche Satz enstand, weil Erasmus in seinem Text πεφυκνῦα an Stelle von πεφυκνίᾳ vorfand').

47 CWE Ep 312:18 (Allen lines 17–18). This is the dedicatory letter, dated 15 Oct 1514.

48 The Latin text is in ASD I-5, 96–320 ed and comm J.-C. Margolin. The English quotations in this chapter are from the translation by Sir R.A.B. Mynors in CWE 23, 135–277. For the history of the text see his introductory note, 125–7.

49 Cf CWE Ep 312:21–5 (Allen lines 20–4): 'Of late, as I reread Aristotle, Pliny, and Plutarch for the enrichment of my *Adagiorum chiliades*, and cleared Anneus Seneca of corruptions ... I noted down by the way these passages, to make an offering for you which I knew would not be unwelcome.' He also took material from Aristotle and Theophrastus, but many of the quotations remain to be identified, cf CWE 23, 219:1n. On the extent of his original work Erasmus informs us: 'In anything under the heading "From Aristotle and Pliny" the application of the image is my own invention. For anything taken ... from Plutarch and Seneca I claim no credit, except for the labour of collection and exposition and such praise as is due to brevity and convenience ... Of Plutarch I have made a very full survey, partly because he wrote in Greek, partly because in this field he is such a leader as to defy comparison even with the greatest authors' (CWE Ep 312:77–88; Allen lines 70–83).

50 CWE 23, 136:6–7 (Plutarch 801A), 144:25 (54E), 142:22–4 (795D)

51 CWE 23, 138:2 (Plutarch 813F)

52 See above note 49.

53 CWE 23, 136:32–4 (Plutarch 804D–E)

54 CWE 23, 148:22–4 (Plutarch 73A)

55 CWE 23, 137:21–5 (Plutarch 793E: μὴ βουλόμενος πιέζειν ἑτέροις ἐπωχεῖτο πρὸ τῆς μάχης ἵπποις), 144:33 (55E: τοῖς μὲν οὖν ταύροις τὸν οἶστρον ἐνδύεσθαι). See also Sir Roger Mynors' note ad locum.

56 CWE 23, 136:16–18; Plutarch 801F: ὁ δὲ πολιτικὸς ἐν ἑαυτῷ μὲν ὀφείλει τὸν κυβερνῶντα νοῦν ἔχειν ἐν ἑαυτῷ δὲ τὸν ἐγκελευόμενον λόγον (the statesman needs to have in himself the mind that governs and also in himself the speech that commands)

57 CWE 23, 147:6–8 (Plutarch 54A). The whole passage is correctly translated in Erasmus' version of 'How to distinguish a flatterer from a friend,' ASD IV-2, 145:718–23: Rursum adulatoris officium nihil habet iustum, nihil verum, nihil simplex neque liberale, sed sudorem, discursationem, clamorem et vultus contractionem ... non aliter quam operosa quaedam pictura coloribus impudentibus, vestibus inflexis ac fractis, rugis et angulis id affectans, ut rem evidenter representare videatur (The flatterer's activity shows no sign of honest, truth, straightforwardness, or generosity, but only sweating and clamour and running to and fro, and a strained look ... like an extravagant picture which by means of gaudy colours, stiff folds in the garments, wrinkles and sharp angles, strives to produce a naturalistic impression).

58 CWE 23, 136:14–15, Plutarch 801C: πίστις ἤθους (confidence in a man's character)

59 CWE 23, 136:20–22 (Plutarch 802D)

60 CWE 23, 136:29–30 (Plutarch 804C)

61 CWE 23, 144:7–9 (Plutarch 52B). Compare the equally incorrect translation in Erasmus' version of 'How to distinguish ...' in ASD IV-2, 128:162–3: aquarum in morem, semper transeuntium ac praeterfluentium, quae ad subjecti soli speciem transmutantur. Plutarch says: ὕδωρ ... συσχηματιζόμενος τοῖς ὑποδεχομένοις (water ... changing its shape to fit the receiver).

62 CWE 23, 145:3–5 (sic adulator laudans diversa vitia in aliis, ASD I-5, 114:253–4); but the passage (Plutarch 57C) is correctly translated in Erasmus' version of 'How to distinguish ...' in ASD IV-2, 136:411–12: clam laudant et alunt eorum vitia, quibus adulantur, dum his contraria vituperant (they covertly praise and nourish the vices of those whom they flatter, by condemning the opposite qualities).

63 CWE 23, 136:36–7 (Plutarch 805E–F)

64 CWE 23, 146:1–8. Plutarch says: 'The flatterer is the sort of person who will say nothing relevant about the actual speech of a poor and ridiculous speaker, but will find fault with his voice and rebuke him severely because he ruins his throat, drinking cold water' (59F–60A).

65 CWE 23, 144:15–16 (Plutarch 53B2)

66 CWE 23, 144:12–13 (Plutarch 52E)

67 CWE 23, 148:1–4 (Plutarch 68E)

68 CWE Ep 312:49–51, 62–3 (Allen lines 44–5, 56–7); but cf Allen Ep

1175: 77–8: 'In writing a commentary there may be some merit, in compiling there is but little glory.'

CHAPTER FIVE

1 Among the studies dealing with Erasmus' approach to translating the New Testament are: Bludau *Die beiden ersten Erasmus-Ausgaben des neuen Testaments und ihre Gegner*; Schwarz *Principles and Problems of Biblical Translation* esp 92–166; L.E. Halkin, 'Erasme et les langues' *RLV* 35 (1969) 566–79; Jarrott 'Erasmus' Biblical Humanism'; Hall 'Erasmus: Biblical Scholar and Reformer'; Holeczek *Humanistische Bibelphilologie als Reformproblem bei Erasmus von Rotterdam, Thomas More und William Tyndale* esp 101–37; Aldridge *The Hermeneutics of Erasmus*; Rabil *Erasmus and the New Testament*; G.B. Winkler *Erasmus von Rotterdam und die Einleitungsschriften zum neuen Testament* (Münster 1974); and Bentley 'Erasmus' *Annotationes in Novum Testamentum.*'

2 Much of what Erasmus says about the aims and methods of Biblical translation is in agreement with the ideas expressed by L. Valla; for specific instances see J. Bentley 'Biblical Philology and Christian Humanism.'

3 For the Latin text of the *Paraclesis, Methodus, Apologia*, and *Ratio* see A. and H. Holborn *Ausgewählte Werke* (Munich 1974). An English translation of the *Paraclesis* can be found in *Christian Humanism and the Reformation* ed Olin, 92–106.

4 *Paraclesis* Holborn 141:20: *pia curiositate singula cognoscimus, disquirimus, excutimus* (we discover, research, and examine each point with pious concern); compare ibid 141:28–9: *fac adferas pium ac promptum animum, et imprimis simplici puraque praeditum fide* (bring a pious and ready mind, and one equipped most of all with a simple and pure faith).

5 CWE Ep 373:62–3 (Allen line 57). The Vulgate translation is ascribed to Jerome, but Erasmus had doubts about his authorship. See also next note.

6 *Comissa sunt permulta et interpretis, quisquis is fuit, vel inscitia vel negligentia* (LB VI**1ʳ). For his criticism of individual points in the Vulgate translation see below 93–100.

7 *Contra morosos* ch 4 (LB VI**3ᵛ)

8 LB VI, 223:36n: *velimus nolimus ad quaedam eiusmodi connivendum est receptiora quam ut citra tumultum mutari possint*, compare 404:11n: *fortassis praestiterit hunc sermonem inter eos numerare quos oporteat peculiari sacrarum scripturarum linguae condonare* (perhaps it would be better to number this word among those which should be overlooked for the sake of the linguistic peculiarities of Holy Scripture).

9 *Apologia* Holborn 170:20–1, compare ibid 169:4–5: *nam qui vertit in alienam linguam longe lateque cogitur discedere* (for he who translates into a foreign language is compelled to diverge far and wide); *Contra morosos* chs 29, 69 (LB VI*4ʳ,***1ʳ), compare CWE Ep 373:69–71 (Allen lines 63–5).

10 CWE Epp 197:15–16 (Allen lines 12–13), 188:25–8, 63 (Allen lines 20, 54–5: *vim ac pondus*)

11 Cf above 32 and below 124–5.

12 *Apologia* Holborn 173:29–30: *ut non affectavimus eloquentiam, ita munditiem si qua in promptu fuit, non respuimus*

13 CWE Ep 373:68 (Allen line 63); compare *Contra morosos* ch 6 (LB VI**3ᵛ): *nec simplicitatem tollimus, sed restituimus* (we are not removing, but have restored, simplicity).

14 *Ratio* Holborn 196:31 (*quibus verbis dicatur*), 272:2–3; cf *Contra morosos* ch 6 (LB VI**3ᵛ): *illecebra quadam … allicere* (to attract with some lure).

15 LB VI 80:26n, 130:20n, compare 66:13n, 71:9n: *hic interpres maluit Latinitati consulere quam voces reddere Graecas* (here the translator preferred to show consideration for Latin idiom rather than render the Greek words literally).

16 Eg LB VI 55:33n, 169:13, 114:41n, 40:8n (*durities*); compare *mollius*: 61:16n, 335:2, 189:30n.

17 LB VI 567:76n (referring to the parallel structure of ἀσυνέτους – ἀσυνθέτους); 630:10n (referring to the root φρον contained in the words ὑπερφρονεῖν, φρονεῖν, εἰς τὸ σωφρονεῖν, which is only partially reflected in Latin); cf 65:6n: *periit apud nos iucunda inter se redditio* ἱερεῖς ἐν τῷ ἱερῷ (in Latin the pleasant repetition of the words 'holy men in the holy shrine' is lost).

18 LB VI 84:12n

19 LB VI 383:9n

20 LB VI 100:10n, 577:4n, 583:5n, 639:4n

21 189:29n, 241:17n, 295:1n

22 553:1n (on the meaning of *apostolus*), 566:66n (on πλεονεξία, 'greed'), 220:13n (discussing ἄμεμπτοι, 'without blame,' which the Vulgate renders by means of two words as *sine querela*), 411:3n (explaining the literal meaning of *Lithostratus*), 224:39 (on the polysemous nature of εὑρεῖν, 'find' or 'discover')

23 See above 24, 77–8.

24 LV BI 84:24n

25 Cf Caesar *Bell Gall* 6.21, Virgil *Aen* 4.328.

26 LB VI 94:4n

27 567:77n

28 Compare Tacitus *Agr* 30 (*affectus*), *Ann* 4.15 (*affectio*).

29 LB VI 5:19n (also 224:39n); compare Plautus *Ep* 4.2.32, Livy 3.4.7.

30 LB VI 91:6n

31 Eg 17:1n on the meaning of μετανοεῖν (repent) and the sacrament of penance; compare below 96.

32 *Apologia refellens quorundam seditiosos clamores* ... (Louvain 1520). See Jarrott 'Erasmus' *In principio erat sermo.*'

33 Cf CWE Ep 373:84–118 (Allen lines 77–107); compare *Apologia* Holborn 171:16–18.

34 LB VI 130:16n, 141:20n, 633:29n

35 222:25n

36 601:7n (*mirum autem cur hic interpres inutilem copiam affectarit*), similarly in 170:23n, 209:48n

37 62:33n

38 210:5n compare 339:10n *primum illud admonendus est lector quod Latinus hic interpres modo lumen vertit, modo lucem, Graecis eandem esse dictionem,* φῶς (first, the reader should be warned that our Latin interpreter translates the same Greek word, φῶς [light], sometimes as *lumen*, at other times as *lux*). At 297:9n Erasmus reproaches the translator for rendering ἐν ἐλαχίστῳ (in the least) in one case as *in minori*, elsewhere as *in minimo: sed amat variare interpres* (but the translator likes to practise variation).

39 40:6n, compare 5:19n.

40 567:75n, 79n. For additional examples illustrating Erasmus' emphasis on accuracy see Bentley 'Erasmus' *Annotationes in Novum Testamentum'* 38.

41 364:13n

42 62:31n, 221:16n

43 126:34n

44 6:22n. The interpretation hinges on the literal meaning of *traducere,* 'to lead across.' For other examples see Bentley 'Erasmus' *Annotationes in Novum Testamentum'* 45.

45 576:28n, compare 573:33n.

46 136:46n

47 81:41n

48 573:3n, compare 288:5n.

49 605:30n

50 114:38n, very similar at 355:9n; compare 228:71n: ὅτι *prorsus hic erat omittendum, cum sermo Latinus huiusmodi genus orationis respuat* (ὅτι should certainly have been omitted here, for the Latin language eschews this kind of construction). 308:215n: *Omittenda erat coniunctio quia,* ὅτι, *quae ex idiomate Graecanici sermonis apponitur aliquoties, affirmandi gratia* (the conjunction *quia,* ὅτι, should have been omitted; it is a Greek idiom sometimes added for the sake of affirmation).

51 222:27n

52 *Apologia* Holborn 168:4: *illustrior, purior, emendatior*

53 Cf CWE Ep 373:55–8 (Allen lines 49–53): *si quid temporum iniuria vitiatum comperimus, id non temere, sed omnia quae licuit, subodorati,*

germanae reddidimus orationi, si quid obscurius dictum occurit illustra-
vimus, si quid ambigue dictum aut perplexius, id explicuimus.

54 *Apologia* Holborn 170:18–19: *num fidelius, num apertius, num signifi-*
cantius expresserim quam vetus interpres

55 *Contra morosos* ch 12 (LB VI**4ʳ), compare ibid ch 19: *ut nihil aliud sit*
commodi certe hoc boni habet sermonis elegantia quod simplex sit et naturalis
cum inemendate loquendi sexcentae sint species (if there is no other
convenience, it has this advantage: pure diction is simple and natural,
faulty speech has six hundred different forms); ibid ch 7: *non offendit*
deum soloecismus is a quotation from Augustine *De doct christ* 2.13
(similarly *Apologia* Holborn 173:30–2); ibid ch 27: *sed dissimulare*
offendiculum ... non est civilitas, sed iniquitas.

56 Cf Thomson's assessment in 'The Latinity of Erasmus' 131.

57 CWE Ep 149:27–30 (Allen lines 23–6)

58 This criticism is found in Erasmus' list of solecisms at the beginning of
LB VI (no pagination), in his remarks ad John 14:12, 7:14, Acts 3:19.

59 He uses this expression in 161:7n, 221:21n, 224:41n, 256:21n.

60 155:34n, cf 349:2n, 48:22n, compare 97:23n: *Decem millia talenta dicit*
pro talentorum, Latinitatis dumtaxat iniuria factum est, sensu incolumi
(he says *decem millia talenta* instead of using [the genitive] *talentorum;*
only Latin grammar has suffered, the sense is not impaired).

61 40:5n

62 59:1n

63 217:3n

64 38:53n

65 169:14n, compare 240:5n, 248:24n, 297:7n.

66 560:27n (referring to χάρισμα, which is sometimes rendered as
charisma, at other times as *gratia*)

67 37:29n, 36:34n

68 76:34n, compare 97:30n (suggesting the alternatives *male* or *sceleste* for
the Vulgate's *nequam,* 'bad'): *Verum huiusmodi permulta praetereo sciens*
ne morosiore diligentia molestus sim lectori (but I deliberately pass over
much of this sort lest I trouble the reader with overly scrupulous
attentiveness); CWE Ep 373:216–17 (Allen line 200)

69 142:33n (speaking of the origin, meaning, and pronunciation of
'Golgotha')

70 601:7n

71 CWE Ep 182:144–5 (Allen lines 129–30); compare LB VI 184:23n: *quid*
est quod tam procul a sacris ablegamus grammaticos de divinis litteris ali-
quanto melius meritos quam sint frigidi quidam ac jejuni dialectici, ne
dicam, sophistae? (why is it that we banish grammarians, keeping
them so far away from what is sacred, although they sometimes
serve the cause of divine letters better than certain frigid and jejune
dialecticians, not to say, 'sophists'?)

72 *nec illud, opinor, inutile fuerit, si theologiae destinatus adolescens, dili-*

genter exerceatur in schematis ac tropis grammaticorum rhetorumque (*Methodus* Holborn 154:10–12)

73 *illic aureum quoddam ire flumen, hic tenues quosdam rivulos, eosque nec puros admodum, nec suo fonti respondentes* (*Methodus* Holborn 154:34– 6), compare ibid 161:3–4: *sed a saepius collectis ac transfusis collectaneis velut a decima lacuna suffuratus ut paene nihil resipiant sui fontis* (but from a collection often gathered and transferred, like a pond ten times removed from its source so that it barely resembles it in anything at all).

74 Ibid 155:5–8: *neque vero me clam est quanto supercilio contemnant poeticen, ceu rem plus quam puerilem, quanto rhetoricen, quanto bonas, ut vocant, et sunt, litteras omnes. Attamen hae quamlibet istis fastiditae litterae insignos illos dedere theologos.* Compare related remarks in Allen Ep 1126:334–5: 'Whatever they themselves have not learned, they call "poetria"' (similarly in Allen Epp 1153:215, 1196:450).

75 *Contra morosos* ch 26 (LB VI**4ʳ), compare *Apologia* Holborn 169:34; *nec indiligenti, nec inexercitato* (neither careless nor inexperienced).

CHAPTER SIX

1 The Latin text is in LB IV 611–16.

2 Cf above 14.

3 Cf Allen Ep 158:6n; for the publication of Agricola's translation *Ad Demonicum* see Erasmus' preface, Ep 677. Agricola also translated *Ad Nicoclem* (published in *Lucubratiunculae aliquot*, Cologne 1539, pp 236–43; I examined this translation and found that Erasmus' version shows no dependence on it).

4 Cf CWE Epp 180:50 (Allen line 46), stating that Isocrates used praise to stimulate virtue, and 222:37 (Allen line 34), listing Isocrates among the authors of paradoxical speeches.

5 It seems, however, that Erasmus did not approve of Isocrates' style unreservedly. While acknowledging him as one of the preeminent Greek authors, he pinpointed as his flaw a certain fastidiousness and artificiality: 'By his imitation of poetical phrases and cadences he ruined the natural charm of the Greek language' (Allen Ep 2611:32– 4).

6 Cf Bolgar *The Classical Heritage* 333, 435; Sandys *A History of Classical Scholarship* II 104.

7 For the genesis of the work see Herding 'Isokrates, Erasmus und die *Institutio principis christiani.*' Erasmus first mentions work on the *Institutio* in CWE Ep 334:178–80 (Allen lines 170–2), dated May 1515.

8 First indications of Erasmus' impending appointment are found in CWE Ep 370:15–20 (Allen lines 16–19), dated November 1515. In 1518 Erasmus revised the book for dedication to Charles' brother Ferdinant (cf Ep 853).

9 Cf Herding 102–3, 113.
10 CWE Ep 393:70–3 (Allen lines 65–8)
11 This was done by Gilles d'Aurigny in the sixteenth century and imitated by the French translator Claude Joly in the seventeenth century. Cf Herding 116.
12 Allen Ep 2431:33–42: 'In this respect we see that the greatest scholars have attempted to relieve the cares of princes by their diligent work. Some, like Theognis and Isocrates, wrote aphorisms ...'
13 611E, 613B, 611D, 614F. All quotations are from LB IV, column and section.
14 614C, 611C, 612D, 613A; on the translation of $\phi\iota\lambda\acute{a}\nu\theta\rho\omega\pi\sigma\varsigma$ see also below 112.
15 613F, 614F
16 614A
17 616D, 61D
18 613A
19 614B, 614E
20 613A
21 616F
22 613E
23 616A; for a similar manoeuvre see below note 91. This was, however, common practice. See De la Garanderie *Christianisme et lettres profanes* I 52: 'Aussi a-t-il [the Rennaisance translator] tendance à adopter trop vite, non point sans scrupule, mais par scrupule, l'hypothese de l'erreur matérielle. Il dépense sa sagacité à substituer la leçon qui lui semble correcte à celle du manuscrit.'
24 616B
25 613C
26 CWE Ep 934:32–4 (Allen lines 32–4), compare Allen Ep 3032:451: 'I who bring forth everything prematurely.'
27 For a synopsis of his controversies see E. Rummel 'A Reader's Guide to Erasmus' Controversies' *Erasmus in English* 12 (1983) 13–19.
28 See above chapter 4.
29 The Latin text is in ASD I-1 639–69, ed and comm Waszink, to whose notes my study is indebted.
30 Cf Bolgar 289–9, 438.
31 John Clement, whom Erasmus knew from More's household, and Georgius Agricola, one of Erasmus' German admirers, were working on the edition (cf CWE 388:185n, Allen Ep 1594:105–7). On 5 October 1525 Erasmus inquired from Asulano about the publication of Galen's *Opera*, which 'was eagerly awaited by scholars' (Allen Ep 1628:3). In Ep 1746:1–2, dated 3 Sept 1526, he acknowledged Asulano's present: 'Nothing as pleasant has happened to me for a long time, dearest Francesco: the complete edition of Galen arrived here, thanks to your generosity.'

32 The dedicatory epistle is Ep 1698, dated 28 April 1526.
33 Cf Brabant 'Erasme, ses maladies et ses médecins' 539–68.
34 CWE Ep 818:9–11 (Allen lines 6–9)
35 Allen Epp 1811:50–64, 2057:5–9; compare Ep 1809:3–5.
36 Cf ASD I-2 358–61, a comparison of fame with other goods.
37 ASD I-4 164:7–9. The first draft of the essay was written in 1499.
38 Cf ASD I-4, 184:366–410, where he depicts the ideal physician as being free of monetary concerns and as obeying professional ethics, ideas also expressed by Galen in chapters 57, 61.
39 Cf Allen Ep 1805:94:3 *dogmatistae personam semper refugi* (I have always shunned the role of the dogmatic). Erasmus defends the study of philosophy and rhetoric in his *Antibarbari*, but quotes Augustine's admonition; *tantum cavenda est ibi libido rixandi* (but there we must avoid the desire for contentiousness, *De doct christ* 2.31.38, quoted by Erasmus at ASD I-1 115:16). Especially the Christian philosopher had no use for 'dialectic subtleties,' 'anxious and frigid quibbling,' definitions and syllogisms (cf *Ratio* LB V 133F, 81B, Allen Ep 858:57–63).
40 Allen Epp 1707:3, 1713:30, 2049:11–12
41 Cf Waszink's apparatus 639:5–7, 640:24, 642:2, 643:25–6, 648:14–15, etc, and his conclusion that 'Erasmus, having only the Aldine as his starting point, has remarkably often hit upon the truth' (635).
42 645:13, 643:8
43 642:10
44 645:7, 647:11, 656:19–20
45 640:20–1
46 641:17, 659:18
47 662:17–19
48 666:17, 657:7, used by Plautus *Aul* 3.5.39; for the translation of φιλάνθρωπος see above, note 14.
49 655:22, 656:2
50 659:5, 18–19
51 639:15, 641:6, 644:23, 641:5, 656:23
52 640:6, ASD I-4, 166:35–7
53 662:24
54 643:8, 649:4
55 640:17, paralleling Virgil *Aen* 1.69
56 650:21, 661:4, 665:19
57 641:21
58 655:17, 660:9
59 665:7ff
60 645:19ff, 668:13ff
61 662:28ff, 663:19ff, 666:7ff, cf Waszink's commentary ad locum.

62 At 663:11 a participle (*dicentes* vel sim) needs to be inserted to restore the sense: *sophistae maxime student sibi reddere incredibile [discentes] nullum esse iudicium naturae* (the sophists strive eagerly to discredit the theory [saying] that there is no natural power of judgment). Cf Niccolo da Reggio's translation (p 8): *quam maxime sophistae incredibile conantur facere discentes quod nullum iudicatorium est natura.* The defective Greek clause runs μάλιστ' αὐτοῖς ἄπιστον ἐργάσασθαι σπουδάζωσιν οἱ σοφισταὶ μηδὲν εἶναι κριτήριον φυσικόν. At 663:22–3 Erasmus mistakenly translates 'began' for 'left off.' Neither verb makes sense in the context. Cf da Reggio (p 9), who omitted the clause altogether.

   Da Reggio translated the essay *De optimo genere docendi* at the beginning of the fourteenth century. Gesner, who included some of his translations in the Latin Froben edition of Galen's *Opera* (Basel 1542), called him a 'primitive but reliable translator' (*rudis quidem, sed fidelis*). The text of his version has been published by Brinkmann in *Programm zur Feier ... König Friedrich Wilhelm III.* A comparison between da Reggio's and Erasmus' versions is interesting, but does not yield any conclusive results because da Reggio used a significantly different Greek text. Cf Gesner's remark: 'I wish his manuscripts which were certainly very clear and uncorrupted had been available to the Venetian and German printers' (ibid).

63 Cf Barigazzi *Favorino di Arelate, Opere* 181:2–4. For Erasmus' translation see ASD 551:1–4.

64 Cf da Reggio's translation (p 5), which is a more likely rendition of Galen's meaning: *sed aliquid aliud petemus ab artificibus praeberi discipulis quod non est aliud nisi ratiocinari quod dicitur a multis discutere* (but we shall require that craftsmen teach their students something else, namely to reason, which the people call 'to examine').

65 The text is in Froben's *Opera omnia* (Basel 1542) vol III, *Libri isagogici* 3–10. For an analysis of Bellisarius' sources see Beaudouin 'Le *Protrepticus* de Galien.' For editions see Durling 'A Chronological Census of Renaissance Editions and Translations of Galen.'

66 Beaudouin 244

67 639:14; 3C

68 53:231–4; 9B

69 3D, 8E, 10G

70 Erasmus' errors have been discussed above 113–14. Examples of Bellisarius' slips are his translation *lege prohibuit ne quis patrem aleret* (he forbade by law that anyone maintain his father, 6E). The correct version is 'that any father demand maintenance' (cf Erasmus 645:18–19). In another passage Bellisarius translates *cuilibet navigationis ministro* (any assistant in the voyage, 7C); the correct version is 'any traveller' (cf Erasmus 649:6).

71 I cannot fully support Beaudouin's characteristic of Bellisarius' translation as 'lâche, redondante, souvent d'une fidélité douteuse et la plupart du temps superficielle,' especially when Erasmus is said by contrast to be 'd'une précision qui va jusqu'à la minutie' (Beaudouin 236).

72 Cf Allen Ep 2145 headnote. The dedicatory letter is Ep 2273, dated 13 February 1530.

73 See Bolgar 435, 492–3.

74 Cf Allen VII 547.

75 Allen Ep 2273:14

76 Ep 2307, dated April 1530

77 Allen Ep 2273:19–22, 25–6; compare CWE Ep 272:7–8 (Allen lines 6–8), praising Xenophon for his sensible advice to princes.

78 *Copia* CWE 24, 614:4–6

79 The following quotations are from the text in LB IV 643–54, col and section.

80 643E, 645A

81 644B, 649F, 652F

82 643A, 647E, 651C

83 645B

84 643D–E

85 648E

86 643A

87 649C

88 See above 79.

89 645C

90 646A

91 644B. The negative is, however, an unfortunate Erasmian conjecture. Xenophon says that kings do not have to listen to criticism.

92 646E

93 The dedicatory letters are Epp 2431 and 2189. The Latin text of the *Apophthegmata* is in LB IV 93–380. On Erasmus' purpose see Cytowska '*Apophthegmata* d'Erasme de Rotterdam.'

91 Allen Ep 2431:11–12

95 Ibid line 58

96 Ibid lines 139–45

97 Ibid lines 73–5

98 Ibid lines 74–6: 'For many reasons I preferred to follow rather than translate Plutarch, to explain rather than give a version of the text: first, to make my speech clearer, that is, less constrained by the wording of the Greek ...'

99 Ibid lines 77–81: 'For these are not written for Trajan, a man proficient in Latin and Greek literature and versed in matters by long experience, but to a young prince, and through you, to all boys and

youths aspiring to liberal studies; nor are they written for that age when sayings and deeds of this kind were common in the talk of ordinary people, in the baths, at banquets, and by groups in the forum.'

100 Ibid lines 85–94

101 Cf ibid lines 145–50.

102 Cf ibid lines 228–33, 270–76, 294–5: 'Material will be found in our work, however, which does not contribute to character formation, but only raises a laugh. And I don't think this is cause for reproach ... as long as it is a subtle and refined joke. For these things entertain and nourish young minds, and make no small contribution to an affable life and pleasant speech ... In my opinion it is more judicious to let schoolboys practise this sort of subject than those common ones which contain tedious aphorisms, yet fail to convey the secrets of the Latin language; but let the teacher explain the methods by which a concise expression can be expanded, and that what is said in jest can be adapted to serious use ... Indeed the wisest men have rightly decided that one must use pleasure to entice the first tender age to love a more serious kind of wisdom.'

103 Allen Ep 2431:324–6; compare Allen Ep 1204:21: 'We want [students] to be exposed to good literature, but in such a manner that they are not infected with bad morals.'

104 Ibid lines 156–67

105 Eg 126D ('and this is a stratagem, not an aphorism'), 113E ('this is not an aphorism'); compare 125B–C, which contain no aphorisms, but are included by Erasmus without comment.

106 Eg 106E = 101D, 110D = 98D, 113E = 95A–B, 107E = 98F; cf 107C and 122D, where Erasmus notes the repetition.

107 Cf 93E, 99A–B, 110C, 101E–F, 121B, 122B.

108 Cf 96F, 118A, 95B, 95F, 104C, 129C, 105A–E, 112A, 102E.

109 96C

110 97C, compare 97E (*solo pallio tectus*)

111 102D, 119D

112 109B

113 Cf 100B: 'and this man was a warrior and a pagan; to the Christian prince every battle ought to be sad if it entails the deaths of many of the host.'

114 110F: 'married women who enjoy attending youthful parties without their husbands, who run off to attend festivals and fairs abroad, who dance in mixed company, and expose their nude bodies to the eyes of any man in the baths ...'; 124F: 'What is seen moves and penetrates the mind more than what is heard'; 129A: 'They pluck and shave parts which nature has endowed with hair'; 132E: 'the greater

part of the troubles is due to physicians, either because they are inexperienced, or negligent, or misled by ambition and greed.'
115 Cf 93C: 'Immortal God, to what men is their [the princes'] formation and education entrusted from tender years on ...?'; 95C: 'Today princes often precipitate war without consulting, or against the will of, their nobles and citizens'; 108E: 'the princes make laws, but are not bound by them'; ibid: 'princes who strive to strengthen their rule in no other way than by weakening their subjects and increasing their own wealth'; 111F: 'they value a mime or jester higher than a trustworthy counsellor.'
116 117C, 112A

CHAPTER SEVEN

1 The text is in LB I 117–64. The translation was dedicated to Johannes Caesarius, cf Epp 428, 771.
2 Cf above 71.
3 For Erasmus' praise of Gaza see Allen I.15:29 ('of all translators the most felicitous'), also Epp 2466:234–5, 2291:49–50 ('without debate, the greatest'). He commented on his command of Latin in Allen Ep 1347:242. On Gaza and contemporary grammarians see Kukenheim *Contributions à l'histoire de la grammaire grecque* 7–45 and Pizzi 'La grammatica greca di T. Gaza ed Erasmo.'
4 CWE Ep 428:17–21 (Allen lines 13–17)
5 CWE Ep 428:23, 26 (Allen lines 19, 22)
6 He sent the translation to Froben in August 1517 (cf Ep 629). When Froben showed no interest, Erasmus sent another copy to Martens, who published it in Louvain, 1518. For negotiations with Afinius see Epp 637–8, for hints to Fisher Ep 667.
7 CWE Ep 771:11 (Allen lines 8–9)
8 Allen I.9:11–13, compare CWE Ep 771:15–16 (Allen lines 12–13): 'I hope the time will soon come when they are full-grown and active in this department of learning and need my help no longer.'
9 Cf Allen Ep 1407:60: 'we beg you to translate that useful book of Theodore, *De mensibus*.'
10 The dictionary was published in Basel, 1524. The preface is Ep 1460
11 Allen Ep 1460:28–32, 36; for Erasmus' effort to promote this thankless, but necessary, work see also Allen Epp 1211:435 and 1233:164–7, where he encourages Budé to compile a dictionary. His suggestion met with some success: Budé published *Commentarii linguae Graecae* (Paris 1529); cf Allen Ep 1233:166n.
12 The publishers, however, had no scruples about misleading potential buyers by implying in the title that Erasmus was involved. For example, a collection of fables, first published by Martens in 1513, lists

Erasmus among the translators. His share consists of eight brief passages, all verbatim quotations from the *Adages*. Demosthenes' works (Basel 1532) had the subtitle 'with notes from the works of Erasmus of Rotterdam …' A closer inspection reveals, however, that Erasmus' contribution consisted of a dozen notes which are little more than cross references to his *Adages*. For other cases of 'false advertising' see below notes 13 and 23, and Allen Ep 2686:14n.

13 Cf Allen Ep 2432:248–66. The edition is listed in Vander Haegen's *Bibliotheca Erasmiana*, but there is no firm evidence for any involvement on Erasmus' part. Gryneus thanks him in a general way for his support: 'I am glad to be advised, to have my mistakes pointed out, to be yours' (Allen Ep 2433:1–2); but in Allen Ep 2434:43–4 Erasmus apologizes for not having had time to provide substantial help: 'You must excuse me, but I was overwhelmed by a great deal of work and had no time to edit it (*hoc recognoscere*).'

14 Allen Ep 2432:2, 264–5

15 Cf Allen Ep 1657 headnote. He also consulted Erasmus on some iambic verses for the title page of Aristotle's *Opera*, cf Allen Ep 2433:28–33.

16 Cf Allen Ep 2686 to B. Amerbach, whose advice Erasmus solicits in this matter. However, when Erasmus was a newcomer on the publishing scene, others were called upon to perform the same service for him. Cf. Fausto's Ep 127 (on the *Adages*) which was 'extorted from him by the publisher' (Allen Ep 1175:57).

17 The preface is Ep 2695.

18 Allen Ep 2695:88–90

19 Ibid lines 34–59: 'I do not consider Demosthenes very suitable reading for those who are seeking to acquire a knowledge of Greek literature, for there is more craftsmanship concealed than is shown prima facie … Just as a man who is not a connoisseur of art takes little pleasure in a painting displaying superior craftsmanship, so readers will not recognize that divine element in Demosthenes, τὸ δεινόν (rhetorical force), which the most eloquent men have always admired in him, unless they are versed in the precepts of rhetoric and equipped with a knowledge of history.'

20 Ibid lines 52–5: 'to discover by comparing passages what one has borrowed from the other, where our Cicero is a match, where he is superior, and where his imitation falls somewhat short of his model. There is hardly an exercise that can be more conducive to developing judgment.'

21 Allen Ep 3130:3–7

22 Allen Ep 1523:208–9, cf Melanchthon's request in Ep 1500:67–8.

23 Cf Allen Ep 2760:8. The work is listed in Vander Haeghen's *Bibliotheca Erasmiana*, but there is no evidence that Erasmus was involved in the edition. Cf Allen Ep 2760 headnote.

24 Allen Ep 2760:25; the other translations were by J. Angelo (Vicenza 1476) and J. Werner (Nuremberg 1514). Cf Allen 2760:22n.

25 Allen Ep 2760:40

26 Ibid lines 17–19: 'among the mathematical disciplines there is hardly any more attractive or essential than geography'; lines 31–3: 'it seems that he did not lack eloquence, but the treatment of this discipline requires precise, sober, and clear language, rather than a splendid and abundant style.'

27 Allen Ep 2422:51–5

28 Ibid lines 43–51. He referred to his *Apophthegmata* in lines 62–5.

29 Ibid lines 65–73

30 Cf above 146 and 72.

31 Allen Ep 2422:75 (quoting Homer *Iliad* 2.325)

CONCLUSION

1 CWE Ep 205:40 (Allen lines 36–7)

2 CWE Ep 177:115 (Allen lines 96–7)

3 Thomson 'The Latinity of Erasmus' 127

4 CWE Ep 293:14 (Allen line 10), Allen Ep 1572:44–5

5 CWE Ep 428:42–5 (Allen lines 37–40); for other instances of this selfless attitude, his satisfaction at being 'outstripped' by a new generation of scholars see Allen Epp 1146:22 ('I certainly am pleased to be put in the shade in this fashion') and 1223:17 ('I would envy them if I did not support with all my heart their service to the public').

Index and chronology

of Erasmus' translations, editions of classical Greek authors,

and study aids

Bibliography

꙰

SHORT-TITLE LIST OF TEXTS USED

Allen P.S. Allen, ed *Opus epistolarum Des. Erasmi Roterodami* Oxford
  1906–58
  ASD *Opera omnia Des. Erasmi Roterodami* Amsterdam 1969–
  CWE *The Collected Works of Erasmus* Toronto 1974–
Holborn A. and H. Holborn *Desiderius Erasmus. Ausgewählte Werke*
  repr Munich 1974
  LB J. Leclerc, ed *Des. Erasmi Roterodami opera omnia* Leiden 1703–6
Opuscula W.K. Ferguson, ed *Erasmi opuscula* The Hague 1933
  Reedijk C. Reedijk, ed *The Poems of Des. Erasmus* Leiden 1956

LITERATURE CITED

Aldridge, J.W. *The Hermeneutics of Erasmus* Zurich 1966
Aulotte, R. *Amyot et Plutarque. La tradition des Moralia au XVIᵉ siècle*
  Geneve 1965
– 'Une Rivalité d'humanistes: Erasme et Longueil, traducteurs de
  Plutarque' *BHR* 30 (1968) 549–73
Barigazzi, A., ed and trans *Favorino di Arelate, Opere* Florence 1966
Baron, H., ed *L. Bruni: De interpretatione recta* Leipzig 1928
Bartelink, G.J.M., ed and comm *Hieronymus: Liber de optimo genere
  interpretandi* Leiden 1980
Beaudouin, M. 'Le *Protepticus* de Galien' *Revue de philologie* ns 22 (1898)
  233–45
Bentley, J. H. 'Erasmus' *Annotationes in Novum Testamentum* and the
  Textual Criticism of the Gospels' *Archiv für Reformationsgeschichte* 67
  (1976) 33–53
– 'Biblical Philology and Christian Humanism: L. Valla and Erasmus as
  Scholars of the Gospels' *Sixteenth-Century Journal* 8:2 (1977) 9–28

Binns, J.W. 'Latin Translations from Greek in the English Renaissance' *Humanistica Lovaniensia* 27 (1978) 128–59

Bludau, A. *Die beiden ersten Erasmus-Ausgaben des neuen Testamentes und ihre Gegner* Freiburg 1902

Bolgar, R.R. *The Classical Heritage* Cambridge, Mass 1954

Boyle, M. O'Rourke *Erasmus on Language and Method in Theology* Toronto 1977

Brabant, H. 'Erasme, ses maladies et ses médecins' 539–68 in *Colloquia Erasmiana Turonensia* Toronto 1972

Brinkmann, A. *Galeni De optimo docendi genere libellus, Programm zur Feier ... König Friedrich Wilhelm III* Bonn 1914

Calderini, A. 'Intorno alla biblioteca e alla cultura greca del Filelfo' *Studi italiani di filologia classica* 20 (1913) 204–424

Chomarat, J. *Grammaire et rhetorique chez Erasme* Paris 1981

Cytowska, M. 'Apophthegmata d'Erasme de Rotterdam, manuel de morale chrétienne du xvie siècle' *Eos* 61 (1973) 123–33

– 'Erasme de Rotterdam, traducteur d'Homère' *Eos* 63 (1975) 341–53

Delcourt, M. 'Erasme traducteur de Lucien' 303–11 in *Hommages à Marcel Renard* Brussels 1969

De la Garanderie, M.-M. *Christianisme et lettres profanes (1515–1535)* 2 vols. Paris 1976

De Petris, A. 'Le teorie umanistiche del tradurre e l'*Apologeticus* di G. Manetti' *BHR* 37:1 (1975) 15–32

Dibbelt, H. 'Erasmus' griechische Studien' *Gymnasium* 57 (1950) 55–71

Durling, R.J. 'A Chronological Census of Renaissance Editions and Translations of Galen' *Journal of the Warburg and Courtauld Institutes* 24 (1961) 230–305

Geanakoplos, D. *Greek Scholars in Venice* Cambridge, Mass 1962

– 'Erasmus and the Aldine Academy of Venice' *Greek, Roman, and Byzantine Studies* 3 (1960) 107–34

Grendler, P. *The Roman Inquisition and the Venetian Press, 1540–1605* Princeton 1977

Halkin, L.E. 'Erasme en Italie' 37–54 in *Colloquia Erasmiana Turonensia* Toronto 1972

Hall, B. 'Erasmus: Biblical Scholar and Reformer' *Erasmus* ed Th. Dorey (London 1970) 81–114

Heep, M. *Die Colloquia familiaria des Erasmus und Lukian* diss Halle 1927

Herding, O. 'Isokrates, Erasmus und die *Institutio principis christiani*' 101–43 in *Im Dauer und Wandel der Geschichte* Munich 1966

Holeczek, H. *Humanistische Bibelphilologie als Reformproblem bei Erasmus von Rotterdam, Thomas More und William Tyndale* Leiden 1975

Hoven, R. 'Notes sur Erasme et les auteurs anciens' *Antiquité classique* 38 (1969) 169–74

Hyma, A. *The Youth of Erasmus* Ann Arbor 1930

Jarrott, C.A.L. 'Erasmus' Biblical Humanism' *Studies in the Renaissance* 17 (1970) 119–52
- 'Erasmus' *In principio erat sermo*: A Controversial Translation' *Studies in Philology* 61 (1964) 35–40
Kukenheim, L. *Contributions à l'histoire de la grammaire grecque, latine et hébraïque à l'époque de la Renaissance* Leiden 1951
Lowry, M. *The World of Aldus Manutius* Cambridge 1979
Lupton, J.H. *A Life of John Colet* London 1887
Mesnard, P. 'La *Paraclesis* d'Erasme' *Bibliothèque d'humanism et Renaissance* 13 (1951) 26–42
Mestwerdt, P. *Die Anfänge des Erasmus* Leipzig 1917
Metzger, B. *The Text of the New Testament* Oxford 1968
Olin, J., ed *Christian Humanism and the Reformation* New York 1975
Payne, J.P. 'Toward the Hermeneutics of Erasmus' 13–50 in *Scrinium Erasmianum* Leiden 1969
Pfeiffer, P. *History of Classical Scholarship 1300–1850* Oxford 1976
Phillips, M.M. 'Erasmus and the Art of Writing' 335–50 in *Scrinium Erasmianum* Leiden 1969
- 'Erasmus and the Classics' 1–70 in *Erasmus* ed T.A. Dorey, London 1970
Pizzi, C. 'La grammatica greca di T. Gaza ed Erasmo' *Studi bizantini e neoellenici* 7 (1953) 183–8
Proctor, R. *The Printing of Greek in the Fifteenth Century* Oxford 1900
Rabil, A. *Erasmus and the New Testament* San Antonio 1972
Renaudet, A. *Erasme et l'Italie* Geneva 1954
- *Etudes Erasmiennes 1521–1529* Paris 1939
Reynolds, L.D., and Wilson, N.G. *Scribes and Scholars* Oxford 1974
Robinson, Ch. *Lucian and His Influence in Europe* London 1979
Rummel, E. 'The Use of Greek in Erasmus' Letters' *Humanistica Lovaniensia* 30 (1981) 55–92
Sabbadini, R. *Il metodo degli umanisti* Florence 1922
Sandys, J.E. *A History of Classical Scholarship* repr New York 1958
Schmitt, W. O. 'Erasmus als Euripidesübersetzer' 129–66 in *Übersetzungsprobleme antiker Tragödien* Berlin 1969
Schwarz, W. *Principles and Problems of Biblical Translation* Cambridge 1955
- 'The Meaning of *fidus interpres* in Medieval Translations' *Journal of Theological Studies* 45 (1944) 73–8
Thompson, C.R., ed *The Complete Works of St Thomas More* vol III, New Haven 1974
- 'Erasmus' Translation of Lucian's *Longaevi*' *Classical Philology* 35 (1940) 397–415
Thomson, D.F.S. 'The Latinity of Erasmus' 115–37 in *Erasmus* ed T.A. Dorey, London 1970
- trans, and Porter, H.C., annot *Erasmus and Cambridge* Toronto 1963

Tilley, A. 'Greek Studies in England in the Early Sixteenth Century' *English Historical Review* 53 (1938) 221–39, 438–56

Vander Haeghen, F. *Bibliotheca Erasmiana* Ghent 1893

Waszink, J.H. 'Einige Betrachtungen über die Euripidesübersetzungen und ihre historische Situation' *Antike und Abendland* 17:2 (1971) 70–90

Wilson, N.G. 'Erasmus as a Translator of Euripides: Supplementary Notes' *Antike und Abenland* 18 (1973) 87–8

Winkler, G.B.N. *Erasmus von Rotterdam und die Einleitungsschriften zum Neuen Testament* Münster 1974

Zappala, M. 'Andrés Laguna, Erasmus, and the Translation of Lucian's *Tragopodagra' Revue de litterature comparée* 53 (1979) 419–31

Index

❦